Chrome Dreams

Automobile Styling
Since 1893

PAUL C. WILSON

Chilton Book Company
Radnor, Pennsylvania

Copyright © by Paul C. Wilson
First Edition   All Rights Reserved
Published in Radnor, Pa., by Chilton Book Company
and simultaneously in Don Mills, Ontario, Canada,
by Thomas Nelson & Sons, Ltd.
Manufactured in the United States of America

Designed by Adrianne Onderdonk Dudden

Library of Congress Cataloging in Publication Data
Wilson, Paul Carroll, 1944–
    Chrome Dreams:

    Includes index.
    1. Automobiles–United States–History.   2. Auto-
mobiles–Design and construction–History.   I. Title.
TL23.W58   1976   629.22'22'0973   76-69
ISBN 0-8019-6352-4

Acknowledgment is made to the following sources for the use of excerpted material included herein:
"Babbitt," Sinclair Lewis, Harcourt, Brace, & Co., New York, 1922. Reprinted with permission of the Estate of Sinclair Lewis and Jonathan Cape Ltd., London.
"My Years with General Motors," Alfred P. Sloan, Doubleday and Company Inc., New York, 1964.
"The Secret Life of Walter Mitty," James Thurber. Copyright © 1942 James Thurber. Copyright © 1970 Helen Thurber. From *My World and Welcome to It*, published by Harcourt, Brace, Jovanovich. Originally printed in *The New Yorker*.
"This Side of Paradise," F. Scott Fitzgerald, Charles Scribner's Sons, 1920.
"The Wind in the Willows," Kenneth Grahame, Charles Scribner's Sons, 1908.

Illustrations by the author
Rendered in ink by Richard M. Clark

Preface

When archaeologists thousands of years from now dig into the stratum containing implements from our time, chances are that their shovels will clang against the rusted fender of an automobile. They will dig it up, clean it off, and when they discover its importance in twentieth century life, they will interpret it as we interpret clay pottery and fragments of statues—as an icon expressive of the culture which produced it. The automobile will not be inappropriate for their purpose. While these future archaeologists will also unearth our buildings, some sculpture, and perhaps a few paintings, these will only reflect the tastes of the individuals or small groups that produced them; the automobile, by contrast, is much closer to being a collective creation of the culture.

Strictly speaking, of course, the appearance of an automobile is determined by its designers, who in turn are influenced by considerations of practicality. But the power of veto exerted by the public by simply refusing to buy an unattractive car is so great that public taste must be counted as the most important single influence on style evolution. A sculptor need only please himself, an architect need only satisfy a committee or a client, but a stylist must often appeal to a million people with a single design. And the appeal must be so strong that the buyer will make the large investment needed to buy a car. As a result, I think it is valid to consider the automobile an object of popular art, and to interpret its appearance as an expression of the culture and period which produced it. What better symbol of the late 1920s, for example, could be found than the original Cadillac V16, which was designed in the late '20s and introduced in 1930? No design of the early '20s or mid '30s celebrates raw wealth with such uninhibited joy; different periods speak visually in different tones.

The assumption on which this book has been written is that the automobile is a "meaningful form" in our culture and deserves serious study. Such a study might move from automobile style in an almost infinite number of directions, however, and to confine the present book within reasonable bounds I have given scant treatment to many subjects that are related to the development of style. This is not an account of the competitive struggles between the automobile manufacturers; not a balanced history of the evolution of the automobile, which would have to include far more information on mechanical development; not a story of the personalities and decisions that contributed to advances in design. Here and there, these peripheral matters are touched upon, but they are not my main theme. Nor is this a purely aesthetic analysis of car styles, because such an approach would remove the designs from the historical context which produced them, and to trace the relation between the designs and their historical context is an important purpose of my analysis.

I have tried to do two main things in this book, both of which are prerequisite for a serious study of the form of the automobile as cultural expression. The first is to pursue, through published comments, cautiously interpreted sales figures, and the influence of original designs on later cars, the vagaries of public taste. My object is to discover the people's true choice, the basis from which generalizations on the cultural meaning of popular art must begin.

My second intention is to educate the reader's eye so that he begins to see nuances in car design. Education is necessarily the intent of all art historians: to the uneducated, all statues in a museum look more or less alike, as do all old cars. Yet to those who know what to look for, the differences are enormous. Looking back, we strain to see things which were grossly obvious to people at the time the cars were built. The 1929 Buick, for example, which people then thought hideous, looks to us now almost identical to the popular 1928 model. I have arranged the illustrations and descriptions to give the reader a sense of development through time, so that, with the images of earlier cars fixed in his mind, he will *see* how modern such cars as the 1901 Mercedes and the 1915 Mercer phaeton looked when they came out. When we are able to see the styling of a car in an historical context, and not merely in relation to personal aesthetic standards, we can begin to interpret the cultural meaning of its form.

In writing this book I owe special thanks to Lynwood Bryant, Professor of Humanities at M.I.T. He hired me to do research under the M.I.T. Highway Transportation Program, during which I had the original idea of this book; he gave me strong encouragement while I was writing, and he read each chapter carefully and made useful suggestions. Without his help and enthusiasm I could not even have begun.

Contents

1

In Search of a Form

At first sight, few people would have said that the newly created horseless carriage was beautiful. There it stood, shivering like a terrified horse being led from a barn fire, burping at regular intervals, and gradually surrounding itself with a hazy halitosis. Its resemblance to a buggy made the differences grotesque: visible underneath were belts, connecting rods, and valve gear, convulsing feebly like exposed intestines. Whatever points the new thing had in its favor, an attractive appearance was not one of them.

Its immediate predecessor, the horse and buggy combination, was far more satisfying in appearance. To start with, it was logical: the motive power obviously came from the horse, and was transferred to the buggy through the harness. It showed the intended direction of travel by the placement of the horse ahead. And in the construction of the buggy itself, years of refinement had made it light and strong and graceful.

In the horse and buggy unit, the horse was the part which really stirred the owner's emotions. The buggy could be elegant and graceful, but the horse gave life to it. Young men of past centuries would talk endlessly about the "powerful shoulders of Geo. Mason's filly Cyclone" and how "that yearling Thunderclap will be fast—he has the small head of his mother." They would dream of driving through town in a light trap drawn by a pair of matched bays; though one horse would easily be able to take the load, the frankly excessive power of having two of them would add dash and excitement to the appearance of the ensemble.

Horse and buggy

1892 *Oneida Buggy*

The buggy was the passive part of the combination, designed for minimum resistance. For easy rolling it had large wheels and very light construction. Not only should it be light, but it must look light: wheels were made as spindly as possible, consistent with reasonable strength; bodies were compact, purposely dwarfed by the wheels; body surfaces were broken up by panel designs, in order to appear still smaller; finally, on some designs, the body was actually perforated by holes cut in the sides. The unworkable extreme of buggy design was shown in the fashion plates of *The Carriage Monthly*: cellophane-covered drawings displayed spider-like vehicles, with absurdly tiny bodies crouched within tall but delicate wheels.

Technically speaking, a buggy is a vehicle designed to be drawn by one horse, with four wheels, a box-type body, and a single seat with room for two or possibly three persons. A dash, usually made of leather, is attached at the front of the toe board, and a folding top is often fitted.

Within these specifications there was considerable variety. Many different springing configurations were used. The buggy illustrated here is a side spring type, with springs mounted longitudinally under each side of the body. There were also variations on the exact shape of the body and seat and in the proportions of the wheels and body.

If an American of 1890 owned any horse-drawn vehicle at all, chances are good that it would have been a buggy. This was not true of his European contemporary. For informal use the European would be more likely to drive a two-wheeled gig or dogcart, while on formal occasions he would recline on the plush seats of a heavy and ornate open carriage while his coachman took the reins. With a few exceptions, early European automobiles were designed for the coach-and-four market, and thus tended to be larger and more pretentious than their buggy-derived American counterparts.

The influence of the bicycle on the fledgling automobile was also strong. Bicycle design was rapidly refined in the '70s and '80s, and by the last decade of the century America was in the grip of a bicycle craze. Everyone had a bicycle. Knowing that aged chaperones could easily be outrun, athletic "wheel men" donned stylish knickers and invited their young lady friends for a ride in the country. Bicycle racing had a wide following, and there were thousands of bicycle clubs. No matter who you were, you could not avoid exposure to the bicycle in the 1890s. It was therefore natural that designers of early automobiles should turn to it for inspiration.

Like the buggy, the bicycle has the appearance of lightness and strength. It is also a mechanism, which the buggy is not. Lacking fenders and chain guard, a bicycle of the 1890s unashamedly displayed its means of locomotion in pedals, sprock-

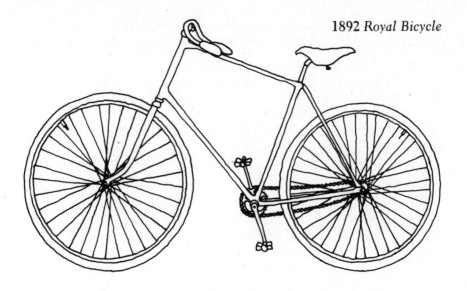

ets, and chain. Its metal tubular frame, formed into a structurally efficient truss, proclaimed its connection with the machine age. Another feature not shared with the buggy was the use of wire wheels with pneumatic tires.

In the late summer of 1893 Frank Duryea operated the first successful U.S. built gasoline automobile. The basis for this vehicle was an ordinary buggy, fully equipped with oil lamps and folding top. The driving mechanism was mounted on a modified and reinforced sub-frame, and was fully exposed. The power was taken to the fragile wheels by chains and sprockets.

In operation the vehicle was a success, but it was not beautiful. The lightness and simplicity of the body belied the growling mass of machinery visible underneath. Next to the exposed machinery, the visual feature of Duryea's vehicle which distinguished it most conspicuously from an ordinary buggy was the steering tiller mounted centrally in front. This helped to make the appearance more rational—at least one could see how it was steered. The uneasiness of contemporaries at seeing a self-propelled carriage was somewhat allayed by visual reassurances that it was under the control of the driver. On early Duryea cars

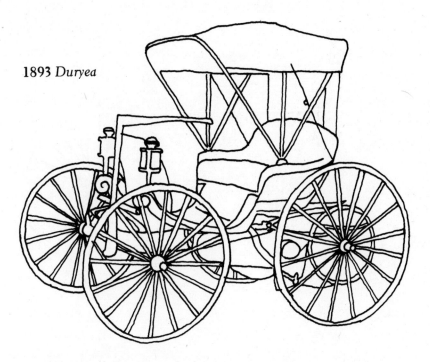

1893 *Duryea*

the tiller was large and prominent, and was used for control of speed as well as direction.

In view of the enormous technical challenges they faced, it is surprising to find that the automotive pioneers were concerned right from the beginning about the looks of their vehicles, even to the point where it influenced the mechanical layout. In January 1894 Frank Duryea wrote a letter to his brother Charles, describing plans for his second car (*Who Designed and Built Those Early Duryea Cars*, by J. Frank Duryea, Madison, Conn., Oct. 15, 1944).

> (I) want to show you then a rough sketch of the new design. It will be good. Shall use a piano-body buggy, side spring. Increase wheelbase what I may without making it unsightly . . . an increase of three or four inches over the greatest length in use will not look bad.

In the same letter he says he had decided not to use chain drive. It makes the frame too long, and "besides the sprockets on wheels look more like a machine than it would be if we drove the axle." It

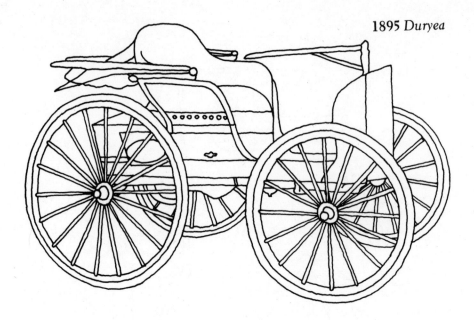

should not be too long, or look "like a machine"; implicit in these comments are the aesthetic standards of the '90s, in which the horse-drawn buggy formed the ideal model.

This second car is the one he drove to win the Chicago *Times-Herald* race of November 1895, the first auto race in this country. The car was much better looking than his first one. The wheels were made thicker and stronger, and the rear ones were reduced in diameter. Pneumatic tires were used. The longer wheelbase made the car look less awkward than before. The most striking change, however, was the enlargement of the body and rearrangement of the driving mechanism so that all the machinery was concealed. This not only made the car look much better, but it also helped to keep grit away from the working parts. After the race Duryea astonished spectators and fellow competitors by washing down his car with a water hose; the others were forced to wipe off each part separately to avoid getting water into the ignition and carburetor.

In the summer of 1894 the first Haynes-Apperson was completed. It had a light body from a buggy, perched above the fully exposed engine and running gear. High wire wheels and a tubular

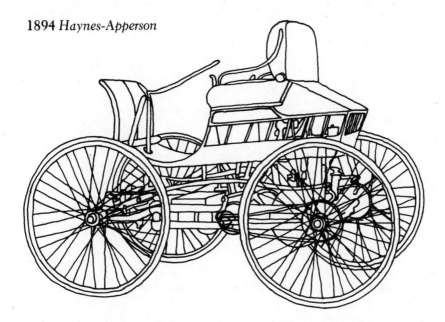

frame gave evidence of bicycle ancestry. Like the first Duryea, the Haynes-Apperson combined active machinery with a passive body in a logical but rather incongruous whole. The parts were not really united in spirit. It gave the same impression as a canoe with an outboard motor—a convenient arrangement but somehow rather makeshift. The division of active and passive parts was accentuated by the positioning of the springs between the body and the frame, as on a baby carriage, rather than between the frame and axles. This arrangement not only looked awkward, but the lack of springing between the heavy machinery and the road put a great strain on the tires and running gear when the car was driven on rough surfaces.

In 1895 and 1896 more than a score of experimental vehicles were built and operated. In the appearance of all of them their ancestry showed clearly. The bicycle influence could be seen in the tubular frame and wire wheels of the Ford and in the bicycle-fork front wheel mountings of the Hertel, while cars like the King were little more than motorized wagons. The sight of exposed machinery was universally disliked. Like Duryea, most inventors first designed an experimental car which was more or less naked of bodywork, and then made efforts on the succeeding models to

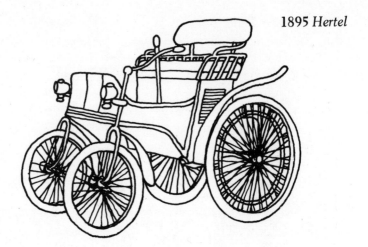

conceal the working parts. There was no movement among
American constructors in the '90s to develop a unique shape for
the automobile: motorists apparently wanted them to look like
neat and symmetrical horse-drawn vehicles. "Most designers
struggle," remarked *The Horseless Age*, May 3, 1899, "to make the
self-propelled carriage as innocent of machinery and as short as
though a horse were to be attached at any time."

In some ways function forced changes from the traditional
carriage aesthetics. Buggies were built high so that the driver
would be able to see past a large horse. On horseless vehicles the
visibility problem did not exist, except for situations when the
engine died and the car was ignominiously pulled home again.
Optimistic builders did not care to design cars with this eventual-
ity in mind, and cars gradually became lower.

Light appearance was the basic aim of bicycle and buggy
manufacturers, and was adopted as a goal by the makers of early
automobiles. The weight and speed of the automobile imposed
strains on the structure which were more severe than most people
anticipated, however, and many constructors came to grief because they balked at using what seemed to them to be excessively
heavy, clumsy-looking components. Features such as thick-
spoked wooden artillery wheels were only accepted when their
necessity was proven beyond question. Year by year, frames,
axles, and wheels were strengthened, gradually losing their resemblances to buggy parts.

The arrangement of the components also caused changes from the basic buggy shape. On the 1897 Winton, the central part of the body was filled with machinery so that a rear seat facing forward would have had no legroom. To solve the problem Winton placed the rear seat so that the passengers faced backwards. This body style was called the "dos-a-dos" and was used occasionally on horse-drawn vehicles such as dogcarts. However logical it was, this solution was unsatisfactory in the long run because passengers in the rear seat complained of riding discomfort and motion sickness. Unable to see where they were going, they tired quickly, probably by subconsciously flinching from an expected collision (not an unlikely possibility in view of the road conditions and the braking ability of the early cars). In any case, backward-facing seating arrangements have never had much success in automobiles.

Another feature of the first Winton which was shared to some extent by most early automobiles was a visual concentration of weight over the rear wheels. While in front the toeboard and dash remained the same as on a buggy, the body box at the rear grew rapidly in order to cover all the machinery. The rearward weight bias was not just a visual effect, either: some early automobiles had as much as five-sixths of their weight on the rear wheels. The dynamics of vehicle balance were unknown then, and though this gave the cars more traction it also gave them treacherous road behavior. Handling was so bad that some of them carried devices called sprags, which looked like reinforced ski poles, mounted under the chassis. When the car began to slide sideways or backwards down a hill the sprag was dropped like an anchor, nailing the car into the road. The device was also needed to hold cars on

1897 *Winton*

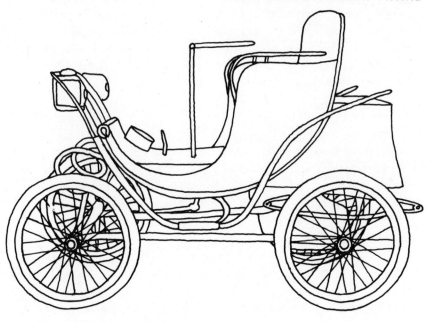

hills, because some early brakes were designed to work only in the forward direction.

The years from 1897 to 1900 saw the gradual emergence of the first standard type of American automobile, the light runabout. If in 1900 a person were asked what a horseless carriage looked like he would describe a car like the 1900 Locomobile steam runabout. This car drew praise from the *Scientific American*, November 17, 1900, for its "clean lines and general light and symmetrical appearance" and is a good example of the type of vehicle that comprised the vast majority of U.S. cars built between 1898 and 1902.

The Locomobile has an engine-under-seat configuration combined with a central chain drive to the rear axle. The body is a simple box construction, neat in appearance, which hides practically all the machinery. One seat, which is wide enough for two people, is mounted midway between the axles. Fairly small, equal-sized wheels are used on the front and rear. On the Locomobile these are the wire type, though wooden artillery

1900 *Locomobile*

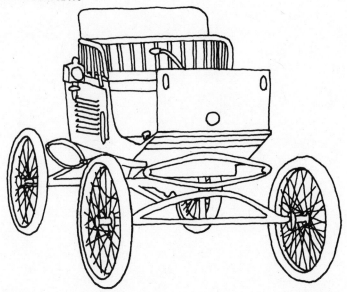

wheels were also common and growing in popularity. The car has pneumatic tires which look fat by bicycle standards.

Like almost all cars of that year, the Locomobile is steered by a tiller. Between the time of the early Duryeas and 1900 steering tillers and control levers had become steadily less conspicuous, to the point where one often had to look carefully to see any means of control at all. A few cars adopted wheel steering in 1900, but its practical advantages were not generally appreciated and its use was thought to be an affected imitation of contemporary practice in Europe. "As to steering," snorted *The Horseless Age*, November 7, 1900, "a few have adopted that foreign freak, the wheel."

Fenders were optional in 1900. They were not a novelty, having been used for centuries on carriages. They were usually made of leather or plywood. Folding tops were sold to some people, such as doctors, who used their cars for practical purposes. Many cars, used just for fun, did not have them. In any case, the tops did not help much when the car was in motion because they were usually entirely open in the front so that the top scooped in the rain as the car ran along.

There were always a few slight variations from one make of car to the next so that they could be identified. The sides of the

1901 U.S. Long
Distance Auto

1902 Oldsmobile

1902 Autocar

body were decorated with moldings of various patterns, and the louvres or grille in the engine boxes were distinctive. Several different types of dash design were used: starting with the simple flat dash of the Locomobile, manufacturers branched out into curved dash designs, such as the Oldsmobile, and the solid box-type used on the Autocar.

Objectively it is difficult to find fault in the design of the 1900 Locomobile or the curved dash Oldsmobile. Their lines are crisp, and the bodies neatly enclose the machinery. There are no frills; the car is utterly functional, yet balanced and pleasant.

What more could one ask? It was hard to say, exactly, but there was a widespread feeling that the standard runabout design was somehow inadequate. Automobile styling contests were held, magazine readers polled, and artists consulted, but no one seemed to have the solution. Suggested changes were usually either functionally awkward (with the driver seated eight feet off the ground, above and behind the passenger compartment) or aesthetic catastrophes influenced by Art Nouveau (with fenders shaped like lily pads and the steering tiller disguised as a jungle growth). They were proffered without enthusiasm and were rejected with loathing by the general public.

The trouble with the runabouts, people said, was that they had a "horse-wanted look." R. I. Clegg, writing in *The Horseless Age*, May 3, 1899, remarked that contemporary vehicles "gave the impression that a horseless vehicle was simply minus the horse," and that, from the expressive standpoint, this was quite unsatisfactory. He continues:

> I can account in no other way for the fear shown by some horses at the approach of a motor vehicle; it is, to them, the very evident lack of something quite essential to the orthodox wagon.

A glance back into the origins of the automobile gives a clue to what he meant. The horse and buggy combination, rather than just the buggy, was the aesthetic unit which the automobile superseded. The components of this unit had a clear meaning to the observer. The power for motion clearly came from the horse's muscles; it was logically transferred through the harness to the buggy, which, as the passive partner in the combination, rolled lightly along behind. The horse gave a sense of power and direction to the static buggy design.

The lines of the runabout were inoffensive, like the modern refrigerator, but they expressed nothing. It needed the addition of a universally accepted symbol of power and direction for its appearance to be satisfactory. Without this, it inspired the same feeling of uneasiness that people now have at the idea of a flying carpet. Before the machine age no one worried about how the carpet flew—they could accept it on faith. By the nineteenth century, however, people felt a need to make even their imaginary creations mechanically logical: Jules Verne's spaceship and submarine, for example, had real-looking rivets and doors in the illustrations, and the technicalities of their operation were carefully described.

It is not surprising that the aesthetic problem of the runabout was so difficult to solve. The refined runabout looked as if it were propelled by magic, since all of its drive mechanism was carefully concealed. Yet the early designs, with fully exposed machinery writhing and thrashing for everyone to see, were clearly even worse. It would not suffice to revert to earlier practice and expose the engine. What the automobile needed was a symbolic substitute for the horse, an easily recognized symbol of power that would combine harmoniously with the rest of the body shape.

The breakthrough came from Europe, where automotive evolution had followed markedly different lines than in this country. France was unquestionably the world leader in car development in the '90s, and its foremost designer was Emile Levassor. In 1891 Levassor first conceived the idea of placing the engine vertically in the front of the car and driving the rear wheels through a shaft-type, centrally mounted transmission. In the summer of 1895 his ideas were convincingly demonstrated by the performance of his car in the famous Paris-Bordeaux race, where it maintained a 15-mile-an-hour average over 732 miles and was the first to arrive back in Paris.

1895 *Panhard-Levassor*

The prestige of the Panhard-Levassor cars and the logic of M. Levassor's configuration persuaded other manufacturers to follow his example, and by the turn of the century the typical French car looked like the 1900 Creanche. Compared with the standard American runabout, it was slightly longer and heavier. The engine was housed in front, under the prominent hood. It had one seat, built wide enough for two people, mounted back on the chassis just forward of the rear wheels. In France a steering wheel was almost universally used by this time, and fenders were usually included.

French cars were fully described in American publications, but before 1900 their appearance found little favor here. An edito-

1900 *Creanche*

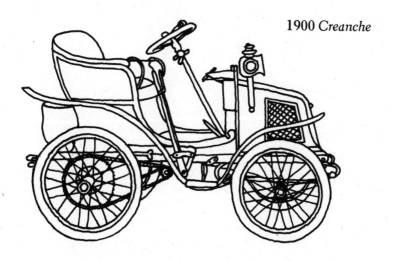

rial in *The Horseless Age* of May 16, 1900, pointed out that "it is common to arraign the French vehicles as being 'hideously ugly,' 'machines all over,' 'too complicated for any use,' etc." The multiplicity of pedals and control levers on French cars struck Americans as being crude and unnecessary. The biggest visual difference between them and the American runabout, however, was the front hood, and at first this feature was very unpopular in this country. It was a blunt reminder of the machinery American designers had worked so hard to conceal. French cars were thought to look like "clumsy road rollers."

The event which marked the beginning of a change in American taste was the first Gordon-Bennett Cup Race, held in France in 1900. On June 14, huge grunting racing machines charged out of Paris on their way to Lyons, 351 miles away. Thousands of people lined the road as the monsters bellowed past. The winner of the race, Charron, drove his Panhard-Levassor over the distance at an impressive average of 38.4 miles per hour.

The success of the first event sent designers rushing to their workshops, and for the Paris-Berlin race of the following summer the cars were greatly improved. Henri Fournier, driving a Mors factory racing car, won the race at an average speed of 47 miles per hour. The speed would have been much higher if he had not

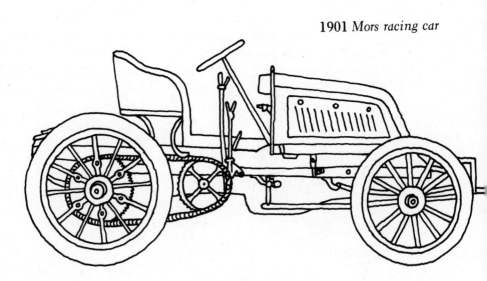

1901 *Mors racing car*

had eleven flat tires on the way; it was said that the faster cars reached 70 to 75 miles an hour on open stretches of road. For unstable, virtually brakeless machines running on poorly surfaced roads, these speeds are breathtaking even today.

In 1902 the course was from Paris to Vienna, in 1903 from Paris to Madrid. Speeds mounted every year, and the crowds grew larger. Mors, Panhard-Levassor, Mercedes, Napier, Renault, and De Dietrich were the cars to watch; the most daring of the men who drove them were Count Zborowski, Jenatzy, Farman, De Caters, Jarott, De Knyff, Fournier, S. F. Edge, and the Renault brothers. Speed, danger, the thunder of exhaust pipes, the smell of hot engine oil—for a taste of these, thousands of spectators crowded the roadsides at the risk of their lives.

Long and well-illustrated articles brought news of these events to Americans. Enthusiasm for motor sports grew rapidly in this country, and the associations of great power and speed suddenly began to sway the American public in favor of the low, stark form of the racing car, with its huge, long hood, thick frame, and heavy artillery wheels. This was a carriage no longer, but a machine. It did not pretend to be propelled by magic: its means of locomotion was expressed directly by the sprockets and driving chains, and symbolically by the massive hood, which was generously louvred on each side to allow the smoke and heat of the engine to escape. No longer did the machine apologize for being what it was, as the discreet, castrated runabout did before: chains, shafts, and levers were nakedly displayed. With the power of the machine brought out into the open, the means of controlling it also had to be made more prominent: one feels that a racing car should require more levers and pedals than a runabout. One would naturally assume that controlling such power required continuous use by the driver of both arms and legs.

It was not very long before a few European racing cars found their way to the United States. An American sportsman named A. C. Bostwick bought a Panhard-Levassor racing car in 1900, and allowed it to be shown at the New York Auto Show in November. Admiring throngs surged around it for the length of the show. During the following summer he drove it in several races and demonstrations. In the fall of 1901 two Mors racing cars were brought over from France. A crowd of 25,000 lined Ocean

Parkway, Brooklyn, to watch them rush past at 75 mph over the one-mile timed course, where they placed first and second over weak opposition.

By the summer of 1901 it was clear that the appearance of front-engined racing cars had a strong appeal for many people, but pure racing cars did not have the comfort or the capacity needed for use on the road. A new form was needed which could combine the look of power and speed of the racing car with adequately large and well-protected passenger accommodation. In 1897 the tonneau body, a tub-like rear seating compartment entered through a rear door, first appeared in Europe. These bodies were fitted to chassis similar to those of front-engined racing cars, and by 1901 they were low and sleek-looking compared with earlier cars.

A good example of a European racing-derived automobile with tonneau body is the 1901 35 hp Mercedes. On August 21, 1901, *The Horseless Age* said:

> The most striking feature about the Mercedes is undoubtedly its lowness of build, and it is safe to say that for the average American road the limit in this direction has been reached in this vehicle.

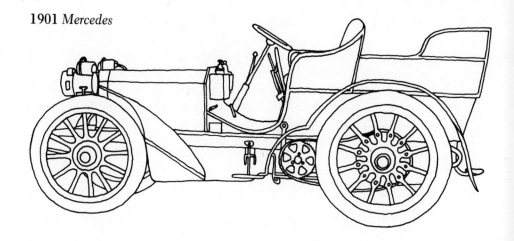

1901 *Mercedes*

A year earlier, February 21, 1900, an editorial in *The Horseless Age* said that "the motor machine must skim the ground like a swallow" and this Mercedes was the realization of the dream. In addition to its pleasing proportions, the new car had a long hood which hinted at great power and speed, and large, flaring front fenders which seemed to be swept back by the wind. The rich paint was set off by polished brass headlights, horns, levers, and instruments. The dazzle and glitter of the machine was awesome.

Public acceptance of the "French form of automobile" was hastened by the enthusiasm shown for them by the Very Rich. Not only were the foreign cars exciting in themselves, but they were considered highly fashionable by the famous "400"—the Vanderbilts, Goulds, Oelrichs, Goelets, Stuyvesants-Fishes and others, families worth countless millions who wintered at Palm Beach and summered in Bar Harbor or Newport. A. C. Bostwick, the sportsman who imported the Panhard-Levassor racing car in 1900, was a member of the circle; he had a mansion on Fifth Avenue only a few doors down from John Jacob Astor and an easy walk from the Vanderbilts.

Between 1900 and 1905 automobiling was a favorite summer activity among the millionaires at Newport. The Vanderbilts were generally considered the most reckless: Alfred Gwynne Vanderbilt was notorious for his flat-out drives from his Fifth Avenue residence to the family "cottages" at Newport such as "The Breakers," a 70-room Renaissance palace. J. J. Astor liked variety: at one time he owned 17 automobiles, all housed in a magnificent garage and tended by uniformed chauffeurs. A favorite event among the ladies was a floral decoration contest, in which the family De Dietrich, Panhard-Levassor, or Mercedes was bedecked with flowers at immense cost.

The New York Auto Show of November 1901 marked the beginning of an American stampede toward front engined tonneau-bodied touring cars of the Mercedes type. As soon as visitors walked through the door to the show their senses were assailed by the sight of low-slung, immensely powerful looking cars, lacquered in gleaming colors and bejeweled with brass ornaments. It made the blood rush to the head. All of a sudden the conventional runabout looked tame; visitors were overcome by the magnificence of the big new models. Deaf to the magazine editorials which criticized the extravagance and impracticality of the big machines, they secretly estimated how much of the price they could raise by mortgaging the house or selling heirlooms.

Foreign manufacturers were the first to take advantage of the shift in public taste, and the lead time that they had over the American builders allowed them to stage a significant "foreign car invasion" between 1901 and 1905. The numbers of foreign cars sold were not large, but the prices paid for them were phenomenal. Smith and Mabley, agents for Panhard-Levassor, Peugeot, and Renault, recorded the following sales at the 1902 New York Auto Show: one 40 hp car, $17,000; one 12 hp car, $8,000; one 24 hp car, $12,500. When one remembers that the dollar was worth several times as much in 1902 as it is today, these prices are fantastic.

Foreign car agents were not the only ones who were impressed by the money being made on the new cars. Domestic manufacturers soon took up the challenge. At first, however, they appear to have misinterpreted the appeal of the new configuration. The 1901 Columbia gasoline runabout, for example, is an unpretentious car similar to the French Creanche. Its engine is in

1901 *Columbia*

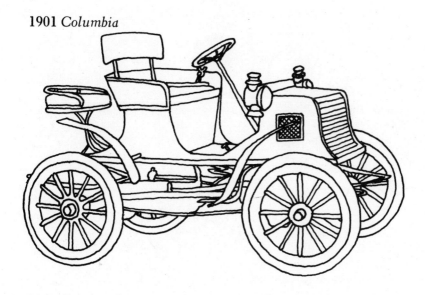

front, but in its small size and sober design it is closer in spirit to the mid-engined runabout than to the big European cars. The American public had been shown pictures of this type of vehicle for several years and had never indicated much interest in it. The front-engine arrangement by itself had little appeal; it was the combination of front-engined appearance and symbolic over-tones of speed and power which made people excited. No one wanted a Columbia; they lusted after a Mercedes instead, and ended up buying the closest visual approximation to it that they could afford.

Unquestionably the most exciting American car at the New York Auto Show of November 1901 was the massive 35 hp Gas-mobile. Its overall weight of 3,300 pounds was twice that of most runabouts. At a time when most cars had one or two cylinders, this one had six. November 16, 1901, *Scientific American* reported breathlessly that:

> [its] ponderous and resplendant appearance . . . has fasci-nated those automobile visitors, who love a big machine and high speed. This leviathan of the "teuf-teuf" family relies for its power on a 6-cylinder engine capable of 35 horsepower—an unusually large amount of power for a touring vehicle of such dimensions.

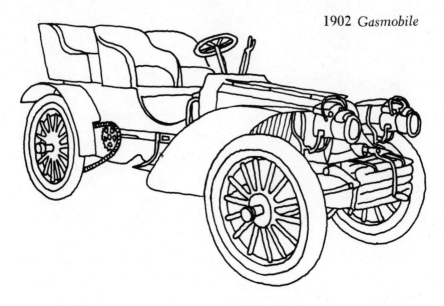

Its price was high and its mechanical design unproven, but nevertheless a "sold" sign appeared on it after the first day of the show.

In addition to its size, the attractive style features of the Gasmobile were its long, louvred hood; huge, ornate, kerosene-powered brass headlights; brass horns; wide, flared front fenders; heavy artillery wheels (by now the same diameter on both ends of the car); and wheel steering. From racing practice came the coiled tube radiator mounted low in front, chain drive, and separate bucket seats for the driver and front seat passenger.

More typical of the new American cars at the Show was the Peerless. Most of the styling features of the Gasmobile were incorporated in it, but everything was on a miniature scale. It had a two-cylinder engine instead of a six, and weighed scarcely half as much. Nevertheless, its proportions and the general effect of its appearance were similar to those of the big cars, and its comparatively low price attracted droves of buyers.

To people in 1902 the first generation of front-engined cars looked big and long and low slung, but this was only true by contrast with the earlier runabout type. Most of them were still pretty small. The 1901 Riker, for example, had a wheelbase of only 66 inches: a tall man could stretch out his arms and place one

1902 *Peerless Tonneau*

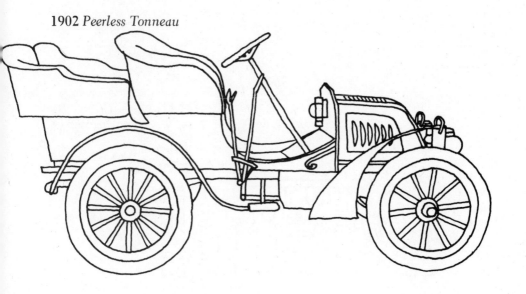

1902 *Peerless Touring Car*

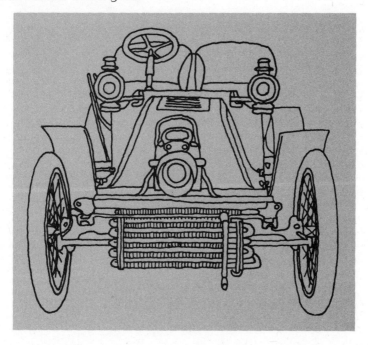

hand on the front hub and one on the rear hub. Height made up for the short length. One really needed the steps provided for climbing up to the driver's seat. Once enthroned, the driver viewed the road from a position more elevated than his ordinary standing height.

The shift in public taste in favor of the front-engined look occurred with startling rapidity. At the beginning of 1900 there were no front-engined cars being built in America, and motorists showed either apathy or active dislike for their appearance. At the end of 1901, however, opinion was almost unanimously in favor of front-engined style, and many people expressed distaste for the old forms. "One would hardly have thought," remarked *The Horseless Age*, November 13, 1901, "that such a revolutionary change of taste could have come about so quickly. The vehicle that does not wear a bonnet in front . . . is not *a la mode*."

The shift marked an important break with the automobile's horse-drawn background. While formerly the word "carriage" was used as a general term for automobiles ("Vanderbilt has five carriages in his garage"), after the new look had appeared the term "machine" was used instead ("one of the new machines at the show is the Gasmobile"). The motorist's dissatisfaction with the flying carpet look of the classic runabout came out in the vehemence of his rejection of it once a satisfactory alternative had been found. The most popular of the new vehicles were those in which horse-drawn lines were least apparent and those which displayed their mechanical nature most overtly. According to *The Horseless Age*, November 13, 1901:

> Nothing better shows the fickleness of public taste, and the complete change of which it is susceptible in a very short time than the enthusiasm that is displayed this year over carriages of the extreme "un-horsey" type, which would have been derided a year or two ago.

The meaning of the change was instinctively recognized by everyone. The prominent front hood gave the automobile a symbol, phallic and aggressive, to express what the horse had stood for in earlier days. The appearance of the new cars was likened to the railway locomotive, with its exposed cranks and long snout. In 1901 this resemblance was often mentioned in derision—front-engined cars were called "hideous road locomotives"—but by 1903 the comparison was welcomed. By then some people seemed to want their cars to look like locomotives: the 1903 Grout Steam Tonneau actually had a cow-catcher mounted in front.

Front-engined appearance coincided significantly with the beginning of a "speed craze." In the early days, cars were designed for people who wanted only enough power in their cars to climb hills safely, to negotiate mud, and to maintain a reasonable pace of 15 miles per hour over most roads. This suited most of their owners, but not all of them. Charles Duryea, in a letter to *The Horseless Age*, May 24, 1899, quotes the opinions of one of his customers on the subject:

> When I first received my vehicle it would do about eight miles per hour, and I was immensely pleased. . . . The satisfaction, however, was short until more speed was desired. By reboring the cylinder and changing the gears I manage to coax out sixteen miles per hour under good conditions now, but I wish it was thirty-five.

When asked if thirty-five was not stretching the matter a little he replied, "Not at all. When one sees several miles of clear road ahead he enjoys shooting it at the highest speed possible."

With the new form of automobile, motorists became insatiable in their demands for power. Six or eight horsepower would not do; they wanted thirty or even forty horsepower if they could get it. *The Horseless Age* commented, February 24, 1904:

> The extraordinary popular demand for high-powered cars is one of the most marked features of the automobile industry . . . it is interesting to conjecture as to the cause of this state of things. . . .
> High-powered cars imply high speed capabilities, but in view of the universality of speed restriction it is impossible legally to make use of this quality. . . .

While the conservative editors of *The Horseless Age* pretended not to know why people wanted power, most manufacturers seemed to understand perfectly the impulses of people like Duryea's customer. In addition to having more power, many of the new cars were equipped with muffler cut-outs which gave a slight increase in power and, even better, allowed the driver to enjoy the ear-shattering noise of the engine while thundering down a country road at top speed.

Newspapers and magazines carried stories of unidentified young men who were seen driving at terrific speed through towns, scattering chickens and terrifying the populace. Their cars were invariably red or yellow, and they drove with the muffler cut-out open. It was described how the local police scarcely had a chance to blow their whistles as the machine rushed past, and the outrage of righteous citizens at such "scorchers" was amply reported. How shocking! How glorious! Thousands of readers secretly wished to have been the anonymous one.

Many manufacturers were reluctant to change the whole mechanical configuration of their cars for something new and untried, but it was clear that the old runabout style would not sell. An interim solution was to graft the appearance of a front-engined car onto an engine-under-seat chassis. Specifically, this

1903 *Oldsmobile Tonneau*

involved the addition of a hood, and usually also an increase in the wheelbase. The great popularity of these peculiar hybrids suggests that the buyers did not care what was underneath as long as the external appearance was appealing.

In 1902 or 1903 the imitation did not have to be very good in order to be acceptable. The only real necessity was for the car to have a hood, whether it looked capable of containing an engine or not. The 1903 Oldsmobile Tonneau, for example, had a small box grafted on to the easily recognizable curved dash body. The radiator is not prominent, and the lever steering and the flywheel visible under the seat indicate at once that this is the same old runabout, thinly disguised.

A more sophisticated duplication of stylish appearance in a small runabout was the 1903 Dyke. This car had the usual single-cylinder engine under the seat, but was fully decked out with a dummy hood of fashionable shape complete with louvred sides and a forward-jutting brass headlight. Note also on this car the folding steering wheel, which facilitated access to the racing-type bucket seats.

Enthusiasm for the look of a front hood led many owners of

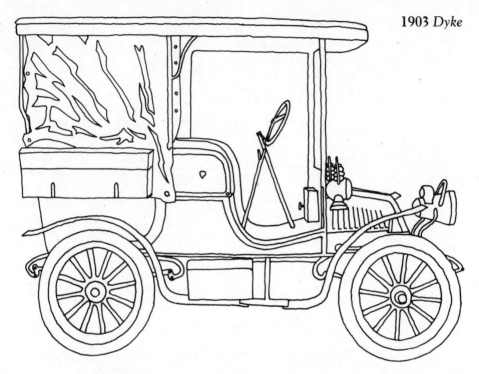

runabouts to restyle their cars. The following letter, written to
The Horseless Age, March 16, 1904, is typical of many:

> Will you kindly inform me in your next issue whether the front
> end of a car, like the Cadillac, Ford, or Knox, can be provided
> with a hood . . . with the object of improving the appearance
> of the car, without injuring the mechanism. . . .
>
> A Subscriber

Some readers sent in descriptions and photos of their modified
cars. Usually their efforts resulted in small appendages similar to
that on the 1903 Oldsmobile, which apparently fulfilled their
symbolic purpose satisfactorily.

Dummy hoods were generally designed to be used as storage
space, but their shape was not very suitable for this. At most, they
were able to contain little more than a simple tool box. One
disadvantage was that, by 1904, the radiator was usually mounted
in front, making the space so hot that it was useless for most forms
of luggage. Sometimes they were used for oil and fuel tanks, but

the radiator heat also caused problems for this. A few realistic manufacturers frankly recognized their function as pure cosmetic, and simply omitted any means of access to the space inside.

Between 1902 and 1904 the style of the new cars was rapidly refined. In 1901, when the front-engined look first came into favor, U.S. manufacturers quickly set out to provide cars which would meet the new tastes. Because their own tradition gave them nothing to build on, most of them set out to copy European designs. Since European cars were rapidly changing in this period also, the alteration of basic forms and the proliferation of new style features were bewildering to the car buyer. From one year to the next, practically nothing which characterized a car's appearance seemed to stay the same.

The most important new motif to appear in this period was the honeycomb radiator. It was first used on Cannstadt-Daimler cars in the late '90s (before they were renamed Mercedes), but it came to the attention of the general public when it appeared on the first Mercedes racing cars. In 1901 these cars staged a startling upset over the favored French machines at the Nice–La Turbie hillclimb, the premier event in a week-long race festival at Nice, and their features were extensively reported. The next summer a refined version of this car, driven by Count Zborowski, placed well in the Paris-Vienna race.

The new radiator was more efficient, which saved weight by allowing less water to be used, but its neat and finished appear-

1901 *Mercedes racing car*

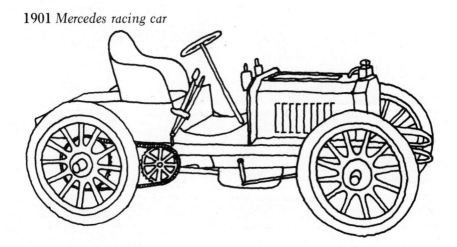

1902 *Mercedes racing car*

ance recommended it even more strongly than its functional advantages. Instead of hanging low near the front axle, like the former flanged-tube type, it was shaped to form the front of the hood. By straightening the hood line it gave a square, aggressive look to the car.

The appearance of the Mercedes radiator, rather than its inner construction, was the first thing to be imitated in this coun-

1903 *Peerless*

try. The 1903 Peerless was thought to be "one of the finest appearing models brought out this year," according to the April 11, 1903 issue of the *Scientific American*, principally on account of its long, box-like hood. Its conventional coiled-tube radiator was raised up to form the front of the hood. The hood sides were extended to conceal the radiator from the side view, but when viewed from the front it still did not have the smooth surface of the true honeycomb type.

The looks of the honeycomb radiator were popular from the first, but initially it was expensive, leaky, and difficult to fix. The idea of making the radiator form the front of the hood caught on immediately, but it was a few years before real honeycomb radiators were used on many cars. The 1904 Rambler, for example, had a radiator surface covered with holes big enough to put a finger into.

In 1903 and 1904 manufacturers developed unique hood and radiator shapes to distinguish their cars. Packard, in 1904, first introduced the famous radiator form that they would keep for half a century. Half-round and rounded top/flat-sided hoods were popular, and a few cars, like the Franklin and National, used fully rounded barrel-like hoods. By 1905 radiators which resembled the Mercedes type were in the majority.

The rear-entrance tonneau body appeared on U.S. cars at the same time as the hood, and the two features were almost invariably combined. More seating capacity was greatly appreciated by owners of two-passenger runabouts. The popularity of touring, or long sightseeing expeditions by car, was rapidly growing; and for this, parents, children, dog, camping equipment, tools, spare tires, and a dozen other things had to be crammed into the car every day for a week or more. This feat was flatly impossible with a runabout, and would be thought impossible with any car but for the undeniable fact that people often did it.

Early tonneau bodies would contain people, but they were often quite uncomfortable. In all but the biggest cars the seats were the size of kindergarten chairs, and passengers sat bolt upright with their chins practically on their knees. "I have often wondered," wrote J. C. Brandes to *The Horseless Age*, April 1,

1904 *Pope-Toledo*

1903, "how people of larger dimensions than Barnum & Bailey's living skeleton could squeeze into such sardine boxes." Because the rear passengers were slightly behind the rear axle, bumps in the road were amplified.

The cramped dimensions were caused by the proportions of the chassis. Builders were reluctant to lengthen the wheelbase too much because it would make the car less maneuverable, and would put more strain on the chassis. The hood had to be long to enclose the engine and also for the sake of appearance. As a result, the steering wheel was at least midway between the axles and usually aft of this, and the front seat was just forward of the rear wheels. The rear seat just had to be wedged into the remaining space as well as possible.

The first major improvement in the tonneau body was the "Roi des Belges" style. Leopold II, the Belgian king who financed Stanley's trip to the Congo, was an avid motorist. When ordering a new body from Rothschild et Cie., the Paris coach-builders, he complained that the rear seats in all the projected designs were too small for his portly figure. Legend has it that his mistress, Cleo de Merode, was the one who suggested that the rear seats be made to resemble some huge stuffed chairs that happened to be in the reception room. The body for the king's new Mercedes was accordingly built with a wide, bulging tonneau which overhung the rear wheels. (*The Horseless Age*, 10/21/13; also see Anthony Bird: *Antique Automobiles*)

Technically, a Roi des Belges body not only had large rear seats, but was built with a voluptuous tulip curve in the rear profile like the 1904 Pope-Toledo. The name had such a rich sound to it, however, that manufacturers quickly extended it to cover any car with a large rear tonneau, and then by degrees to any car with a tonneau body at all. Only by 1905 or 1906, when curvaceous bodies on automobiles began to go out of fashion, was the term again restricted to bodies with double-reverse-curved backs.

In 1902 the public suddenly began clamoring for tonneau bodies, just as they did for front hoods. The builders of small runabouts dutifully supplied them, though the combination of this body with an engine-under-seat chassis was often dangerous and impractical. The first problem was footroom: the engine took up the space where the feet should have been, so the rear seats practically rested on the floor. This is an early example of "design for the legless," which later was to become an American automotive tradition.

Another problem was weight. The feeble single-cylinder engines of the runabouts were sometimes hard pressed when carrying only two people. The added load of the empty body was enough to slow the car noticeably, and when the rear seats were occupied the performance was reduced even further, so that, in the driver's mind, a slight upgrade loomed like the skyward inclination of a yak-trail in the Himalayas. Even so, it was all right if the trip was successfully completed, but sometimes it was not.

1903 *Ford Model A*

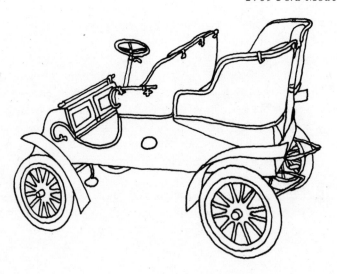

Two extra passengers put such an added strain on the chassis that a big bump often broke the frame or the axle.

Efforts to compromise created the most frightening problem of all. Manufacturers designed a convenient removable body, which could be put on when passengers were carried. Ordinarily it was left in the garage, and the car was then a light, sporty runabout with a stylish sloping rear deck. Advertisements stressed the ease of detachment ("only three bolts to undo"); unfortunately, these rear tonneaus had a terrifying tendency to self-detach at high speed, dumping the hapless passengers into the road. This lugubrious incident was common enough to inspire editorial comment in *The Horseless Age*, August 13, 1902.

Even though the rear entrance tonneau body was a lot better than having no rear body at all, its shortcomings were clearly seen even in the early days of its popularity. The "Roi des Belges" curves and bulges helped, but it was still uncomfortable and cramped. The rear door let passengers out into the road, which was often covered with ankle-deep mud. Another problem was that the placement of the door made it impossible to design a light and practical folding top.

The advantages of side-entrance bodies were recognized early, and in fact many were built on early mid-engined chassis. Their design came straight from the surrey, a horse-drawn vehicle with front and back seats which could carry from four to six

1904 *Packard*

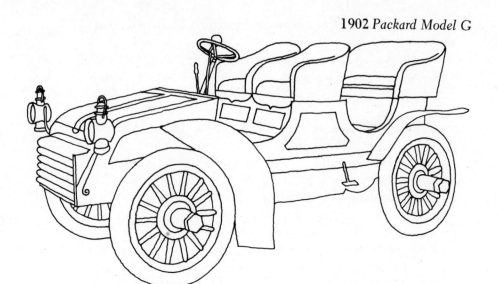

people. A late example of a surrey-bodied automobile is the 1902
Packard Model G. Following the fashion, this car had a dummy
hood in front, but the engine was under the floor. The front seat
was mounted ahead of where it would be on a front-engined car,
and this allowed room for a side entrance to the rear seat forward
of the rear wheel.

Several things related to the change in mechanical configuration combined to make the surrey obsolete and to delay the introduction of second-generation side-entrance bodies. One has already been mentioned: the standard proportions of front-engined
chassis pushed the body way to the back of the frame. Also, wheel
diameters had increased between 1900 and 1904. A third problem
was the use of side-mounted chain drives, which had come into
use by 1904 through European racing influence. Passengers enter-
ing from the side into a chain-driven car were likely to be smeared
with grease, even if they were agile enough to clamber over the
obstruction of the housing.

An early solution to the problem is the arrangement used on
the 1904 Regas. This front-engined car had the customary proportions of that year and used chain drive. Access to the tonneau was
through a side door which formed the bottom of one front seat;
when the seat was tipped forward, an opening appeared. This did

let passengers out at the side, but it was not satisfactory: a movable front seat would have complicated the design of a folding top, and the passengers still had to be athletic to climb in and out. The Regas had few imitators.

The real impediment was the short wheelbase. If it could be extended another foot or two there would be ample room for a side door. Arguments of practicality were put forth by manufacturers to justify short wheelbases, but perhaps the most important reason was that they were afraid people would not like the looks of a longer car. The rear-entrance type already looked radically elongated compared with a buggy, and they felt that a car that was much longer still would be rejected as freakish. To a motorist of 1903 it might look as awkward as an airport limousine looks to us now.

As it did so often in this period, the impulse for change came from Europe. As early as 1902 a few side-entrance tonneau bodies were made for Panhard-Levassor and other European luxury cars which already had long enough chassis to allow room for a side door. The trend gradually spread to lower-priced cars, and most European touring cars of 1904 had side entrances. Pictures of these cars were shown in the U.S., and soon the fears of domestic makers were found to be groundless. After a short adjustment period, American motorists decided they liked the looks of the new long cars with side entrances much better than the old style.

As in the winter of 1901–1902, U.S. manufacturers in 1904 had to develop new and quite different models almost overnight in order to keep pace with public tastes. Feverishly they worked out new steering geometries, stronger frame designs, and the exact arrangement of the body that they would use. Wheelbases were stretched an average of 15 to 20 inches. In some cases, chain drive was dropped in favor of shaft drive to allow more room for the rear door. New tops were designed to take advantage of the absence of a central rear door. In early 1904 side-entrance touring cars were still thought to be a novelty, but at the New York Auto Show in January 1905 they had swept the field. The exhibits included sixty-six side-entrance types and only fifteen rear-entrance types.

One can appreciate how much the appearance changed in this year by comparing the 1905 Thomas with the 1904 model. The new car is much longer, and when seen on the road it looks comparatively huge. The frame rails are practically twice as deep as before, and the folded top extending out at the rear increases the visual effect of length. The 1905 car is also notable for its Roi des Belges body, its sporty searchlight mounted inside the dash, and the combination of a windshield with a folding top, which was unusual for that year.

The enlargement of cars for 1905 can only be partly explained by the need to have a side door to the tonneau. It also represented a new concept of how big a car should be. Sometimes a change in scale can be as startling as a change in proportions. One gets a strong feeling of this when walking through a chronologically arranged exhibit of old cars. Those built after 1905 seem nearly as long as modern cars, and of course are much higher; most earlier ones are tiny by comparison.

Up until 1903 very little progress had been made in weather protection for motorists. Early runabouts sometimes had buggy tops, but since they were open in front they did not help much. Accessory makers offered rubber lap robes, but these were messy and inconvenient. In the early days, effective protection from the

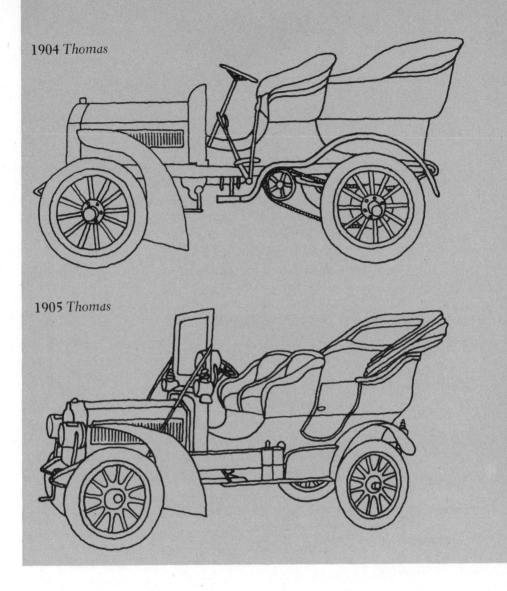

1904 *Thomas*

1905 *Thomas*

elements depended primarily on one's choice of foul weather gear.

In 1903 the canopy top first appeared, and was welcomed by motorists. One of these is shown on the 1903 Autocar. Also called a surrey top, it is a semipermanent wood frame construction supported by metal rods mounted on the body. A "glass front"

1903 *Autocar*

1903 *Duryea*

1903 *Packard*

or windshield was mounted on the dashboard, and sometimes a second windshield was placed behind the rear seat to protect the passengers from eddies of dust. In bad weather curtains could be hung on the sides. Generally these were made of rubber, making it impossible for tonneau passengers to see out, but at least the interior was kept dry. Weather curtains are mounted on the 1903 Dyke shown earlier in this chapter. As well as the more obvious advantages of the canopy tops, touring enthusiasts appreciated the additional luggage space provided by the roof rack, which supplemented the meager capacity of wicker baskets hung on the sides of the tonneau.

Also in 1903 the first U.S. built closed passenger cars appeared. One of these was the 1903 Duryea Doctor's Vehicle, designed to be a convenient and comfortable all-weather vehicle for doctor's use. More popular, however, was the limousine, another European invention. This car was designed to be driven by a chauffeur. It had a closed rear body compartment with a central rear door, and a canopy or canvas top over the driver's area. The 1903 Packard is an attractive example of this type.

These early closed cars had many disadvantages. One was cost: they were entirely handmade, and were so expensive that only the very rich could afford them. They were also very heavy. Usually the bodies were made with wood framing covered with, sheet aluminum. In any case, their weight had the effect of a manacled ball and chain on the performance of even the most powerful cars. Elegant limousines invariably seemed to sink hub-deep in mud when they strayed beyond well-paved city streets.

Some shortcomings of the limousine were shared by cars with canopy tops. Windshield wipers, for example, were far in the future, so when it rained the driver who was in a hurry had the awkward choice of either opening the windshield and receiving the torrent in his lap or keeping it closed and plunging blindly onward, trusting to luck that no one equally foolhardy was coming the other way. Visibility to the rear and rear quarters was nonexistent in a canopy-top car with its curtains up, and was poor on most limousines. Though lighter than a full limousine body, the canopy top weighed enough to hurt the performance of some cars. Also, it had to be either left in the garage or mounted in

1905 *Rambler*

position; it could not be taken down and stowed in the car on sunny days.

On the side-entrance touring cars of 1905 a new kind of top appeared. Called a Cape Top or Cape Cart Top, it was made of fabric and was mounted on a folding frame. One of these is shown here on a 1905 Rambler. Compared with the canopy top it was light and inexpensive, and its folding feature endeared it to tourists. Even though the protection it gave from rain was still not very good, its users seemed to be fairly satisfied. The same general design remained in use for nearly ten years without major changes.

With the arrival of the front-engined, side-entrance touring car, automobile appearance reached the first major plateau in its evolution. In the previous decade the auto had rapidly developed from a motorized buggy, through the intermediate stages of a small, neat runabout and a lumpy-looking rear-entrance tonneau machine, to the graceful shape exemplified by the 1905 Packard touring car.

Generalizations on the role of style in this early development are hard to make. Sometimes public tastes accelerated functional improvement, sometimes they retarded it. Frank Duryea and others worked hard to conceal the working parts of their vehicles, an aesthetic improvement that was also unquestionably a functional one; but the overall influence of style considerations on automobiles built before 1900 must be considered a negative one. The conservative public wanted automobiles to look like horse-drawn vehicles, and in yielding to this pressure, builders made their cars too light for adequate strength, and too short and high for either riding comfort or directional stability. Early preference for the "horse-drawn look" also delayed the introduction of the "French form" of the front-engined car, which gave better weight distribution and accessibility and allowed more freedom in body design.

After 1902 style preference had a more positive influence. The great switch in taste in favor of the "French form" accelerated its adoption in this country. The new configuration must be counted as a functional advance, though the fad for dummy hoods on mid-engine chassis, which also resulted from violent public enthusiasm for the front-engined look, certainly cannot be. As might be expected in this formative period, a great many of the changes in auto appearance before 1905 cannot be related to style considerations at all, but were due entirely to functional needs.

The addition of fenders, windshield, and top, and the strengthening of the frame and wheels, giving a heavier look to the automobile, had little to do with style, and the adoption of the tonneau body was prompted by the practical desire to carry more passengers. In retrospect, the obvious and rapid functional development of cars in this period tends to overshadow the role of style, making it seem as if functional improvement were the only goal of the automaker; but the maker had to sell cars to stay in business, and *The Horseless Age* remarked, August 19, 1903:

> The fact is that the average purchaser of today . . . sees only the general form of the car, and the outside finish. . . . the bulk of orders, therefore, go to the maker who offers a car of satisfactory appearance . . . at the lowest possible price.

Then, as always, considerations of style and function went hand in hand.

2

The Age of the Touring Car

From the introduction of the side-entrance tonneau in 1905 to the development of the popular-priced closed car in the early '20s, the open five or seven-passenger touring car reigned supreme. Its form was so well suited to its function that, for more than a decade after its inception, no one seriously proposed any alternative to it for basic transportation needs. Not only was it overwhelmingly the best seller, but the concept of the touring car was at the back of the designer's mind all through this period when he set out to design a new car: closed cars were conceived as touring cars with tops, and smaller open cars were regarded as touring cars which happened to be on a reduced scale. Only the sporting two seater, the electric, and the motor buggy were unique types rather than touring cars with added or subtracted bodywork.

Before 1906, most style changes were at least partially the result of functional requirements, but with the stabilization of the basic touring car shape people's attention turned toward more decorative than functional aspects of car design. The average buyer of a car in 1906 was quite pleased with the looks of his new car. Rapid progress had been made in the previous few years in evolving a functional form and refining its proportions. This was only the second year of the side-entrance tonneau, and its novelty had not yet worn off. Wheelbases had continued to grow, and his car was longer and sleeker looking than the same model of the previous year. Certainly it made even the most expensive rear-entrance car of 1904 look dumpy and old-fashioned.

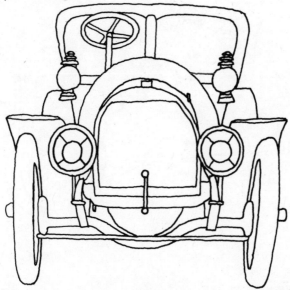

There was still room for improvement, however, in both the decorative themes and the general proportions of the new cars. Around 1906 people decided that the exuberant use of brass and bright colors which had characterized the appearance of the earliest front-engined cars was in bad taste. On August 22, 1906, *The Horseless Age* observed:

> . . . signs apparent of a tendency toward more modest body colors and a little less lavish use of bright work of all kinds . . . the use of (brasswork) in excess is nothing less than vulgar.

The first full cycle from sobriety to flamboyance and back again was thus completed, following the ancient laws of fashion long since established in the fields of art, architecture, and dress.

Motorists also began to dislike the appearance of cars with radiators set well ahead of the front axle. On earlier cars where the engine and body were heaped onto a short chassis this problem was unavoidable, but in 1905 and 1906, when wheelbases grew longer, people began to object to cars which looked like the 1906 Grout. They gave the impression of lumbering heavily onwards headfirst, and looked clumsy and truckish compared with a

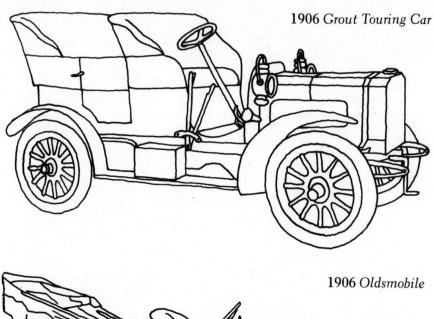

1906 *Grout Touring Car*

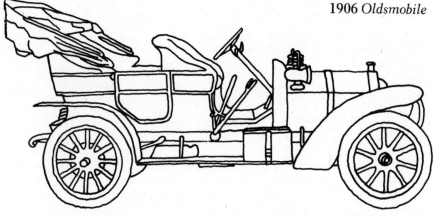

1906 *Oldsmobile*

car like the 1906 Oldsmobile. The front wheels of the Olds seem to reach forward eagerly while the rest of the car crouches behind.

Public preference for the radiator-over-axle position slowly gathered momentum, until by February 4, 1909, *Motor Age* could say that:

> . . . the old custom of having the radiator anywhere from 6 inches to a foot in front of the axle is practically obsolete . . . the maker has realized the importance, from a

standpoint of car control, appearance, and other ways, of locating the radiator either directly above the axle or to the rear of it.

The adoption of this radiator position had little to do with functional considerations, in spite of the vague implications of the *Motor Age* writer. Moving the radiator (and the engine) backward in a chassis of a given length actually reduced "car control" or stability by giving the car a tail-heavy weight distribution. It made the body cramped, and forced the rear-seat passengers to sit in an uncomfortable position right over the rear axle. In short, it was an anti-rational development in defiance of practicality. Nevertheless, it was so compelling from an aesthetic standpoint that, once established, it became an inviolable standard of appearance for almost a quarter-century.

Another thing in need of improvement in 1906 was the design of front fenders. Most cars of that year used fenders similar to those on the 1906 Grout. On earlier cars they had looked all right, but as cars grew longer and sleeker their abrupt rise over the wheels began to look out of place. A more pleasing shape was introduced on the 1907 Mora, in which the fender was extended back past the dashboard. On September 5, 1906, *The Horseless Age* made special note of the "peculiar racy type of front mud-

1907 *Mora Touring Car*

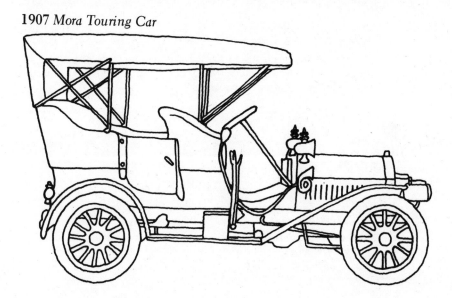

guards" on the Mora, and motorists were enthusiastic about their graceful appearance. In a year or two the new style had almost swept the field.

To the dismay of the editors of *The Horseless Age*, and to the secret joy of almost everyone else, the speed craze which had begun with the introduction of front-engined cars had intensified by 1906. Cars rapidly grew bigger, faster, and more exciting looking, and motorists became more wasteful in their purchases and more reckless in their driving. Hordes of people seemed to have utterly abandoned themselves to their lust for fast cars. "Glorious, stirring sight!" murmured Toad, in *The Wind in the Willows*:

> The poetry of motion! . . . Here today—in next week tomorrow! Villages skipped, towns and cities jumped—always somebody else's horizon! O bliss! O poop-poop! O my! O my!

By this time the large touring car had lost much of its sporting associations and young "scorchers" wanted a more expressive machine in which to make their illegal and exhilarating high speed runs. The result was the "High Powered Runabout" or "Gentleman's Roadster," which was a veritable catalog of symbols expressive of power and speed.

> Their appearance is in itself an advertisement that they were built for unlawful speeds. No doubt such cars are capable of legitimate employment . . . . Nevertheless, the presumption seems reasonable that in the vast majority of cases the purchaser of one of these rather ridiculously overpowered rigs acquires it solely that he may travel public highways at extremely high rates of speed.

So sniffed *The Horseless Age*, January 2, 1907.

An early example of this type is the 1906 Thomas Runabout. It was made primarily for two people, who sat in racing-type bucket seats, and it had a large engine with a lot of power. It could do all that a "scorcher" required in the way of performance, but it did not look right: the radiator hung heavily over the front axle, the front fenders were too abrupt and the rear ones too delicate, and the overall proportions showed that it was only a reworked

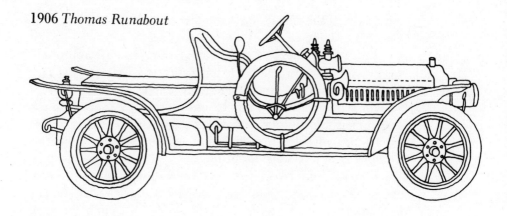

touring car after all. It had a practical air about it which was fatal—one suspected the folding seats in the rear deck even before they were shown.

By 1909 designers had learned to make the Gentleman's Roadster as exciting to look at as it was to drive. Every line and detail of the 1909 American Simplex spoke to the emotions. Its long, sweeping front fenders lunged forward past the radiator, which was mounted in a rakish position behind the front axle. The steering column was set at a low angle, and the seats hugged the frame just forward of the rear axle. There was no compromise with practicality in this car—it was made for two passengers who wanted to go fast, and considerations of comfort and weather protection were beneath the attention of its designer. Racing practice was recalled by the oversized gas tank mounted in a conspicuous place behind the seats. To give a windswept look to

1909 *American Simplex*

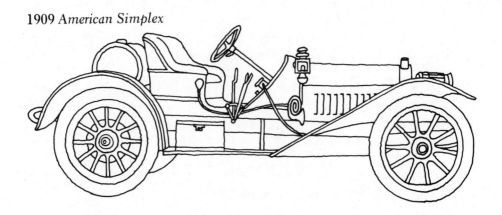

the middle of the car, and to add to the visual length of the hood, a metal cowl curved back past the driver's feet.

In 1906 the country was in a wave of prosperity, and newly wealthy motorists rushed out to buy flashy and exciting cars. This use of money seemed unsound to many conservatives: it was very well for people to buy sober and useful touring cars, because these gave honest value for the money, but to spend $3,000 or $4,000 on a machine built solely to gratify emotions seemed rather immoral. The owner of a touring car could look you in the face and give you his reasons for buying the car: there was room in it for the wife and family, it had a reputation for reliability, it would help him in his business, and so forth. All the owner of a High Powered Runabout could do to explain his choice was to mumble "I liked it because it was red" and gurgle engine noises in his throat. What kind of foundation was this, people wondered, on which to build a giant industry?

The economic slump of 1907 seemed to justify the conservative attitude. The unstable condition of the auto industry which made it susceptible to economic fluctuations was blamed on the unsound principle of buying cars for emotional reasons, and the High Powered Runabout was the symbol of this habit. An editorial on December 11, 1907, in *The Horseless Age* gloated:

> After a sound scourging the automobile industry will soon revive. Not so the methods of its past. They are gone. . . . Automobiles can no longer be sold by the beating of tom-toms, the smashing of speed records, and . . . windy puffery. . . . The people who are now buying want efficient service and useful work for their money. . . .

Written less than a year before the introduction of the Model T Ford, this piece was in some ways prophetic, but in predicting the elimination of emotion from car buying it was quite wrong. After a very brief lull the tomtoms were heard again, and the sale of Gentleman's Roadsters regained a brisk pace by 1909.

Parallel to the development of expensive machines like the Thomas and the Simplex was the creation of small, low-priced imitations. Some of these were outright copies, which exactly reproduced all the features of the big cars in miniature. Others were basically economy cars which had a few racy details added on.

1906 *Ford Model N Runabout*

1908 *Buick Model 10*

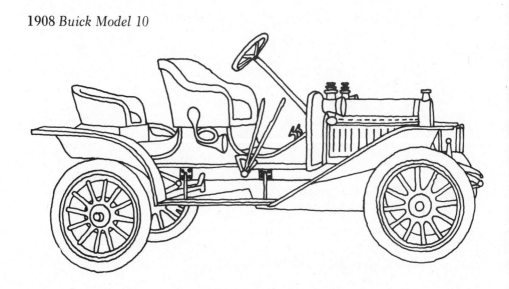

An example of the latter type is the 1906 Ford. This car has a stylish boat-shaped rear deck, but it was far more suitable for a country doctor than for a hot-blooded "scorcher." A compromise type is the 1908 Buick, which is obviously a simple variation on the touring car chassis, but which succeeds better than the Ford in giving a sporty impression. The long fenders help in this, as does the mother-in-law seat in back. This seat was originally built so that a mechanic could accompany wealthy gentlemen on their high speed runs. But then its function changed. On June 17, 1908, *The Horseless Age* commented:

> As body design was developed, it became recognized that this seat, if properly proportioned, added greatly to the appearance of the runabout, and it is probably as much for this reason as on account of any useful purpose it serves that this type of seat has been adopted on so many recent runabouts.

Outright imitation of expensive runabout appearance is shown by the rakish 1909 Hupmobile. Costing only $750, it included almost every style feature of the Simplex.

Because its design was not closely tied to practicality, the Gentleman's Roadster was sometimes used as a proving ground for new styling ideas. An interesting example of such a "dream car" is the 1907 Aerocar, introduced in the summer of 1906. The stated purpose of this design was to reduce wind resistance, and by contemporary standards it looked wild and futuristic. The "original shape of the body . . . is hard to describe in words," said *The Horseless Age*, May 23, 1906. Its most notable features were the way the hood smoothly flared out at the rear to blend with the body, the revolutionary front doors, and the fenders. "The fenders are best described by the term used by the designer, Mr. Dietrich, who calls them 'sail shape.' " All of these things were generally disliked in 1907. After only one year the body was scrapped, and the succeeding model was thoroughly conventional.

There were many men who longed for a High Powered Runabout but whose consciences forbade them to buy a car of such evident impracticality. Nor did they want a large, comfortable touring car, because a car like this, which is truly practical, always has a depressing way of looking so. What they really

1909 *Hupmobile*

1907 *Aerocar Runabout*

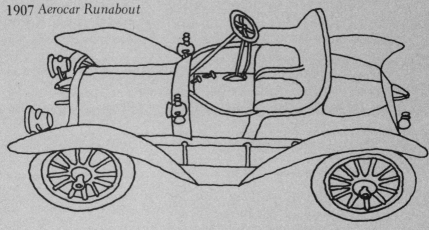

1908 *Aerocar Runabout*

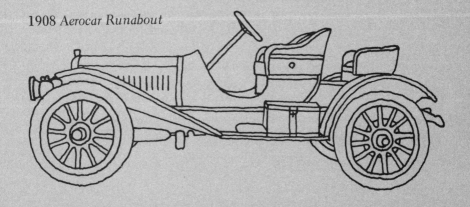

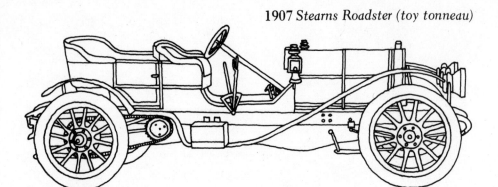

wanted was a High Powered Runabout masquerading as a touring car: a wolf in sheep's clothing. Some small suggestion of utility had to be included for the sake of the buyer's conscience, but the basic car could be as close to his unbridled imaginings as his pocketbook would allow.

Such a car was the 1907 Stearns. This type was variously called a toy tonneau, baby tonneau, or pony tonneau. It embodies the essential symbols of speed: the driver is well aft of the wheelbase midpoint; the steering column is set at a low angle; the front fenders are long and graceful; and the radiator is set well back. One hardly notices the miniature tonneau tucked in behind the front seats. The tonneau seats were child-sized even on a big car like the Stearns, but nevertheless they qualify it as a four seater, which, in theory at least, makes it a suitable car for family use.

Between 1907 and 1910 toy tonneaus grew rapidly in popularity. Sometimes they were High Powered Runabouts with small rear appendages, like the Stearns, and sometimes they were essentially touring cars which had slightly abbreviated bodies, like the 1910 Marion. Either way, from a functional standpoint they were less satisfactory than a standard touring car. There was usually little legroom and no luggage space in the tonneau. Motor magazines probed the motives of people who bought them and concluded that most owners had only slight familiarity with any seat other than the driver's, since practicality was often cited by owners as one of the strong points of the toy tonneau style.

1910 *Marion Toy Tonneau*

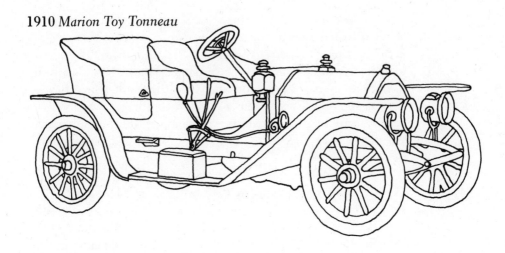

In 1907, after several years of behind-the-scenes development, the high-wheeled motor buggy creaked its way onto the American scene. Powered by a feeble one or two-cylinder engine and driven by a crude chain or rope drive, it seemed to deny all the automotive developments of the previous decade. Its arrival was sudden, and its popularity grew rapidly. By 1908 thousands of the wheezing, spidery vehicles were pouring out of hastily built factories all over the country.

1908 *Menard Auto Buggy*

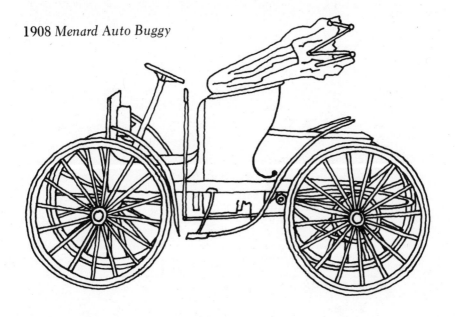

In their public statements, the designers of motor buggies claimed to have been motivated by purely practical considerations. Casting aside current tastes in auto appearance, they set out to make the best possible vehicle for farmers and others who lived in rural areas, and the motor buggy was the result. One of their central arguments was a dubious claim that buggy wheels gave better traction than conventional automobile wheels. Aside from this, the vehicles were certainly lighter, simpler, and cheaper than the usual type of car.

On the balance, however, their practical shortcomings were overwhelmingly greater than their advantages. The basic construction was not nearly strong enough, and the tall wheels with hard tires were particularly unsuited for a motorized vehicle, both because they were too weak and because (in spite of claims to the contrary) they gave too little traction. The whole scale of the design was wrong: if the vehicle was capable of more than about 20 miles an hour it would collapse on rough roads, but if it had less power than required for this it could not drive itself out of mudholes and up hills. Its light weight could not compensate for its fragility and lack of power.

Advertisements for motor buggies mentioned only utility, but the impractical design of the vehicle suggests that the reason for its popularity lay elsewhere. Its most enthusiastic supporters were farmers, particularly in the Middle West. They had viewed the arrival of the automobile with distrust, but as time went on they were forced to concede its usefulness as a means of transportation. Nevertheless, its complexity made them uneasy, and they especially disliked its unfamiliar appearance.

It was a happy day when the farmer opened a Sears Roebuck or International Harvester catalog and saw the motor buggy. The sales talk printed under the picture was reassuringly sensible, but it was the picture that really sold him. There it was—a buggy! Its high wheels and piano-box body made it unmistakable, yet it had the useful features of an automobile. A buggy was something the farmer knew. Maybe these had motors attached, but even so they were fundamentally the same vehicle as the type he had used all his life, and their low price removed the last doubt from his mind. He ordered one.

In 1907 and 1908 the outward appearance of motor buggies

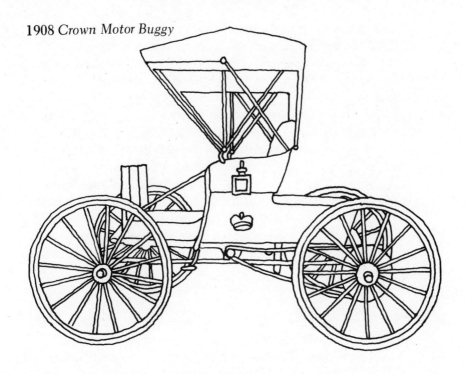

was characterized by close imitation of horse-drawn vehicles. Not only were the high wheels the same, but they used piano-box bodies, flat (usually leather) dashes, and buggy-like moldings around the seat. The engine was usually well hidden, but the drive mechanism to the rear wheels was exposed in most cases. The mechanism was clearly not entirely integral with the buggy part. The split personality of the original Haynes-Apperson, with the active part separated from the passive, was duplicated here. If the two had been merged it would have become an automobile, but the open chain or belt showed that it was still just a motor-driven buggy.

In 1909 and 1910 some manufacturers of motor buggies changed the appearance of their vehicles in the direction of standard automobile practice. Inconspicuous steering levers were replaced by steering wheels, and sometimes the whole front-engine configuration was used. The one unalterable feature was the wheels, which were invariably high, frail-looking, and solid-tired.

The Age of The Touring Car 59

If all the features of a buggy that do not carry associations with the good old times are pruned off, it seems that only the wheels remain. These are the symbols of a buggy, and their familiar appearance was a comfort to the farmer in his first experience with the automobile.

In 1910 the demand for motor buggies slackened, and by the end of 1911 they were almost entirely out of production. Reasons for their demise are not hard to find. By 1910 thousands of farmers had discovered that the step from the horse to the automobile was not as difficult as they had expected, and much of their former prejudice had disappeared. Also significant was the introduction of the Model T Ford in 1908. The supremely practical design of this car threw the deficiencies of the motor buggy into glaring relief. When the Ford agency opened in Gopher Prairie the motor buggy was doomed.

The styling of electric cars was another retrograde movement which ran counter to the general course of development. Up through the turn of the century there was no real difference in appearance between gasoline, steam, and electric cars: all were built on the standard runabout pattern. Then, in 1901 and 1902, public tastes swung strongly in favor of front-engined touring cars, and makers of gasoline and steam cars remodeled old designs or introduced new ones to conform to the change.

With very few exceptions, the makers of electric cars did not. One reason, of course, was that their cars would not benefit functionally from a similar alteration in configuration, but aesthetic considerations had even more influence on their decision. The masculine, aggressive appearance of front-engined touring cars was not suited to the personality of the electric. Compared with steam and gasoline cars, electrics were clean, quiet, and easy to drive, but their top speed of about 20 miles an hour and range of 50 miles or less made them decidedly unappealing to the sporty set. Most electrics were used by women and old people, and few were seen outside of cities.

The years immediately following the introduction of the frong-engined touring car were bad ones for the electric car. Electric commercial vehicles, such as delivery vans and milk trucks,

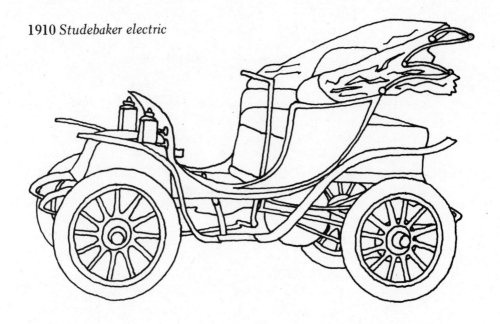

found a ready market, but the sales of passenger cars declined. No one could decide what the "image" of an electric should be. Certainly it could not be a powerful road-devourer like the gasoline car. Magazine editorials doubtfully suggested that it be considered a "park vehicle" to replace the carriage in Sunday tours around the park. This would indicate that associations of wealth and dignity were suitable for it, but the role was not concrete enough for the image to take hold.

After the initial excitement over touring cars had died down, it appeared that there was still a small but regular market for conventional electrics. From the manufacturer's standpoint, the best policy seemed to be to pretend that time stood still. In 1910, for example, Studebaker blandly presented a car which, except for its modest front hood, would not have turned any heads in 1898. Year after year, the most successful makers of electrics were those who seemed impervious to the passing of time.

The market was small, however, and it took nerve to resist innovation. Every season some manufacturer would panic and bring out an electric powered imitation of a gasoline car. January 20, 1909, *The Horseless Age* noted that:

The Age of The Touring Car 61

. . . there is a very strong tendency towards the production of electric cars which look as much as possible like gasoline rigs and are controlled in a closely similar manner. . . . There is something rather artificial and modish in all this. . . .

The type of gasoline car most often imitated was the High Powered Runabout, and the duplication was quite exact, even to the details of the radiator. Not surprisingly, the public recoiled from such gross deception, and these vehicles were never popular. Throughout the electric car era, when a manufacturer of electrics was about to fold, its corporate death-rattle was usually signaled by the introduction of an imitation gasoline car.

A reprieve for the electric car came when it was mated with a closed body. By 1908 or 1909 the cost and weight of a closed body had been reduced to the point where its use was feasible on an electric chassis, and by 1910 electrics which looked like the Baker were quite common. Electric coupes had the distinct "image" which open electrics had always lacked: they were rolling boudoirs, highly suitable for fashionable women to drive.

Their design showed an emphatic renunciation of the masculine values on which gasoline car appearance was based. The gasoline car was built to express power and speed: the massive

1910 *Baker electric*

hood was its muscles and the exposed levers, chains, and shafts were its genitals. The electric, by contrast, was modest and discreet. It had practically no hood, and did not show either direct or symbolic means of motion. The "flying carpet" look which men found unpleasant delighted the sort of woman who wanted fig leaves put on statues in the museum. To her the noiseless movement of an electric was an expression of feminine mystery.

Once the essentially feminine character of the electric coupe had been recognized, it was quickly refined to make the image more complete. Curtains were made for the windows, which even when drawn back gave some suggestion of modesty and aloof seclusion. The interior was upholstered in brocade or other elegant material, and flower vases were invariably supplied. Appointments and interior decoration were the focus of annual style changes in electrics, because the negative spirit behind their external design removed the impetus for development there.

The Prince Henry Tour, organized in the hope of forming friendships among European royalty, turned out to have more effect on car design than on international relations. Like the Newport money-aristocracy of America, European royalty included many ardent motoring enthusiasts, and the Tour provided a way for them to meet and talk over their motoring experiences. Or so the theory went; but in practice the automobile has rarely been successful as a catalyst of human relations, and it was not so then. Noses raised high, the monarchs arrived on the scene with the finest motorcars their countries' industries could produce.

The trouble was that the Tour was competitive, *very* competitive. In its general scheme, it was similar to the American Glidden Tour—a test of reliability. The Prince Henry Tour, however, had a special test where the cars were timed over a high speed run, and success in the speed test made a significant difference in the car's overall point score. The result was an emphasis on high-speed performance that was absent in the Tour's American counterpart.

The most dramatic product of this competition was the streamlined "torpedo body," featured on a German Daimler which participated in the Tour in 1908. The innovation created

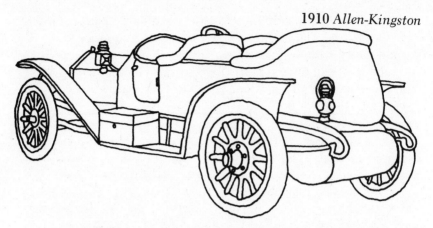

much excitement, and was soon copied by enthusiastic American designers. One of the first American versions was the Allen-Kingston, introduced in September 1909. The general shape of the body is influenced by hydrodynamic principles, and its smoothly flared cowl and its rounded, tapered back express speed in an unmistakable manner.

The most revolutionary feature of the body, however, was its front doors. Before this time doors were never used for the front seat of a touring car, except for low half-doors on a few Oldsmobile models. Part of the reason was the sporting spirit of motoring that still existed at that time. Many motorists felt that if you wanted always to be comfortable, you should stay at home, and if you wanted to go motoring, you should do it in a properly vigorous manner. They regarded front doors with the same condescension that many people felt fifty years later for the golf-cart. Their stated arguments against front doors concerned only practicality, however: they contended that the doors would make the front compartment hot and stuffy in the summer and that this was worse than being cold in the winter.

By the time of the New York Auto Show, in January 1910, several other manufacturers had joined Allen-Kingston in offering torpedo bodies. All of these featured front doors, and many of them had round, bulging backs on the tonneau. More complete enclosure of the passengers was accentuated by the use of very high sides on some models. While body sides usually came approximately to the height of the bottom of a man's rib cage as he sat in the car, on some new torpedo bodies the sides reached up to shoulder level. Another development in the spirit of streamlining was the omission on most torpedo bodies of outside door handles.

Torpedo-bodied cars at the show were surrounded by crowds of gaping people, and were photographed and described by a thousand newspapers and magazines, but after the initial uproar had subsided it was discovered that very few people had actually bought them. The focus of the dissatisfaction was the rear end: long, tapering tonneaus like that on the Allen-Kingston were almost universally loathed.

The motoring public was also uneasy about what seemed to be a slurring of the distinction between the body and the hood. The Allen-Kingston showed some flat dash area, but its tapered cowl came uncomfortably close to the shape of the hood. In people's minds the body and hood were two quite separate things: the former was the part which descended from the buggy, the passive container of passengers; the latter was the horse part, the source of motive energy and symbol of power. Most people liked the way this separation in function was shown by the abrupt divider of a flat wooden dashboard.

The most popular product of the excitement over torpedo bodies was the "fore door body." This was little more than the earlier "straight line body" (top line of hood and body sides on the same level) equipped with front doors. If a fore door body had no side moldings or external door handles it was called a "flush-sided body." The effect of the change can be seen by comparing the 1910 Haynes, which has a straight-line body, with the 1911 Stafford, which is the flush-sided type. Both cars have a flat wooden dash running across the body at the back of the hood. The only

1910 *Allen-Kingston Torpedo Body-cowl area*

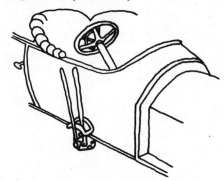

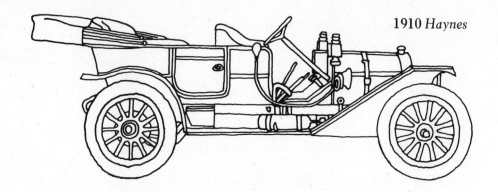

1910 Haynes

real difference between them is in the body sides: the Haynes carries moldings which define the separate elements—the rear door, seat, and seat support—and has no front door, while the sides of the Stafford are one smooth plane, broken only by the narrow cracks around the doors. Front doors helped the appearance of a car by eliminating the "chopped in two look" of earlier designs, and the combination of this and their practical advantages made them nearly universal on touring cars by 1911.

1911 Stafford

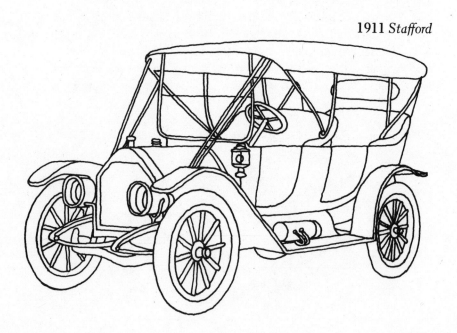

On the clean panels of the flush-sided body, exposed side levers looked messy and out of place. It was clear that they must be moved inside the body, but at first there was some confusion about where they should go. Drivers liked to work levers with their right hands, and since most cars had right-hand drive, this meant that the levers had to be squeezed between the driver's right leg and the body side. This was uncomfortable and inconvenient. Some makes mounted the levers in the middle of the car, but right-handed drivers protested. By 1912 manufacturers realized that with American traffic regulations, where cars keep to the right, it was easier to maneuver with left-hand drive anyway, and in that year most cars had the wheel on the left and the levers in the middle.

The clean lines of the torpedo body also drew attention to the clutter which had accumulated on the runningboards. When the first "continuous fenders" appeared in 1903 and 1904 they were free of obstructions except for the chain drive housings on some cars. Then around 1906 the Presto-o-Lite system of acetylene lighting came into general use, and the cylindrical gas generator was put on the runningboard. By 1908 bodies had become so low that there was no longer enough room under the seats to put the tools, and tool boxes appeared on the runningboards as well. By then the area was a jungle of odd accessories, such as scissor-

1911 *Packard Touring Car*

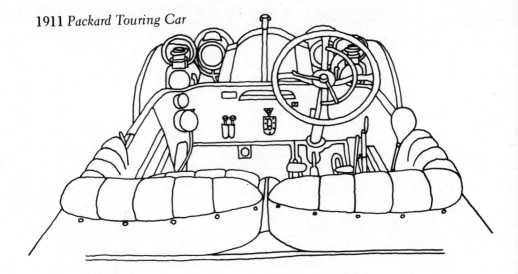

action extending fences which kept luggage from falling off, boot scrapers, extra horns, and much else.

One reason for the haphazard appearance of the accessories was that they were often not supplied as standard equipment by the manufacturer, but either offered as factory options or purchased by the owner from an auto accessory maker. When lights, windshields, and horns were adopted as standard equipment they were integrated into the total design. In 1912 the runningboards were swept clean: tool boxes were usually sunk in the apron, and when Prest-o-Lite tanks were used they were put there also. As a side benefit of electric starting systems, many cars switched to electric lighting in that year, making the Prest-o-Lite tank obsolete.

In Europe, evolution from the torpedo to the "streamline body" took place rapidly. In 1912 an Opel shown at the Brussels Show had a completely smooth taper from the body to the hood and showed no flat dash area at all. In this country the development was much more gradual, moving through several clearly defined intermediate stages toward the same end result.

In 1911 and 1912 practically all American touring cars had flush-sided bodies like the 1911 Stafford. By 1913 most cars had adopted electric dash lights, and usually these were countersunk in the dash, as on the 1913 Premier. By this time the term "torpedo body" was out of fashion; stylish cars like the Premier were said to be the "streamline type." The changes in the basic body

1912 *Opel Torpedo*

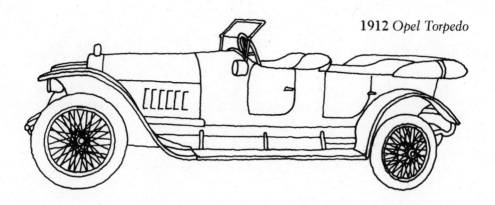

shape from the Stafford to the Premier were in lengthening the cowl about six inches and rounding off its square corners. In 1914 the exposed dash had become too small to carry lights, and running lights were either omitted or built into the headlights. Some cars had a vestige of the old flat dash, like the 1914 Winton, but others took the final step to the "fully streamlined body," like that on the 1914 KisselKar.

In this country it was clear that designers would not give up the flat dash without a struggle. On the 1914 Winton, for example, it would have been just as easy to build the body with no break at the cowl, but a smooth transition was not wanted. "The streamline effect," remarked *Motor Age*, January 30, 1913, "in its extreme form . . . seeks to have an unbroken line from the extreme front back to the very rearmost point. The beauty of such design is to be questioned." Associations from the past again intruded on present aesthetic preferences: originally the dash was the leather front of the buggy which shielded passengers from road mud and the filth of the horse. When front-engine hoods replaced the horse the dash remained in its old place, now protecting passengers from the grease and fumes of the engine. From 1902 to 1913 the flat wooden dash was a sturdy demarcation between the "horse" part of the car and the "carriage" part. There was a kind of logic in its presence, and people were reluctant to part with it.

In 1910 and 1911 renewed interest was shown in wire wheels. They were nothing new, of course, having been used on many early runabouts, but the strength and simplicity of the wood artillery wheel had pushed them off the market by 1902 or so. Their revival first came in England, and the Daimler and one or two other makes supplied them as standard equipment in 1911.

Initially the argument in favor of wire wheels centered around their supposed practical advantages. Their advocates made loud claims for their strength-to-weight ratio, and backed them up with pseudoscientific experiments in which wheels of both types were crushed in hydraulic presses. There were equally loud replies by supporters of wood wheels, who were photographed triumphantly lifting crushed wire wheels out of their own

1913 *Premier Little Six*

1914 *Winton Six*

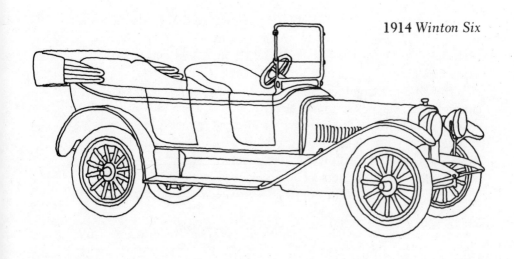

hydraulic presses. A parallel claim was made that they improved tire life 15 percent, 50 percent, or 100 percent, depending on the test. Phrases such as "up to XX percent," and "as little as XX percent" appeared frequently in these presentations. The main reason given for better tire life with wire wheels was that they were more resilient. But then someone "proved" that wooden wheels were actually more resilient than wire ones! The weight of the lightest possible wire wheel was compared with the heaviest wooden wheel, and so on.

All of this had a negligible effect on public preference. Their widespread adoption on passenger cars depended on their aesthetic appeal. People would not buy them if they thought they were ugly, and at first this was the case. *The Horseless Age*, September 14, 1910, pointed out that:

> . . . the most important objection . . . is probably the question of appearance . . . it becomes a very open question whether it is worth while spoiling the appearance of the car to a very large extent . . . few people consider the appearance of the wire wheel attractive.

As time went on, however, this view began to change. Their associations with very high-priced and impressive European makes like Daimler and Rolls-Royce helped. Also, because they actually were slightly lighter for a given strength, they began to be used on racing cars, and this gave them a sporting flavor. In 1913, when they first appeared in appreciable numbers in the U.S., public reaction was hesitantly favorable. In a description of one 1913 car, on January 5, *The Horseless Age* remarked, "The sporty appearance of this car is topped off with wire wheels." An article in the same journal on April 30 gave a good summary of the general feeling at that time:

> From a selling standpoint, perhaps appearance is of as great importance as economy. Many people at first object to the wire wheel, probably because they are not accustomed to it. At the same time the very novelty of the thing attracts many others. Certain it is that wire wheels attract much attention wherever they are seen.

By 1915 they had been accepted as the most stylish type of wheel, and were used on high-priced limousines and all sporty models. They were optional on most medium and high-priced cars, and on cars which did offer them they were always shown in advertisements instead of wood wheels.

They never quite conquered the field, however. At the auto shows a large proportion of the cars were exhibited with wire wheels, but the number of cars so equipped which were seen on the street remained low. One reason was price, another was practicality: even at this time, most of the average man's driving was done on dirt roads, which turned to mud at the first drop of rain. Cleaning mud out of wire wheels was a tedious job.

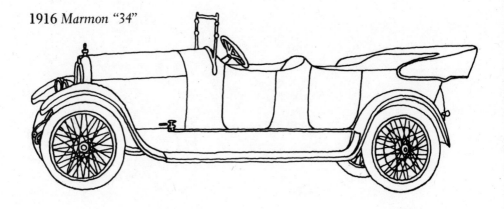

1916 *Marmon "34"*

Equally important, perhaps, was the aesthetic problem. Many people were never persuaded that the wire wheel looked as attractive as a wood wheel. The appearance of the 1916 Marmon partially explains this feeling. Cars were looking heavier every year, and the deep, barrel-chested appearance of the Marmon's hood and its thick crowned fenders made it look as massive as any. The light, delicate wire wheels clash with the heaviness of the rest of the car in a way that artillery wheels do not. To overcome this problem, some makes offered optional artillery wheels finished in their natural wood color. Like wire wheels, these were exotic and expensive-looking, but their substantial appearance blended well with the rest of the car.

Official disapproval by the press and vehement opposition by wives and magistrates failed to stunt the evolution of the High Powered Runabout. In 1911 Simplex built a car that could accelerate from rest to 60 mph in under 20 seconds and reach a top speed of nearly 90 mph. In a slightly less expensive class was the Mercer Raceabout, a direct descendant of the successful Mercer team racing cars. When new it was guaranteed to do a mile in 51 seconds, which works out to a fast 70 mph. Compared with the 1909 American Simplex mentioned earlier, its seat is still lower, hardly more than a thin cushion set on the floor, and its steering column is even flatter. The Mercer shown here has a huge searchlight mounted on the dash. Another option was a rakish-

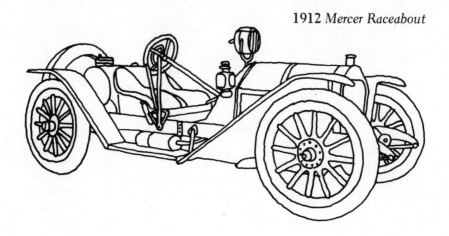

looking and quite ineffective round "monocle" windshield clamped to the steering column.

The Mercer was the culmination of an earlier visual tradition in which the relations of the components—hood, seat, steering column, and wheels—and the curve of the fenders were the expressive elements. This tradition was superseded on touring cars by the streamlining school, which was principally concerned with the flow of lines running from the front to the back of the car. This caused a dilemma for designers of cars like the Mercer: as the years went by, the bare-essentials, completely open sports car would inevitably begin to look old-fashioned. Yet the addition of a larger, streamlined body to the classic model would rob it of some of its essential character.

For several years manufacturers simply avoided making changes. The 1915 Stutz Bearcat, for example, does not look very different from the 1912 Mercer. But as time went on, the appeal of these cars gradually waned, and sales dropped. Stutz and Mercer, the two principal makers of High Powered Runabouts in the teens, took the inevitable step of clothing the old chassis with more enveloping bodywork, but the tough, rugged look of the earlier models was gradually lost. The companies increasingly turned their attention to more popular and prosaic body types. By the late teens, the High Powered Runabout, the racing car with fenders and lights, was almost extinct.

74 *Automobile Styling Since 1893*

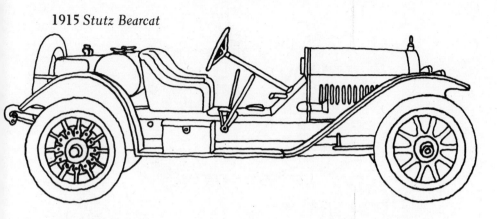

1915 *Stutz Bearcat*

The history of early automobile styling was periodically marked by outbursts from a reactionary segment of the motoring public, which had viewed the automobile's noisy intrusion into the world with dismay. They resented the swift and unsympathetic way that it had put the horse out to pasture and the carriage into storage. In the boisterous progress of the automobile they felt that the dignity and charm of horse-and-carriage days were lost.

While granting the practical advantages of the automobile, they expressed their dissent in retrospective styling motifs that recalled the good old days. For the farmer, the motor buggy had been such an expression; for the city dweller, the electric had served a similar purpose. The conservative factions watched grimly while the motoring world was shaken by torpedo bodies and streamline cowls; finally, in 1911 and 1912, unable to stand it any longer, they retaliated by introducing the "Colonial Style."

According to *Motor Age*, January 30, 1913, these designs, in spirit, recalled "the features of the old colonial equipages. They suggested the days when men wore lace cuffs and powdered wigs." In appearance the Colonial Style reflected an attempt to graft onto the automobile the old-fashioned elegance associated with Early American architecture and antique furniture. The style was only applied to closed cars. The 1911 Chalmers Colonial Coupe carries most of the distinguishing features of the style. The side windows are made up of small square panes of glass, beveled at the edges to look thick. Old-fashioned lamps hang near the roof. The basic body shape is reminiscent of a stagecoach, and its emphasis on verticality and sharp edges is a vehement rejection of

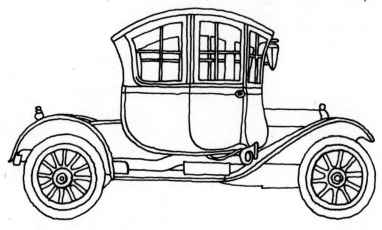

the theme of motion and power, on which most body designs were being developed. Small details continue the resemblances: the door handles are like drawer handles on an antique bureau, and the interior decoration suggests antique furniture. Names such as "Martha Washington Coach" were used. The Colonial Style never attracted a wide following, but it was popular enough to last until 1916 or 1917.

What people wanted, at a time when car appearance was still evolving rapidly, was some link with the past which would make the new styles more familiar and thus easier to accept. For this purpose some early horseless vehicles were equipped with whip sockets; and the carriage-like adornments of the Colonial Style helped also. But these were reversions to the static forms of buggy and carriage, and as time passed, they risked looking ridiculous. For many motorists it was enough that a new car had a family resemblance to earlier models; as long as the evolutionary steps from one model to the next were plainly evident, the buyer was reassured that the apparently radical trend of car design was not out of control.

For this type of motorist Packard had the most attractive appearance. From year to year it was instantly recognizable by its distinctive radiator shape, first used in 1904. Also, beginning around 1909, Packards began to have a calculated out-of-date look: they never looked really old-fashioned, the way the Colonial

Style did, but neither were they the first to employ advanced styling motifs. In 1909, for example, when long front fenders were in vogue, Packard retained the old-style flared fenders. By 1911 the fenders had been changed, and a fore-door body was introduced, but instead of smooth body sides the Packard had new "Victoria Lines" which defined the front and rear seating compartments. These heavy moldings, which became known as "Packard Pillars," recalled similar lines on early rear-entrance tonneau bodies. As the rest of the motoring world was rocked by one fad after another, Packard stood fast. In the December 30, 1915, *Motor Age* annual pictorial review of the 1916 cars, the Packard is the only one shown which has heavy moldings on its sides and which does not have a smooth transition from hood to body.

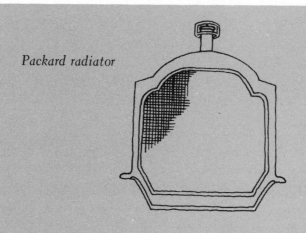

Packard radiator

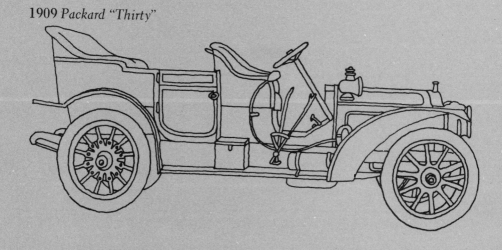

1909 *Packard "Thirty"*

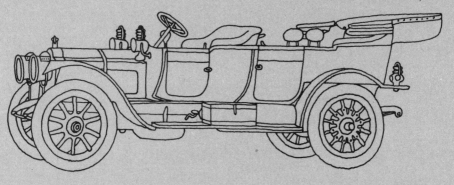

1911 Packard "Thirty"

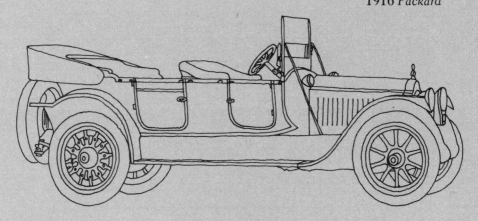

1916 Packard

By lagging slightly behind the latest developments, Packard offered the perfect balance of good taste and aristocratic disregard for mere novelty. Year after year it was praised for its handsome appearance, and sales were consistently good. The difficulty of this achievement should not be underestimated. Although it worked very successfully for Packard, as a general rule outdated body styles are the quickest way to bankruptcy for an automaker. The details must be carefully chosen. Packard delayed changes in fender shape, side decoration, and cowl design, but kept pace with the competition in making the body lower. It is also significant that the Packard was a luxury car, competing with Peerless and Pierce-Arrow in the upper price ranges. Its conservative policies probably would not have been successful if applied to a medium or low-priced car.

Excitement over the development of the streamline body between 1910 and 1914 drew attention away from variants of the basic touring car. The toy tonneau, which had been very popular around 1910, had disappeared by 1912, and the sort of light runabout with a mother-in-law seat exemplified by the Buick of 1908 had also become scarce. By 1914 the practical, newly streamlined, five or seven-passenger touring car dominated the field.

By 1915 the drama of the streamlined body had been acted out, and the public was ready for something new. In low-priced cars the demand was partially answered by the sweeping sides of the boat body, an attractive style shown on the 1915 Saxon. This, however, was just a slight variation on the touring car theme; also needed was a new general type of car, a new size or configuration which could escape the utilitarian associations of the touring car and express what the powerful and aggressive-looking toy tonneau and High Powered Runabout had before.

One solution was offered in the dual-cowl sports phaeton body, as shown on the 1915 Mercer. The second cowl running across the car behind the front seat divided the body into two exclusive compartments. The low overall height of this car was enhanced by crowned fenders which wrapped closely around the wire wheels. The hood met the body without the quick flare at the

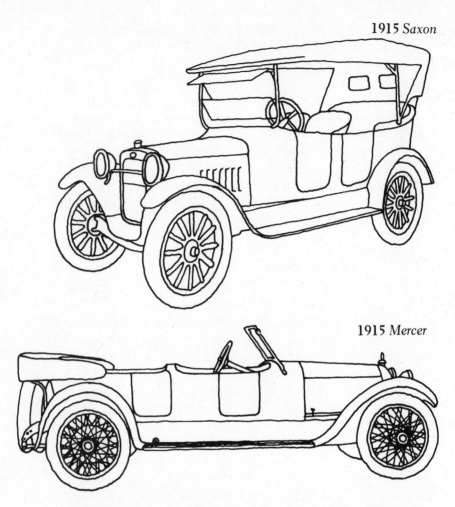

cowl that most streamlined cars had, and the body surfaces flowed smoothly around the passenger compartment openings. A raked-back windshield continued the general effect of speed. Instead of the usual color scheme of black for the fenders and color for the body, it had fenders and body the same color.

Even though the Mercer could carry four or five people in comfort, it had none of the workaday personality of a touring car. In spirit it was the descendant of the toy tonneau, having most of the sporting flavor of the 1907 Stearns while offering more room and comfort for back-seat passengers. It was one of the sensations of the 1915 season, and was widely imitated in the following year.

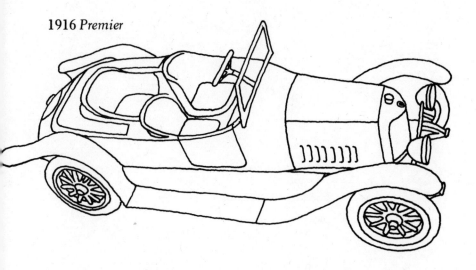

In spite of the imitation, however, the beauty of the original design continued to make it stand out. On January 11, 1917, *Motor Age* said, "The Mercer might perhaps be classed as having one of the best touring body designs in the show . . ." even though it had been changed very little in the two years since its introduction.

Another new type of car was the cloverleaf roadster. It got its name from the placement of its three seats in the form of a cloverleaf, as on the 1916 Premier. Although its configuration recalls the runabout with mother-in-law seat like the 1908 Buick, in spirit it was a more practical type. All seats were placed within the wheelbase and could be enclosed by a top. Unlike the dual-cowl sports phaeton, it was as successful on low-priced cars as on high-priced ones, and it enjoyed great popularity in 1915 and 1916.

In 1917 many cloverleaf roadsters were enlarged so that they could carry four passengers, like the 1917 Liberty. This made a stylish car which could carry two people in comfort and two more in more-or-less acute discomfort. The seating arrangement was just the same as the toy tonneau, except that the newer car had only two doors, making it necessary for passengers to clamber over a folding front seat or squeeze through the center aisle in order to get into the back. Editorials on the four-passenger roadster, like this one in *Motor Age*, January 11, 1917, used almost the same words as those of 1910 on the toy tonneau:

The Age of The Touring Car 81

These four-passenger jobs are not four-passenger touring cars. There is not sufficient comfort in the rear seats to warrant taking a week's tour with four passengers. These vehicles have practically no space for baggage. As two-passenger jobs they are very satisfactory. . . .

To enliven the appearance of the practical everyday car, designers have always tried to graft onto it associations with more exciting vehicles. The most common source of inspiration has been the racing car, and several style features of the late teens can be traced to it. A representative racing car of the time is the 1917

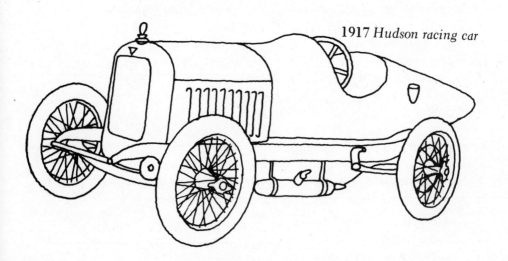

1917 *Hudson racing car*

Hudson. Its appearance is dominated by a high hood and radiator. The driver's seat is so low that he can barely peek over the top of the cowl. Wire wheels are used, and from one side of the hood protrudes an exposed exhaust system.

The appearance of a high hood such as the one on the Hudson had wide appeal, and every year the hoods on production cars grew higher. The most popular cars were those on which the hood looked high without being freakish. At first it was enough simply to raise the hood and radiator, but by 1916 they had become so high on a few cars that they began to block the driver's view of the road, and other visual means had to be used to emphasize the same effect. One successful solution is shown on the handsome 1916 Stutz Bulldog, in which the body sides are cut slightly lower than usual to make the hood look higher in contrast. Another common way of creating this appearance was to lengthen the runningboards forward and make the front fenders very short and closely wrapped around the wheels. The powerful, rugged effect this gives is shown by the 1916 Marmon.

Racing practice had an influence on more superficial aspects of passenger car appearance as well. Some fancy sports models like the 1918 Velie carried racing type exposed exhausts. This car also has individual fenders over each wheel and no running boards, following the practice of some European sports cars. Omission of the runningboards gives the same deep-bodied look as the runningboard and fender design of the Marmon.

1916 *Stutz Bulldog*

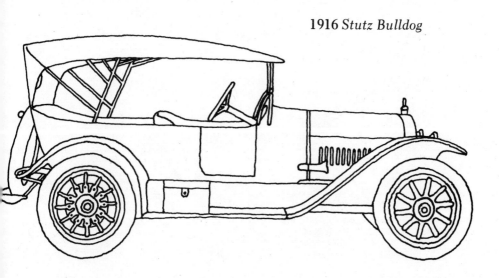

1918 *Velie Sport*

The great increase in overall size that began with the first front-engined cars and continued through the introduction of the side-entrance tonneau, carried on all through the period covered in this chapter. The quickest growth was in the years up to 1908. The Model T Ford, which was introduced in 1908, had a 100-inch wheelbase, which was as long as many very expensive cars in 1904. It was also lower than most cars built four years earlier, but the change in this respect was not so readily apparent.

The 1913 Knox shows how big some luxury cars had become by then. The Knox did not compete with Packard and Pierce-Arrow but was in the upper-middle price range. Its 130-inch wheelbase was not unusual for such a car in 1913, though it was longer by

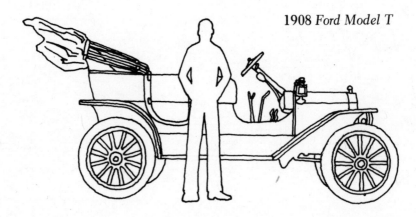

1908 *Ford Model T*

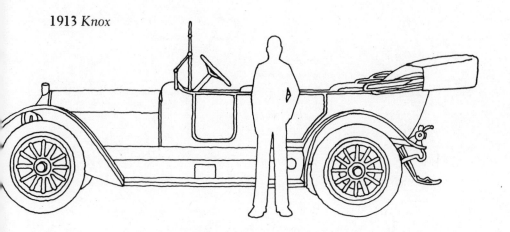

a foot or two than a comparably priced car of 1908, and would dwarf even the biggest domestic cars of 1903.

The 1920 Tulsa was an average-sized car for that year with a 117-inch wheelbase. It was fairly low in price, competing with a large number of cars in the range just above the Ford. Comparison of the Ford with the Tulsa gives a fair idea of the median growth between 1908 and 1920.

In 1917 closed cars constituted less than five percent of total auto production. The rest of the cars made were open models, and an overwhelming majority of these were five or seven-passenger tour-ing cars. Under these circumstances, it is curious to find that many

1920 *Tulsa*

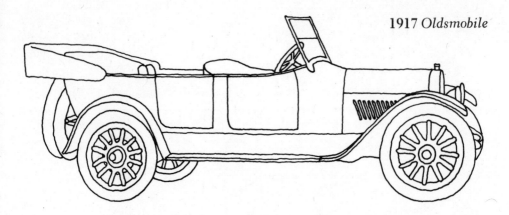

people were then predicting the replacement of the touring car by the closed sedan for everyday use, and even suggesting its extinction as a distinct type. What were the causes of this growing disenchantment with the touring car?

In a roundabout sort of way, part of the problem was aesthetic. The 1917 Oldsmobile, a typical touring car of that year, is well-proportioned and generally pleasing, but it is simple to the point of severity. It has no door handles or side moldings, no air scoops or lights in the cowl, no tool box or other interruption in the line of the running board. On most cars the radiator and headlight shells were enameled, and there was no brightwork at all on the body, but the Olds had an unusual nickel-plated radiator.

Sporadic attempts were made to enliven the touring car design. The bevel-edge body, which had a crease running from the radiator or the windshield to the rear seat, appeared in 1918, and is shown here on the 1918 Studebaker. Like the boat body and the dual cowl, the bevel-edge body helped temporarily to win back interest in the touring car, but in the long run it was no use. People had been looking at more or less the same thing for too long, and they were tired of it.

Even more important than the aesthetic problem was the growing awareness people had of the practical shortcomings of the touring car. The style which in 1906 was thought to be highly satisfactory was criticized in 1919 for being drafty in cold weather, leaky in rain, and generally spartan. This was in spite of the adoption of windshields and side curtains in the intervening years. The reason for the changed attitude was the wider experience of

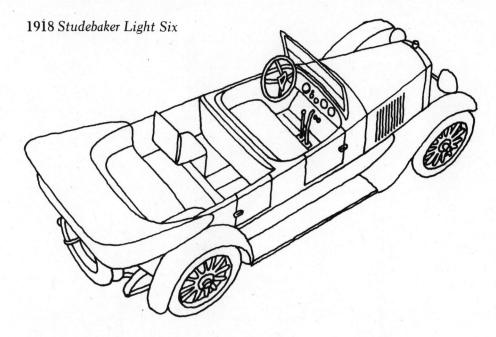

the later motorist. In 1906 few people had ever ridden in a closed car, and by comparison with completely open or canopy-topped cars, their touring car with folding Cape Cart Top was a marvel of comfort and convenience. By 1919, however, almost everyone had ridden in a closed car and could imagine what it would be like not to struggle with ill-fitting side curtains and endure a leaky top whenever the rain came. Most motorists still could not afford a closed car, but they would dream of one. With expectations of increasing personal income and reduction of closed-car prices, many buyers of touring cars in 1919 knew that this was the last open car they would own.

As the price of closed cars came down, the feelings of the motorist about open and closed cars began to alter. Up until the late teens, the closed car was regarded as a luxury type and associated with wealth and distinction. The open car was the cheap, practical working car. By the early '20s, however, this view had changed completely. Then the closed car was the practical one (though it had not lost all its luxury associations) and the open car was looked upon primarily as a sporting type. The decline of a body type from the exotic to the everyday has been common—the

The Age of the Touring Car 87

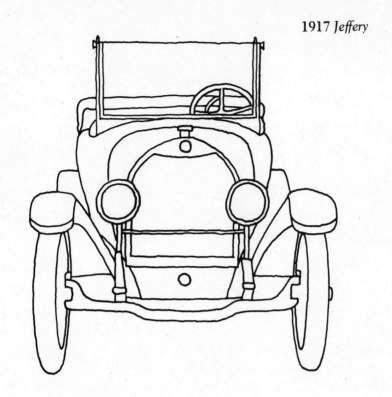

1917 *Jeffery*

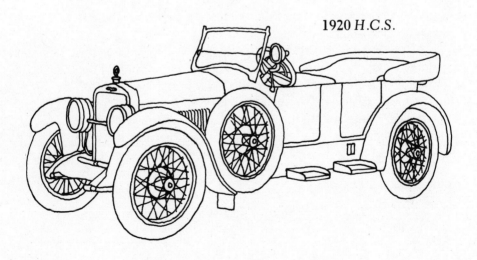

1920 *H.C.S.*

1920 *Amco*

touring car itself had undergone this change—but an instance where the process worked in reverse was unique. "We have no other comparative case," pointed out *Automotive Industries,* January 11, 1923, "in which a model has been superseded by a conversion that changes it from the reliable standby to a pride of fashion."

The altered status of the touring car could be seen before 1920. Though they were still the basic model of most manufacturers, touring cars were shown less and less often in advertisements and magazine articles. Closed cars got the most space, and when open cars were shown there was heavy emphasis on rakish sports models like the 1920 H.C.S. Although touring cars were produced by some companies through the '20s, their concept was fading from the motorist's mind by 1920. As an open type, the touring car was beginning a metamorphosis into the open sports phaeton, while its spirit of economy and practicality was being absorbed by the closed car. The age of the touring car had passed.

3

Closed Cars
and a Touch of Class

Up until the mid-teens, the automobile was generally considered to be a fair-weather vehicle. When winter came, most people jacked their cars up on blocks in the barn, drained the water from the radiator, and waited for spring. A few cars were left on the roads, driven either by fresh air enthusiasts or by very rich people who could afford a closed car. Even these die-hards were city-bound, due to impassable rural roads. In the country, the mare was harnessed up to the buggy, and for a few months it was 1890 again.

The creation of a moderately priced closed car suitable for year-round use was the most important evolutionary development of the 1920s. In the late teens motorists discovered that they could no longer consider the horse and buggy as a reasonable alternative to the automobile. A year-round car was a necessity, and discomfort was not thought to be an essential part of the experience of motoring, as it was in the early days. They wanted a closed car at a price that the average buyer could pay.

The public clamor for cheap closed cars was not at first taken seriously by automakers. Closed cars, they thought, were a luxury, and like other inessential things, subject to fads. Though fashionable this year, they might be forgotten the next, leaving volume makers of closed bodies stranded. But sales figures soon convinced them: from 1919 to 1927 closed cars made up these percentages of total production: 10, 17, 22, 30, 34, 43, 56, 72, 85.

The '20s also saw a basic change in the nature of the automobile business which brought body design into greater prominence. In the early days the main problem for manufacturers was in making cars, not in selling them. Almost anything on four wheels would sell, as long as the price was right. Since a low price depends on high volume, success went to the optimists like Durant at General Motors, who commenced on a sufficiently grandiose scale, or like Ford, who with the assembly line led the industry in production efficiency.

In the '20s the industry came of age. As the supply of cars approached public demand, small builders concentrated on sports or luxury cars or else went out of business. Volume manufacturers adopted Ford's production methods and even improved on them, and expanded to the immense scale that was needed for survival. Good used cars began to take over the low-cost transportation market, pushing new cars up to what was really an intermediate price range, for people who wanted something extra.

The extra they wanted most was, predictably, better styling. As early as 1906, perceptive observers noted that, aside from low price, style was a car's biggest selling point. According to *The Horseless Age*, July 18, 1906:

> So far as the mechanical parts of automobiles are concerned, the great majority of manufacturers have been constantly approaching a common type, and today the differences between the individual makes of cars relate mostly to small details. . . . A tastefully designed body . . . has probably more effect on the commercial success of a model than any other feature of its design. . . .

As production costs became more similar, the prices of cars of comparable size and quality were also necessarily similar, and the appearance of the car became a critically important determinant of a car's sales fortunes. While the changed circumstances did not immediately result in a transformation of the appearance of the automobile, they did force motor executives to take body design more seriously. Designers were gradually enfolded into the corporate bosom, and the importance of their activity was recognized by the creation of styling departments. Car styling was not invented in the '20s (though the word was), but it was made organized and rational.

In 1903 the first American-built closed cars appeared. They were chauffeur-driven limousines, following the European vogue. The limousine was quickly joined by the coupe, an owner-driven closed car for two or three passengers. These two body types dominated the closed car field in the first decade of its development.

Early closed car styling was closely derived from the more popular open body types. The limousine, for example, was simply

1905 *Packard Model N Brougham*

a touring car with a roof built over the tonneau, and the coupe was little more than a boxed-in roadster. One can clearly see the High Powered Runabout which underlies the 1905 Packard coupe.

Even when closed cars first appeared, people objected to the tall and unstable-looking effect of the superstructure. An extension of the roof over the windshield was often used to emphasize the horizontal lines. A lower, longer appearance, plus the addition of sweeping fenders, made the 1909 Packard coupe far more handsome than its predecessor of 1905.

The public image of the closed car made the course of its evolution uncertain in the early years. It was exclusively a car for the very rich, because its hand-built body put its price out of the range of the average buyer. The owner of a closed car was often rich enough to have several cars, so that no single one was needed for all-around use. The open touring car could be used on excursions into the country, the coupe used for errands in town, and the limousine could be reserved for formal occasions like a trip to the theater. For general use the touring car was unpleasant in bad weather, the coupe too small, and the limousine too big. The limousine had the extra drawback of either requiring a chauffeur or isolating the owner-driver from the rest of the passengers.

1909 *Packard*

It was not until around 1912 that a practical-sized closed car designed to be driven by the owner was introduced. The 1912 Cole was one of the earliest and best looking of this type. At the shows in 1913 these cars, variously called berlines, sedans, or coaches, attracted much attention. By 1915 the term sedan was used to describe this body style by all but the most pompous of manufacturers; those who considered the word too vulgar for their elegant vehicles used such terms as "owner-to-drive coach" and "town berlin."

The introduction of the sedan was partly overshadowed by the rapid multiplication of other closed and semi-closed body

1912 Franklin 25HP Landaulet

types at that time. Almost all of these were variations on the limousine theme. One could buy a limousine with a folding roof over the chauffeur and a solid roof in back, or the reverse combination, or one of several other alternatives. The 1912 Franklin Landaulet has a folding rear quarter, a closed center section, and a chauffeur's compartment roofed-over but open on the sides.

Perhaps the most popular model in the early teens was the fully enclosed seven-passenger limousine like the 1914 Haynes. Even though the roof of this car towered nearly eight feet off the ground, complaints were already being heard about the discomfort of low cars, and the Haynes had an arch built over the rear door so passengers could step in without ducking their heads. On January 30, 1913, *Motor Age* said:

> Contrary to the decreasing of body height, there are some designers who are of the opinion that it should be somewhat increased so as to accommodate the aigrettes of the women and the silk or opera hats of the men. . . .

1914 *Haynes*

There was diversity also in the seating arrangements used in closed bodies. Most limousines had a bench-type seat in front for the chauffeur, a large sofa-like seat in back, and two folding jump seats in the forward part of the rear compartment. Sedans usually had separate seats in front to allow access between the front and rear without getting out of the car. But there were many other arrangements, also: sideways facing jump seats, staggered seats to allow more shoulder room, and others. A Peerless show car described in *Motor Age*, January 8, 1914, set a new standard for originality:

> Instead of seats, this beautiful car has individual colonial arm chairs within, which are movable. . . . To get rid of any tendency to jump around due to jarring the movable chairs are heavily weighted in the seats. The construction is said to be entirely practical and at the same time it gives a greater possibility of sociability.

One suspects that the social possibilities of the arrangement would be quickly forgotten on a rough road, with heavily weighted colonial arm chairs leaping and crashing against the sides.

Even though on January 30, 1913 *Motor Age* remarked that for the owner-driver the sedan "leaves nothing to be desired in the closed car field," they caught on with the public rather slowly. The rich customers, as pointed out above, had little use for a general purpose closed car. Less well-to-do motorists were intimidated by the price, and were also reluctant to forego the pleasures of an open car. The development of roll-up windows in the early teens somewhat improved the ventilation of the passenger compartments in closed cars, but it was still pretty bad. One could either roast in the summer or freeze in the winter, and at half the price, most people chose the latter alternative, especially since bad road conditions often made winter driving impossible anyway.

The Springfield Top was one attempt to provide an ideal solution. As shown on the 1912 Stevens-Duryea, this was a folding top with side windows and window frames like a sedan. When closed, it was warm and weather proof; when open it allowed passengers to breathe fresh air and enjoy the view. The problem lay in the process of changing from one to the other. The top itself was not much more complicated than the usual folding top

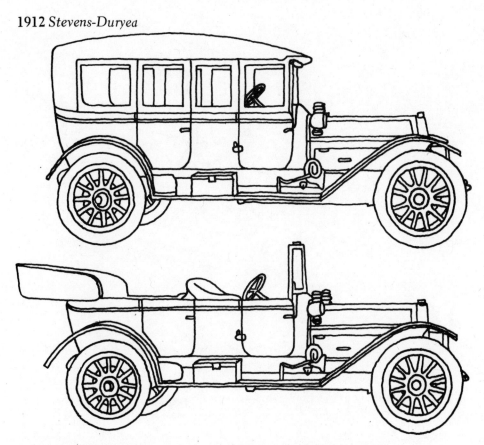

(such a thing being next to impossible) but the windows marked a new high-water mark for complexity. Manipulation of a series of latches, hinges, clips, and sliding tracks allowed them at length to disappear into concealed compartments, from which they provided an infinite variety of rattles and squeaks. The procedure for raising or lowering the roof took so much time and patience that the Springfield Top never had wide popularity. Its price did not help, either: sometimes such a car cost even more than a sedan.

The detachable or convertible sedan body was another attempt to combine the virtues of open and closed bodies in one car. This was a sedan roof which could be attached to a touring car during the winter. In the summer the car carried the usual type of folding top. First introduced on a KisselKar in 1915, this feature quickly caught on with other makers, and in 1916 there

Closed Cars and a Touch of Class 97

was a wide selection of convertible sedans to choose from. Although the basic idea was a good one, and the price was reasonable ($350 extra on a $1,650 KisselKar), this type of body enjoyed only a brief popularity and was almost extinct by 1920. Its principal drawbacks were the inconvenience of installation, removal, and storage; its near-total lack of ventilation when mounted; and the creaks and groans it generated on anything but ideal roads.

The open or touring sedan was yet another approach to the same problem. This was a body with a permanent sedan roof built with folding side pillars like the Springfield Top. Its price was even greater than an ordinary sedan, but with the windows lowered and the pillars removed it provided good ventilation and visibility. Without the pillars, the oblong side openings made the car look long and handsome. One of the first examples of this body was on a Locomobile limousine shown in 1915, and it was offered by a few high-priced makes for several years after this. Unfortunately, the problems encountered with the Springfield Top were also present in the open sedan. As recorded by the *Journal of the* SAE, April 1918, a speaker at an SAE meeting became rather heated on the subject:

A year or two ago somebody thought it a great idea to build a sedan type of body with the center pillars removable. It has not been discovered who originated this, but from a builder's point of view he had better keep it secret, because we are all looking for him. . . . I venture to say that no man who ever bought one ever had the removable pillars out more than once. . . .

A late effort to solve the problem was the California Top, which appeared at the national shows in 1920. As shown on the 1922 Leach, this was a semipermanent top built on a light wooden framework, neatly padded and covered with fabric. Since it was fixed in place it facilitated the design of relatively weatherproof side curtains, which in good weather could be removed and stored in the usual manner. California Tops first appeared on luxury cars and were richly finished with varnished wood framework inside and nickel fittings. In this form they were very expensive (some cost as much as $500 extra), but in a year or two after their introduction cheap versions were being sold on low-priced cars.

The restless search for an all-purpose closed car form was not accompanied by comparable aesthetic advances. Comments on

1922 *Leach*

new closed cars were mostly confined to descriptions of up-holstery material and interior appointments, some of which were indeed remarkable. Interiors were done in suede, broadcloth, leather, or brocade, and the list of luxury features was almost endless. Virtually all limousines had cut-glass flower vases near the doors, curtains for privacy, reading lights, and a speaking tube (sometimes a miniature telephone installation) between the rear compartment and the driver through which one could cry, like one of Fitzgerald's spoiled young things in *This Side of Paradise*, "Turn down this side street, Richard, and drive straight to the Minnehaha Club!"

In designing appointments it was assumed that the owners would use the limousine principally for trips to the opera, and furthermore, that they would invariably be late in getting ready and thus be forced to dress en route. The lady's side was equipped with mirrors, vanity cases with perfume and smelling salts in-cluded, and pockets specially designed for ballroom slippers. One car included gold hairbrushes stamped by Tiffany as standard equipment. The gentleman was assumed to have completed his dressing before departure; on his side was a full smoking set, in-cluding electric cigar lighter, leather tobacco pouch (with to-bacco), pipe rack (with pipe), ash tray, and miscellaneous small drawers for cigars and cigarettes. He was apparently envisioned as a nervous man who chain-smoked to relieve the tension created by his wife's last-minute preparations.

None of this had any effect on the car's external appearance, however. Before 1920 open cars set the pace in styling progress, and the public seemed not to expect dramatic styling in closed cars. In the teens, remarked the *Scientific American* in March 1922, closed cars looked like "a combination of a grand-opera house and a hearse." The people who actually bought them—New York millionaires, Boston Grande Dames, and such people—liked the stately dignity of the vehicles as they were and were reluctant to exchange it for something more modern.

Aesthetic development of closed cars in the teens was con-sequently slow. The only problem egregious enough to stimulate any action was the windshield. It rose like a wall from the back of the hood, presenting to the wind a flat face which looked as big as the side of a house. A vertical position emphasized its height; but

1917 *Franklin*

if it was raked back, it shortened the length of the hood and roof and often made the car look even worse. One unhappy solution, significantly without imitators on production cars, was the vee-windshield introduced on the 1917 Franklin, which looked like the blunt bow of a wooden battleship. The windshield problem was not solved in the teens, and was a source of discomfort to designers all through the '20s.

Public reception of the original Lincoln, introduced in the fall of 1920, indicated the growing influence of body design on sales success. The Lincoln was designed by Henry Leland, whose brilliant engineering ability had given the Cadillac a reputation for excellence. The Lincoln was to be his masterpiece: every component was refined beyond the ordinary standards of the day in order to make the car quieter, smoother riding, and more durable than any other.

Innovation in other areas of the car's design did not extend to its body. As *Motor Age* put it, September 9, 1920, "The body styles

Closed Cars and a Touch of Class **101**

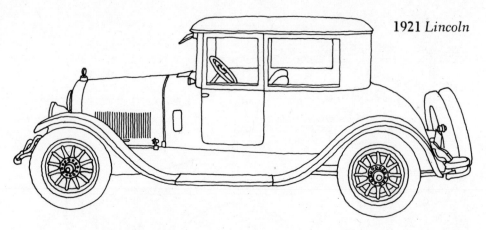

might be described as conservative without radical innovations. . . ." Less tactful commentators would have said it was
dull. Its high roof gave it a dowdy, dated look that was utterly
lacking in distinction. The economic recession which coincided
with the Lincoln's introduction explains only a few of the cancel-
lations of advance orders after the car appeared: practically no
one wanted to pay a high price for a plain car, no matter how
good it was supposed to be. Partly because of this, the Lincoln
Motor Company was in financial trouble within a year of its first
sale. The company was bought by Ford, who immediately expanded arrangements for special bodies to be made by Brunn and
other custom body makers.

In 1922 most motorists dreamed of owning a car with a closed
body. A family discussion in Sinclair Lewis' *Babbitt* sums up the
sentiment of the time. Babbitt has just remarked that he was
thinking of buying a new car:

> Verona, the older daughter, cried "Oh, Dad, if you do, why
> don't you get a sedan? . . . A closed car is so much more
> comfy than an open one.
> ". . . It's got a lot more class," said Ted.
> "A closed car does keep the clothes nicer," from Mrs.
> Babbitt; "You don't get your hair all blown to pieces," from
> Verona; "It's a lot sportier," from Ted; and from Tinka, the
> youngest, "Oh, let's have a sedan! Mary Ellen's father has got
> one."

The opinions of the Babbitt menfolk were divided, but the women were unanimously in favor of the closed car, and in the '20s their views finally began to have some influence on the purchase. The trend toward sedate and refined looking cars certainly owed something to the feminine touch.

Most men wanted closed cars too, however. The obstacle was price: most sedans still cost between 50 and 75 percent more than comparable open models. In the fall of 1921, however, the Essex coach was introduced—a closed car which in many ways was the answer to the motorist's dream. To start with, the closed body at $1,495 cost only $300 more than the touring car. To achieve this amazingly low price the maker abandoned the usual nineteenth century methods of closed body construction and drastically simplified the design. Only two of the wooden frame pieces were curved, and the body had no compound curves; elimination of rear doors, the use of equal-sized windows front and rear, and simpler upholstery design further cut the cost.

The Essex was not only cheap, but it was also unusually good looking, due to its shortened "close coupled body." Smaller than the usual bus-like seven-passenger sedan, but larger than a cramped coupe, its compact shape had an exclusive air about it. December 8, 1921, *Automotive Industries* said.

> The close coupled body has many advantages. It is more sociable. It brings the rear seat forward of the rear axle and therefore makes the riding easier; it . . . offers a more pleasing appearance. . . .

1922 *Essex*

Of the benefits listed, improved appearance was perhaps the only significant one: counterbalancing the stated functional benefits were cramped legroom in the rear seat and difficult entry and exit.

The proportions of the Essex were immediately seized upon by other manufacturers, and in their roster of body types for 1923 most makes had a close coupled sedan. The 1923 Buick shows the handsome effect of this style. In place of the usual ponderous, overhung rear body this car has a trunk which nicely balances out the side view of the car.

In the first years of the automobile, when inadequate wheel strength had been a problem, automakers investigated the potential of the disc wheel. Since it had an even distribution of strength over its whole circumference, it seemed a logical solution, but it was never used on early passenger cars. November 9, 1904, *The Horseless Age* said:

> From an engineering standpoint, there appear to be absolutely no objections against a disk wheel, but we fear that strong aesthetic reasons will be urged against its adoption on pleasure cars. . . . It would appear almost like a reversion to the most primitive form of vehicle wheel, the flat wooden disk, as still used in China, for instance. The disk wheel conveys the impression of great weight and clumsiness and of being, therefore, ill-adapted for use on a fast moving vehicle.

1923 *Buick*

Motorists preferred to have wheels of possibly inferior strength rather than spoil the looks of their cars. Disc wheels did come into use on trucks, where the loads were greater and the appearance less important than on cars.

In the late teens disc wheels came into vogue on fancy show cars, and subsequently (as an option) appeared on a few production cars. Since 1904 cars had become better suited to them: the bulk and apparent weight had greatly increased, making the heavy-looking disc wheels look less out of place. Also, partly as a very distant influence from cubism (which was fashionable to talk about but little understood), severely rectilinear body shapes had come into vogue, which the bare geometric shape of disc wheels complemented nicely.

Disc wheels became one of those things, like escargots or caviar, which it is unfashionable to admit a dislike to: such an admission was taken to be a mark of uncultured tastes. By 1924 they were a common sight on classy middle-priced cars like the 1924 Nash, and they were also adopted by Packard. Most luxury cars relied on wire wheels, and wood wheels were still used on cheap cars.

In 1925 a statistical study done on show cars by *Automotive Industries* showed that for the most sophisticated class of buyer disc wheels had passed the peak of their popularity. Some of the people who had loudly defended their aesthetic merit in earlier years began to find fault in their appearance; it was also discovered that they had a tendency to drum on rough surfaces, which

1924 *Nash*

somehow had been overlooked before. For buyers of low-priced cars, however, they were still the highest mark of fashion, and they remained popular for several more years.

On his way to the Zenith Athletic Club one day Babbitt bought an electric cigar lighter for his car. He was worried that $5 may have been too much to pay for it, but, as the advertisement said, it was "a dandy little refinement, lending the last touch of class to a gentleman's auto."

In the early '20s motorists wanted more individuality in their cars, not so much in the general design as in small accessories which, like Babbitt's lighter, would "lend class." Manufacturers had not given them much choice before: in the early years all production cars of a given model were equipped exactly alike. One Packard touring car, for example, would have the same kind of upholstery, top, horn, and lighting equipment as every other one sold, and would even be painted the same shade of blue. If the owner wanted nonstandard equipment he had to buy it from one of the thriving accessory companies.

On February 6, 1919, *Motor Age* reported that ". . . the demand for individuality . . . is gathering force year by year." In the early '20s the lists of factory options grew rapidly. Choice of wheel type and body color, and optional use of bumpers, spare tire covers, and rear trunks gave some variation among cars of one make. Minor decorations helped to distinguish one make from another: radiators, radiator cap ornaments, cowl lights, and moldings were the most frequent objects of ingenuity in design.

From the new trend inevitably came the "loaded" deluxe model, bejewelled and glistening, carrying every imaginable option. Such a car was the 1925 Marmon shown here. In front it had a plated radiator and headlamps, and cowl lights which duplicated in miniature the shape of the headlamps; at the rear were a trunk and double spare tires flanked by stylish half-bumpers. Its leather-covered top had a long visor extension at the front and oval windows in the rear quarters, behind which were nickel-plated, nonoperative "landau irons." The side moldings were arranged to give the fashionable "double belt line effect."

The new taste for individuality was helped greatly by the

introduction of Duco finish. Auto paint had been a problem for some time. In the early days, before 1910 or so, cars were often painted in bright tones, but owners soon found that the brighter the color, the more faded, discolored, and unattractive it looked after a year or so. Black enamel was the most durable finish, but it tended to give a depressing, funereal look to the car. Paint was also a problem for manufacturers: by 1920 the mechanical parts of cars could be assembled in a few hours, thus reducing parts inventory, but bodies had to be kept for several days while the paint dried. Body inventories were huge: one motor magnate remarked that if a fast-drying paint were not developed, every square foot of the state of Michigan would soon be covered by partially finished automobile bodies.

Duco finish was developed by G.M., and first appeared on the Oakland (a G.M. car) in 1924. In 1925 it was used by almost everyone. It dried fast, and was far more durable than earlier finishes. Best of all, it gave a wide color range: motorists could buy a red or yellow car without having to expect rapid deterioration. Green, tan, and gray replaced black as the most popular colors, and many cars used two or three-tone color combinations.

The '20s are often portrayed as a decade of flappers and speakeasies and wild parties at Jay Gatsby's mansion on Long Island. These things existed, surely; but they stood out with such prominence partly by contrast to the conservatism of the major-

Closed Cars and a Touch of Class   **107**

ity. It was also the decade of "normalcy" and Warren G. Harding. In the matter of buying a car, "normalcy" generally prevailed.

One car which caught the spirit of the age was the first Chrysler, introduced in 1924. The success of its styling was due to a perfect combination of proven motifs rather than the creation of anything really new. It was "distinctive"—a magical and elusive quantity—without departing from the conventional idiom. Alfred P. Sloan, the president of General Motors, in a letter to H. H. Bassett, general manager of Buick, suggested that its wheels were the feature which set it apart:

> (For) the first Cadillac car that I ever had . . . I purchased small wire wheels in order to get the car down nearer the ground . . .Chrysler, in bringing out his original car, certainly capitalized that idea to the fullest extent and I think a great deal of his success . . . was due to that single thing.

The Chrysler also took advantage of the growing preference for heavy-looking cars, with details like fat wheel spokes, thick balloon tires, and extra deep crowned fenders which emphasized the appearance of weight. The popularity of the heavy look was something new in the '20s. In the days of the engine-under-seat runabout, cars were made to look as light as possible, as buggies had before. Heavy-looking cars were thought to look clumsy. By the teens, the lightweight look had gone out of style, but an overly

1924 *Chrysler Phaeton*

heavy appearance was also avoided: the ideal balance was achieved on a lean, rangy-looking car like the 1915 Mercer sport phaeton.

By the early '20s strong preferences for heavy cars began to take hold. Terms such as "substantial" and "massive" were used to praise new cars. To justify the new tastes a large body of ignorant opinion came into existence, voiced in such clichés as "Gimme a heavy car that will hold the road," and "them new Packards are real solid—you could drop a pile of bricks on one without making a dent." From the practical standpoint, excessive weight in such places as body panels is a waste: a heavy car is worse than a light car of comparable design in all aspects of performance, such as acceleration, braking, and handling, and also in gas mileage, tire life, and mechanical wear.

Because of the practical disadvantages, few makers actually built their cars heavier than necessary, but to satisfy the buyer's irrational desire for weight they began to make them look heavy. The Chrysler benefited by being the first car in its price class to take up this theme. It was also unusually low. By looking conventional without being dull, the Chrysler had phenomenal success.

The conservatism of the mid '20s was shown by the controversy caused by the looks of the redesigned 1925 Auburn. For the average motorist, this car represented the outer limits of good taste. In most respects it was quite an ordinary looking car, but there was one conspicuous exception: on the hood it had a curved

1925 Auburn

molding similar to the one used on the expensive Italian Isotta Fraschini. Division of color along this curve gave a spear-like thrust to the hood lines. In an editorial written many years later (February 1, 1932), *Automotive Industries* singled out this car for special comment:

> The original Auburn body design developed under E. L. Cord's regime brought definite reaction from almost everybody who saw it. Some disliked it violently. Others liked it. But hardly anybody was indifferent.

After some deliberation, motorists cautiously decided that they liked the effect, and Auburn sales improved.

For the car buyer of the late teens who wanted a reliable low-priced car there was no real choice: he had to buy a Ford. One car out of every two sold was a Model T, but few were purchased with any great eagerness. Though style changes were made from time to time they never brought the appearance of the car up to date: on the average, it looked about two years behind the times. The small brass radiator was retained long after owners had grown to loathe it, as was the vestigial dash. As it came from the factory, in

1916 Ford

its primitive black paint, it had the same hopelessly utilitarian look as an army truck.

The virtues of the Model T could not be denied, however. Its design and materials gave it exceptional strength, and its 22-hp engine had plenty of power for climbing hills and driving through mud. It was usually reliable, and when not, was easy to fix. Any farmer could be taught to drive it in five minutes—there were no difficult techniques like gear shifting to be mastered. The dealer network was so vast that wherever you happened to be, Ford parts and service were sure to be available nearby, and this was true for no other car. Yet even these things might have been discounted if it had not been for the price.

In value per dollar, nothing could approach the Ford. In the *Motor Age* annual pictorial review of American cars for 1916 (the December 30, 1915 issue), the Ford roadster (the cheapest body type) was listed for $390. The only one below it was the Woods Mobilette at $380, a flimsy overgrown motorcycle with half the horsepower. Upwards from the Ford were such cars as the Metz 22, Fastoria, Partin-Palmer, and Sterling; the first car on the list that might last more than a year was the Overland 75 at $595, but the Overland had only 15 hp, seven less than the Ford. For a car of acceptable quality which had the power of the Ford one would have to spend $635 for a Maxwell 25 or $725 for the larger Overland 83. No wonder most people bought the Ford: the wonder is that other makers stayed in business at all.

In 1916 there was no choice, but there was by 1923 or 1924. The Ford was still there, mechanically unchanged, offering all it always had. But at the same price one could buy a reliable used car (which earlier had been hard to find) with more power and comfort than the Ford. And in the new car field, there was no longer a huge price gap between the Ford and a car which had a "touch of class," like the new Chevrolet.

Under its new president, Alfred P. Sloan, G.M. had foreseen the altered conditions of the '20s and in 1923 introduced a drastically redesigned Chevrolet. The new body featured a lower roof line, 4⅜-inch higher radiator, stylish drum-shaped headlights, and more deeply crowned fenders. Even though the appearance of the Ford was improved in 1924 and the Chevrolet was not changed, the latter remained by far the better looking. For the

1923 *Chevrolet*

1924 *Ford Model T*

coupe, the prices were $525 for the Ford and $640 for the Chevrolet, still a large enough difference to make the buyer pause but small enough to tempt him.

Even more appealing were the special deluxe models introduced by Chevrolet in 1924. These cost even more ($625 for the touring car—almost half again as much as the Ford) but for the price, no car had ever offered more style. Gone was the black paint universally used on low-priced cars before; the new car was finished in brightly colored Duco. It also had stylish disc wheels, painted to match the body; bumpers front and rear; nickeled radiator; cowl lights shaped like the headlights; windshield wings;

and much else. In 1925 many of these features were included as standard equipment on the redesigned K model Chevy, which also had a one-piece windshield and automatic wipers on all closed models. The Chevy still cost more than the Ford, but with its colors and bright trim it was hard to resist, especially when G.M.'s newly instituted installment plan made it easy to buy on time.

The battle was between Ford, who assumed that car buyers act rationally, and G.M., who based the appeal of their car on the buyer's emotions. Ford cut prices, Chevrolet added style features, and the outcome was not long in doubt. In 1925 Chevy sales rose 64 percent while Ford's held about even. "But," as Sloan wrote later, "since the market as a whole in that year rose substantially over 1924, Ford's share declined relatively from 54 to 45 percent, a sign of danger, if Mr. Ford had chosen to read it.

Chevy's concentration on closed cars also began to have an effect at this time: to meet the growing demand, Chevy's production of closed cars rose from 40 percent of its total output in 1924 to 73 percent in 1926 and 82 percent in 1927. The light Ford chassis was less suitable for closed bodies than the Chevy's, and by 1926 production of closed Fords was only slightly more than 50 percent.

Henry Ford's contempt for style changes, which was responsible for the previously glacial evolution of Model T body design, was lessened during the '20s by the influence of his style-conscious son Edsel. A face-lifted Ford came out in early 1925, and a more drastically redesigned version was introduced in the fall of the same year. Each time, the car was lowered, the radiator raised, and the use of colored finishes extended to more models. For 1926 a nickeled radiator was introduced, and wire wheels were offered as an option. But the changes were too slight, and too late: the Chevy was still far better looking, and Ford sales continued to drop.

If Chevy held an edge in 1926, there was no comparison in 1927. While the Ford was virtually unchanged, the Chevrolet was completely redesigned: it was lower, seemed longer, and was much more expensive looking, while actually costing a lot less than before. Ford was in serious trouble. "And yet," wrote Sloan, "not many observers expected so catastrophic and almost whimsi-

1927 Ford

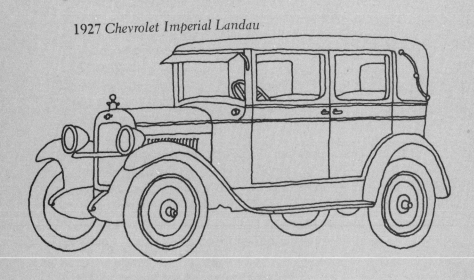

1927 Chevrolet Imperial Landau

cal a fall as Mr. Ford chose to take . . . ." In May 1927, with no specific plans for a new model yet developed, he ordered production of the Model T to cease.

In the automotive field, the early years of the Roaring Twenties had less roar in them than ever before. In this time the American sports car reached a new low point in popularity. Some commentators saw this as a mark of improving taste and growing maturity in the motorist. In September 1922, *Arts and Decoration* said that "it is an encouraging sign of the times to note that our thoroughfares are afflicted with fewer of those highly colored juggernauts which we used to term 'sporty cars'. . . ."

Sports cars are an expression of the irrational side of man, and in the "age of normalcy," the display of feeling was not fashionable. The Indianapolis race reports from 1920 up until about 1927 carried this attitude almost to absurdity. Gone were the descriptions of noise, dust, and smoke that filled the reports of a decade earlier. On May 5, 1921, *Motor Age* declared:

> To those who have the automobile industry close at heart automobile racing no longer is considered a sport. If this were so, we should not find men connected with the industry devoting their time to the designing and construction of a fleet of race cars. . . . An event like the Indianapolis race is a great laboratory. . . .

It was unthinkable that grown men would devote time and money to a project simply because it was exciting; the advancement of science or the amassing of profits were the only explanations such commentators could imagine.

The large sport phaeton had become the fashionable sporty car, and, though many of these were undeniably handsome, they were too sedate to express the power and aggressiveness of a two-passenger sports roadster. In the early '20s the Kissel Speedster came about as close as any to the appearance of a real sports car. Appearances, in this case, were deceptive, because the car's performance did not keep pace with its styling. Nevertheless, its low,

brightly painted body, crouched between deeply crowned cycle fenders, kept alive the styling tradition inherited from sports cars of the teens.

With a few exceptions such as the Kissel, the roadster had gone into decline. Not only were there no High Powered Runabouts worthy of the name, but even the less pretentious roadsters still being made were selling badly. Commenting on an auto show in January 1923, *Automotive Industries* noted that "roadster models are conspicuous by their absence."

Part of the problem was in the image of the roadster. In order to sell in large numbers, a body type must not only fulfill a functional requirement but it must also serve an expressive purpose. Few people needed the capacity of a limousine, for example, but ownership of such a car connoted wealth and social standing, thereby justifying its large price tag. For specialized body types the expressive function was particularly important: sales of sport phaetons, for example, depended far more heavily on an image than sales of ordinary sedans or touring cars.

Ever since the mid-teens the roadster had had a blurred image in the public mind. Open to the fresh air, and displaying its occupants to advantage, it had good potential as a sporty car. The trouble was that it was always the cheapest model available in any manufacturer's lineup, and therefore was widely used by country doctors, salesmen, and other equally unglamorous people. Too many rusty roadsters, driven by dirty and unshaven farmers, were seen carrying haybales and chickens for a high-class sporty image of the type to remain in focus for long.

In the mid '20s the new popularity of golf and the country club brought, as a side effect, a revival of the roadster. The country club was a symbol of middle class aspirations: it represented money, status, and refined tastes, without being in any way bizarre or unconventional. Around 1924 advertisements began to match the roadster with the country club: introductory pictures of the 1924 Kissel speedster, for example, included a golf bag attached in front of the rear fender. To emphasize the role, makers began to provide small doors for golf bags in the body just forward of the rear fenders.

A roadster became an essential part of the businessman-golfer's equipment. Natty clothes and expensive golf clubs meant nothing unless one rolled up the driveway to the club in a roadster. Country club associations suddenly gave a sharply defined and very desirable image to the body type, and sales quickly rose. "(T)he roadster is the accepted sport model, or sport type, of today," one manufacturer could say by December 1925 in *Motor Age*, only two years after the type had been almost forgotten by the public.

Favorable associations were not the only reason for the revival of the roadster: they had also become better looking. Roadsters of the late teens had narrow bodies, skinny tires, and generally a flimsy home-made look. The rear end was especially unsatisfactory: compared with the proud hood and radiator in front, the rear end was low and forgotten-looking. The new roadsters of the mid '20s looked much heavier and more powerful.

1925 *Jordon Playboy*

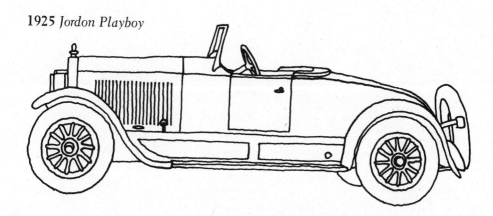

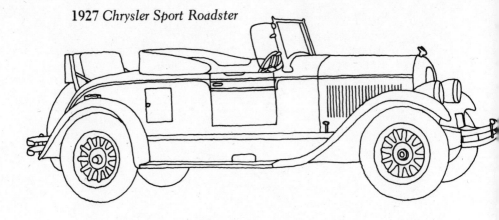

1927 Chrysler Sport Roadster

Their bodies were wider than earlier types, to the point where no connecting apron was needed between the rear fender and the body. The rear deck was made higher and broader, which made a better visual balance with the hood. Enlargement of the rear portion also allowed room for a folding rumble seat, which by 1927 was almost universal. Tops were also more attractive: tan material was available as well as black, and, instead of being left to sprawl over the rear deck when lowered, they now were either concealed or neatly enclosed in a cover.

Progress in body design had always depended to some extent on the existence of fabulous cars built for the very rich, which though far beyond the means of an ordinary man could nevertheless form the substance of his daydreams. They made him dissatisfied with the looks of his present car and inspired manufacturers to make low-priced imitations. The classic example of such a car was the original 35 hp Mercedes, the model after which virtually every American car was patterned in 1904.

Before World War I most of the cars which set the pace in style came from Europe. The front-engine configuration, the rear-entrance tonneau, the limousine, the side-entrance tonneau, and the torpedo body all originated in Europe and were subsequently copied here. In 1914, however, European firms were forced to stop work, and without outside inspiration, American designers confined their attention to refinements and detail improvements while leaving the basic form unchanged. On January 23, 1919, *Motor Age* commented that:

> Since the United States entered the World War, the motor car body has undergone no radical change. In fact, to date back to 1914, the car has much the same general appearance. . . . We have always looked to the European carrossier to bring forth radical changes in styles and designs. . . .

As a result of the long hiatus of the war and its economic aftereffects, however, Americans seemed to forget about European cars. Before the war, novelties on European cars were eagerly noted by both motorists and manufacturers in this country, but when production of high grade European cars resumed around 1920 few Americans paid much attention, in spite of the fact that products of European custom body builders were as far ahead of domestic producers as ever.

In the early '20s there was less European influence on American car design than ever before. Without external pressure for basic changes, American manufacturers settled back into a conservative routine. Every year the cars became fractionally lower, and trim lines, color combinations, and radiator shapes were constantly varied, but very little change was made in the overall appearance.

In the meantime the European "carrossiers," or special body makers, had been busy working on new designs, especially for the luxury market. At first little notice was taken of them here, but suddenly around 1925 Americans discovered that foreign luxury cars with special bodies had become far more handsome than the domestic makes. There was panic in the Packard and Lincoln showrooms as celebrities began to buy Hispano-Suizas or Isotta Fraschinis instead. The number of foreign cars sold was never threatening (only 820 were imported in 1927), but it galled domestic manufacturers that so many highly conspicuous people drove foreign makes: everyone knew, for example, that film idol Rudolf Valentino owned an Isotta Fraschini.

The lethargy of American designers was shaken off quickly as they tried to match the elegance of the European makes. But in the meantime the foreign cars held an edge in both appearance

and snob appeal. It was fashionable for a car to look like a Hispano-Suiza: new style features on a 1928 Moon, for example, were said to "lend a decidedly European touch to the car and set it off to advantage," according to *Motor Age*, January 12, 1928. The car was said to "typify the new Franco-Spanish school of automobile design."

In a similar way the pace of styling development was quickened by the domestic custom body trade. Custom body makers were directly descended from the carriage-making firms of the nineteenth century, and had built automobile bodies (particularly closed bodies) in small numbers right from the beginning. Up until the war, however, the styles produced by these firms were generally retrospective and dowdy, built to please the elderly buyers of limousines.

At the 1921 show at the Hotel Commodore in New York, where foreign and special-bodied cars were exhibited, there were fourteen custom body makers represented: Brewster, Brook-Ostruk, Pease, De Causse, Derham, Fleetwood, Healey, Holbrook, Locke, Murphy, New Haven, Rochambeau, Smith-Springfield, and Waltern. In spite of the number of firms, their total output in 1921 was not large, but in 1925, as the economic boom got under way, a flood of orders came in. Between 1925 and 1930 was a busy time for the custom body makers. On February 3, 1927, *Motor Age* entitled its report of the custom body salon in Chicago, "Salon Reveals Huge Growth of Custom Body Market—Leaders Estimate Their Industry Had Trebled in Last Two Years." By 1927 a few of the firms exhibiting in 1921 had gone out of business, but their places had been taken by the great names of Dietrich, Judkins, LeBaron, Willoughby, Weymann, and others.

The difference between a production body and a custom-made one did not, at first glance, seem enough to justify the difference in price, which was usually quite large. Many of the features which gave the car its basic appearance, such as the fenders and radiator shell, were the same on both. When both types were seen side by side, however, the difference came out. The custom body was better proportioned, and the design of the trim at the belt line and around the windows always looked more attractive. The quality of finish was breathtaking, and the color schemes were always in excellent taste: often a dark color was used for the fenders and above the belt line, with a lighter color, or lighter shade of the same color, for the body and hood. Inside the car, the upholstery and interior appointments were the finest that money could buy.

A custom body, like a custom-made suit, gave the owner status in the most sophisticated circles. The uninitiated may have seen little difference between it and its mass-produced equivalent, but to those who knew what to look for there was no comparison. The actual number of bodies made by these companies was quite small, and the growth of the custom body trade was felt directly by only a few luxury car manufacturers. Indirectly, however, the custom built cars influenced the whole industry by setting a high standard of appearance.

Foreign cars and domestic custom cars thus began to make regular production models look unexciting and cheap by contrast. For most luxury car manufacturers, whose largest profit came from the chassis rather than the body, the answer was to make fewer

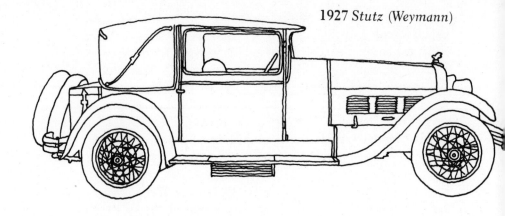

1927 *Stutz* (*Weymann*)

bodies themselves and send more chassis out for custom-made bodies.

The general manager of Cadillac, Lawrence Fisher, took another course. Through a Cadillac distributor in Los Angeles named Don Lee he met Harley J. Earl, who was the director and chief designer of the Earl Carriage Works, a custom body shop associated with Lee's Cadillac dealership. As well as being a talented designer, Earl was an insider in the custom car business and also had a flair for management. In early 1926 Fisher arranged for Earl to come to Cadillac as a special design consultant, in the hope that he could give production Cadillacs the elusive custom built look.

The effect of his presence was first seen in detail changes on the 1927 Cadillacs, which had had an all-new body the year before. The dual-cowl phaeton was the handsomest car in the

1927 *Cadillac Dual Cowl Phaeton*

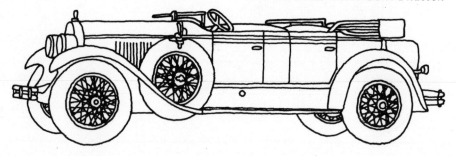

lineup. For a production car its color scheme, with inset color panels on the doors and a different color on the hood than on the body, was an innovation, and the folding windshields both front and rear started a fad. Though it was hardly practical to drive the car with the front one folded, the owner could always put it down when the car was standing in the driveway and admire its appearance. From custom car practice came the dual side mounts sunk in front fender wells and topped by rear view mirrors and the oversized, nickel-plated headlights. Special wire wheels with big hubs and thick spokes tastefully completed its styling. Even for the connoisseur, the new Cadillac was easy to mistake for a custom-made job.

Though the new Cadillacs provided custom car features at much less than one would have to pay for the real thing, at prices ranging upwards from $2,985 they were hardly cheap. There were vast numbers of motorists who yearned for a car with these features but could not afford the Cadillac. In March 1927 G.M. introduced a new car for them—the LaSalle, which was priced between the Cadillac and the Buick "Six" at $1,295.

The La Salle was the first car built by a major company in which appearance was the principal design goal. The mechanical side was not neglected: the engine, drive train and chassis were well engineered, with many parts borrowed from the Cadillac. But the body, styled by Earl and his associates, was what mattered most. No apologies were needed: even at its low price, it had all the subtle touches which previously had distinguished custom cars from production models.

1927 *LaSalle*

Like a custom car, the La Salle was not unusual in its overall appearance—both were built for conservative tastes. But as one looked closer, one noticed dozens of small details that set it apart. The introductory article on it in *Motor Age*, March 3, 1927, had far more space devoted to style features than for any other car of that year. Like the Cadillac phaeton, it had dual side mounts in fender wells with mirrors, folding windshields on phaeton models, original color combinations, and optional wire wheels. A chrome band divided the hood from the cowl, and a plated cross brace with a beautifully designed La Salle emblem ran between the headlight stanchions.

Many of the La Salle's styling details seem trivial in themselves—longer front fenders with arrow-shaped beading in front, roofs with gently rounded rear quarters, more elongated side windows—but their tasteful combination made the car really distinctive. In this car, the triumph of the designer was not so much in the importance of specific features he included as it was in the sheer range of his attention. The La Salle was meticulously styled from front to back.

The introduction of the La Salle caused a sensation. A year afterwards, on March 1, 1928, *Motor Age* could report that "(t)he immediate success of the new La Salle was one of the outstanding high points of the industry during 1927." In the same way that foreign or custom models had done in other years, it became the model of fashion. Reversing the usual procedure, many of its features subsequently appeared on custom bodies, and it was slavishly imitated by other volume manufacturers. In 1929 practically every car on the road had a cross brace with emblem between the headlights and a chrome band around the cowl.

The success of the La Salle convinced G.M. management that body design should be approached in a systematic way. In the summer of 1927 the G.M. Art and Color Section was organized, with Harley Earl at its head. This was an important event: the task of designing the appearance of the company's cars was finally given to full-time design specialists, working as an official part of the general staff.

In 1929, after a decade dominated in spirit by the tastes of George Babbitt, expressed attitudes toward the automobile began to change. Car buyers began to show what they had been afraid to admit earlier in the decade: that the automobile is more than transportation, more, even, than a weapon in the war of status-seeking. It is an expression of power, of youth, of escape. Race reports hinted at this: the sober analogies to a laboratory were gone, and in their place were descriptions full of sensory appreciations of cars. A report in *Automotive Industries*, March 23, 1929, on land speed record attempts has a different quality than the one quoted in 1921:

> Whatever the basic objective of the designers of such vehicles as the Triplex and the Golden Arrow, it is hard not to believe that the spirit of adventure predominates over that of research in those men who actually drive these cars.

The roadster of the mid '20s was given a big boost in performance and more flamboyant styling, reincarnating the spirit of American sports cars of the teens. It was generally larger and heavier than the European type of sports car, but its extra power was sometimes enough to make up the difference in performance. In 1928 a high standard of performance was set by a Stutz which placed a close second in the 24 Hours of Le Mans, while the two-tone, boat-tailed Auburn speedster brought the appearance of the American sports car to a new level of exuberance.

Joining in with the new enthusiasm, automakers began to build special two-seaters to exhibit at shows, partly as a way of lending glamour to the production models and partly as a testing ground for new ideas. The DuPont speedster, shown in 1929, served as both. It was spectacular. Every line expressed speed: its headlights were rounded to reduce wind resistance, as were the graceful wing-like fenders. But its most unusual feature was its grille. On most cars the functional component itself was exposed, but all one saw on the DuPont was mesh and sheet metal—the actual radiator was hidden inside. This separation allowed greater latitude in front-end design: the front of the DuPont grille was curved to suggest better streamlining and the shell painted the same color as the hood, emphasizing that it was part of the body rather than an exposed working part. The same appearance could

1928 *Auburn Speedster*

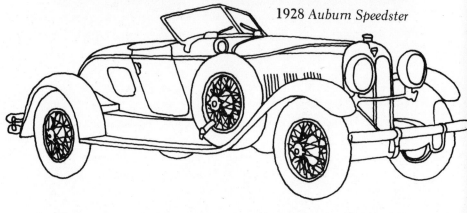

1928 *Auburn Speedster*

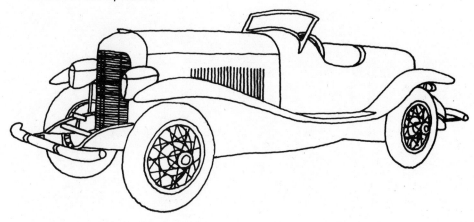

have been given by a modified radiator, but it would have been far more expensive.

DuPont followed Stutz to LeMans in 1929 with the object of earning a high-performance image for the make. Since its 3,500-pound bulk was propelled by only 75 hp, the prospects did not appear bright, but publicity for the expedition was so well managed that, from the prestige standpoint, it was impossible to lose. The chassis was stock, the drivers were gentlemen, and the car was exceptionally handsome—what else could one ask? The car rumbled slowly around for only a few hours before expiring, but even so the venture was praised as a "sportsmanlike attempt." An entry at Indianapolis in 1930, done in a similar spirit, was also thought to be "a superb sporting gesture." This time, after qualifying next-to-last, the car staggered around for 22 laps and then hit the wall.

The Auburn Cabin Speedster, also shown in 1929, had few if any features worth imitating on production cars, but by exaggerating characteristic Auburn styling motifs such as the hood spear it drew attention to the company's regular line. At 58 inches overall it was very low (the frame actually ran under the rear axle) and its steeply raked vee-windshield gave it a look of speed. *Automotive Industries*, on February 9, 1929, was moved to describe it as "one of the most daringly designed motor cars that has ever been offered," and it drew large and appreciative crowds.

Closed Cars and a Touch of Class   **127**

With the triumph of the LaSalle giving them confidence, Harley Earl and his associates turned to the design of the 1929 Buick. 1929 was Buick's Silver Anniversary, and to celebrate the company's twenty-fifth year of business a new car was planned which would bring the flavor of custom styling to an even larger market than the LaSalle's.

The general appearance of the new Buick was conventional—perhaps a bit lower than usual, but not in any way radical. The custom look depended on nuances, small touches here and there which added up to a distinctive appearance, and the Buick had plenty of these. Its most unusual feature was the

1929 Buick

elimination of the conventional molding along the belt line. In its place there was a slight bulge in the side, running from the bottom of the windows forward into the radiator. Earl felt that the highlight created by the bulge would be a more subtle way of emphasizing length than the usual molding.

When the car was introduced in the summer of 1928 its initial reception was not as warm as had been hoped. In November, 1928, the motoring editor of *Country Life* reported on the car. He liked its performance and comfort, but not its styling: "The appearance of this model . . . is not as fortunate as it might be. Too bad, for the model just preceding it was such a swell looking turnout. . . ." As time went on it became clear that the new design was a catastrophe. Buick called the car the "Silver Anniversary Buick," but because of the bulge at its belt line it was quickly dubbed the "Pregnant Buick," and the latter name stuck, to the despair of Buick dealers. The car became a joke, and in the year it was introduced Buick's share of the market fell to less than half of what it was the year before.

In explanation for the failure of this car Earl claimed that between his specifications and the production model, and without his knowledge, other departments had added five inches to the overall height and had changed the curvature of the sides. Without these alterations it certainly would have looked sleeker, but the fact remained that its general proportions were no less attractive than the popular 1928 model, and its cataclysmic failure was due almost entirely to the seemingly trivial belt-line bulge.

The failure of the pregnant Buick temporarily checked the adventurousness of car stylists. On January 25, 1930, *Automotive Industries* reported that:

> The experience of one of our largest car builders in introducing a distinctly different body style which failed of public acceptance has led all other manufacturers to be extremely cautious.

No wonder; if the Buick had been a radical departure from the ordinary, with weird proportions or outlandish contours, one might have predicted failure, but in most respects the 1929 model was nearly identical to its predecessor. Even its innovations were fairly conservative—Earl's belt line treatment had been used before on European custom coachwork without raising any protest. Public reaction could not have been predicted, nor could it be rationally explained, but at least it was unambiguous: people hated the car. When the 1930 model appeared it had flat sides again, as in 1928.

In the late '20s front wheel drive was in fashion. Rumors flew around about new FWD cars about to be announced, and one journal after another extolled the merits of the system and predicted that in twenty (ten, five) years all cars would have it. European makers were the first to put such cars on the market, and the Bucciali and others were given extensive publicity in this country.

In the magazines, FWD benefits such as safer handling and better traction got the most attention, but there was another which was perhaps more appealing to the customer. By eliminating the drive shaft and moving the transmission out in front of the engine, body designers were free to lop a foot or more off the overall height while keeping the same interior dimensions. In one step the car could be made dramatically low, giving it proportions that had invariably been popular.

One new body which received a lot of publicity was designed by Baker-Raulang for the proposed Gardner front-drive car. In an article on June 22, 1929, in *Automotive Industries*, its designer wrote:

> . . . there is one thing which the front drive car, aside from any mechanical merits, can provide the automobile industry, and that is something new in body design.

He set a good example: the front end of his car, in particular, was revolutionary. It had a grille which, from the side view, ran in a smooth curve forward from the hood down to a point even with the front of the tires, or more than a foot in front of the usual radiator position. In the same article, he explained:

> . . . we provided a curved shroud, serving both as a radiator cover and as an enclosure for the front drive

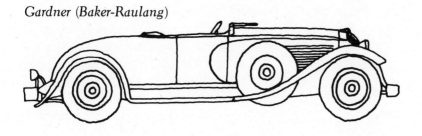

mechanism . . . (This also) eliminated the abrupt vertical lines of the conventional radiator shell.

The Gardner front-drive was stillborn, however, and the Ruxton, which came out in late April of 1929, had few styling novelties other than its extremely low overall height.

The magnificent Cord L29, introduced in June 1929, took better advantage of the styling possibilities of front-wheel drive. It was a brilliant extension of conventional practice, managing to look dramatic and new without being so different as to turn people away. From its front-drive configuration it was naturally very low, and placement of the engine and transmission forced an extremely long hood, giving it a racy and powerful appearance.

1929 Cord

Partly due to a different frame construction, the trough between the hood and fenders was not as deep as usual, which, in the front view, exaggerated further the already immense breadth of the fenders. The Cord front fenders were the biggest yet seen: not only were they wide and full, but from the side they looked incredibly long, carrying back the full length of the hood and meeting the running board at a point directly below the windshield.

Another notable thing on the Cord was its vee-shaped grille. In its construction it was similar to the one on the DuPont speedster, being actually part of the bodywork. As on the DuPont, the shell was painted the same color as the hood. Even the grille bars were painted, leaving only a narrow band of bright trim around the opening.

Like the designer of the bodies for the proposed Gardner car, many people had hoped that the new front-drive cars would break away from conventional styling and thus dispel the stagnation which was felt to have settled on car design. The Gardner car, if it had appeared, might have done this, but the cars which were actually produced did not. Though certainly beautiful, the Cord's styling was more a summary of current themes than a step in a new direction.

In the period from 1929 to 1931 activity among the custom body builders was at a peak. The special shows for custom coachwork drew large and perceptive crowds, and until the full effect of the stock market crash was felt, orders remained at a high level. At the Chicago Salon in 1929, the following body makers exhibited: Baker-Raulang, Brewster, Brunn, Derham, Dietrich, Fisher, Fleetwood, Holbrook, Judkins, LeBaron, Locke, Murphy, Rollston, Weymann, and Willoughby; and there were still others in business which were not represented. Demand for special bodies was increased by the growing tendency of prestige car makers to farm out bodywork. The extremely high quality, immensely powerful (265 hp) Duesenberg, which was introduced in late 1928, used custom bodies exclusively—the parent company made only the chassis (for $8,500, f.o.b. Indianapolis).

The conditions under which custom body designers worked

1931 *Duesenberg (Rollston)*

gave them opportunities which production car designers did not have. Since they produced for a prestige market in which cost was of little or no object, they were free to use any materials they chose, and they did not have to restrict their designs to something which could be produced simply and with little labor. Each car received individual attention, and the design could be changed at any time.

Also an advantage was the organization of the custom body shop. The director of the firm was almost always the chief designer, and the overall size of the average company was very small. The designer, therefore, was in complete control, and often supervised the actual construction of the body.

1930 *Duesenberg (Murphy)*

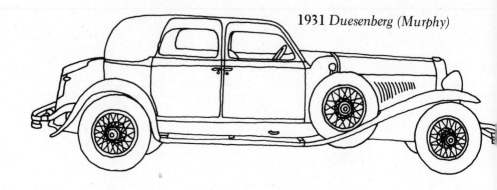

There were also limitations on the designer of custom bodies, however, and in the long run they were as restrictive as those on the designer of production cars. Custom cars were built for a market full of elderly and conservative people who in the teens might have bought towering, black, seven-passenger limousines. Styling evolution in the '20s had brought some enlightenment, but except for such people as movie stars, the customers for special-bodied cars were still rather reactionary. The customer was also in closer touch with the builder and could nip innovation in the bud, while on production cars the theory of anticipation of public tastes gave some latitude.

Though designed within the conventional idiom, the creations of the custom body firms in these years easily justified the "classic" label later given to them. Never before had cars looked so rich and elegant. Their immensely long hoods suggested vast power, which in most cases the straight eight, vee-twelve, or vee-sixteen-cylinder engines were able to substantiate. The sweeping, winglike front fenders which stretched nearly half the length of the car symbolized motion and exaggerated the already enormous length of the wheelbase. But the final triumph of the classic custom bodies was in the nuance—the proportions, finish, and detail that somehow made every car look unusually handsome.

Because of their enforced conservatism, however, the custom body makers gradually lost their position as pace-setters in styling for the industry after about 1930. In a report on special bodies, February 8, 1930, in *Automotive Industries*, the chief designer of an influential coachmaker, Mr. Willoughby, was reported to be

. . . of the opinion that the higher class cars would continue to show the same refinements and dignity but that still bolder combinations would be attempted in certain other productions. . . .

The other productions were clearly meant to be low and medium-priced mass-produced cars, whose buyers had less conservative bias and might be more receptive to new features which changed the basic appearance of the automobile.

Around 1930 there appeared in the General Motors lineup a phenomenon which might be called "hand-me-down styling." Under this system, styling evolution is carefully planned in advance: new features, first introduced in the expensive lines, gradually sift down to the low-priced ranges over the period of a year or two. By the time the process is completed, other new and appealing touches have been added to the expensive car, so that it always stays a few steps ahead.

For this process to work successfully, several conditions are necessary, both within the company and in the general state of styling development, and these were optimum only for a brief period between about 1929 and 1931. Before this time, the industry had not given styling change the rational study that was needed to plan such a campaign. Also, even if the planning had been done, to carry it out one had to have a very highly developed corporate organization, and even G.M., which was way in advance of the others in this respect, was not up to such a task until the end of the decade.

Another prerequisite was reasonable stability in the general trend of design. Through the '20s the average car's appearance changed only slightly from year to year, so a fresh idea offered on a luxury car in, say, 1926 would still be new and appealing on a low-priced car in 1928 or 1929. With a more rapid pace of evolution this does not work: a feature that is one or two years old will look outmoded no matter what class of car it is offered on.

The "hand-me-down" process can be seen very clearly in the way new styling was passed on from Cadillacs to Chevrolets between 1930 and 1932. In 1930 Cadillac announced a magnificent

1930 *Cadillac* V16

new sixteen-cylinder prestige model, a veritable cathedral of a car. Even when burdened by three tons of machinery and luxurious bodywork, its acceleration and top speed were well above average, but it was most impressive in the way it could climb steep hills, silently, in high gear, at any speed down to 5 mph, with the inexorable progression of a glacier.

In keeping with the power of its gigantic engine, the appearance of this car was utterly overwhelming, particularly in the front view. Its towering radiator, shielded by the plated tracery of a stone guard, was flanked by heraldic trumpets in chrome, and pillars supported the enormous headlights. Huge fenders arched outward from the radiator. Notable in the side view were the dual side-mounted spares sunk in fender wells and the adjustable chromed doors which replaced louvres in the sides of the hood.

For people who could not raise the price of a Cadillac in 1930, Chevrolet offered many of the same features on their 1931 model. For example, the radiator shape of the new Chevy was identical to the Cadillac's, and a plated stone guard was available on deluxe models. And if the 1931 Chevy looked like a standard Cadillac, the 1932 model looked like a miniature V16. By this time virtually everything except the size was appropriated. All models had a "built-in grille," an integral chromed grid which looked like the Cadillac-type radiator and stone guard. Adjustable doors

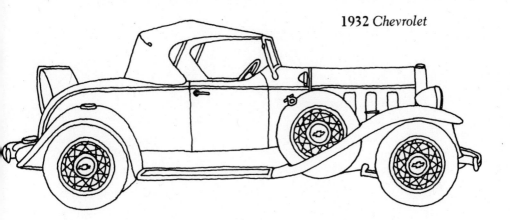

(chrome-plated on deluxe models) took the place of hood louvres, though the Chevy maintained a respectful distance by using only four instead of the Cadillac's five. One trumpet-type chrome-plated horn was mounted under the left headlight, not quite as fancy as the dual horns on the Cadillac but close enough.

Those who thought the Chevy did not look enough like a Cadillac or were too impatient to wait for Cadillac influence to sift down to the Chevrolet could always buy a more expensive G.M. car. As the price tag grew, the similarity to a new Cadillac became more pronounced. The LaSalle, for example, looked almost the same as a Cadillac of the same year; Buick was similar to a new Cadillac in some ways and in others it was a year behind; Olds-mobile was still farther behind, and so on. Not every styling idea came from above, but there were enough handed down so that by 1931 G.M. cars had a strong family resemblance to one another.

In the '20s manufacturers awoke to the importance of styling for sales, and as a result, the sheer number of style changes was greater than ever. Most of the changes, however, were details in the execution of the standard form which did not affect the over-all appearance of the car very much. By the end of the decade some people became critical of the trend. In the March 23, 1929 issue a critic for *Automotive Industries* argued:

> The designer's problem is essentially one of mass. Rotation of design, and by that we mean the periodic change in the

Closed Cars and a Touch of Class   137

shape of lamps, type of wheels, location of accessories, and the like, offers little, if anything, to the fundamental advancement of design.

A year later, on January 25, 1930, an editorial in the same publication put the case even more bluntly: "one must conclude that automobile body appearance has reached a state bordering standardization, or perhaps we should say stagnation." The impatience of the critics was not caused by cars which were actually ugly: a commentator, writing in *Automotive Industries*, January 12, 1929, on the New York Show remarked that "the uniformly attractive appearance of all cars . . . (is among) . . . the things that impressed in the show itself." The average 1931 car was not bad looking, but it just looked too much like cars built five or ten years earlier. The time had come for something really different.

4
Toward an Aerodynamic Form

Human beings have always been highly susceptible to the lure of speed. Before the automobile appeared, fast travel by horseback or horse-drawn vehicle gave people many of the same sensations. In the eighteenth century Boswell reported in his *Life of Johnson* (under 19 Sept. 1777; Hill, George Birkbeck (ed.): *Boswell's Life of Johnson*, Vol. III; The Clarendon Press, Oxford, 1887, p. 162):

> Johnson strongly expressed his love of driving fast in a post-chaise. "If (said he) I had no duties, and no reference to futurity, I would spend my life in driving briskly in a post-chaise with a pretty woman."

A hundred years later William Dean Howells, in *The Rise of Silas Lapham* (Houghton, Mifflin Co., 1928; originally published 1884) described the way his hero went out on weekends to "speed his horse":

> The Colonel said, "I'm going to let her out, Pert . . ."
>   Nothing in the immutable iron of Lapham's face betrayed his sense of triumph as the mare left everything behind her . . . the muscles of her back and thighs worked more and more swiftly, like some mechanism responding to an alien force, and she shot to the end of the course . . .

Before the machine age, winter sports such as tobogganing and skating also fulfilled this need, and early descriptions of these activities often mention "faces flushed with the excitement of swift motion." The bicycle allowed more people to share the experience: speed was an essential part of the bicycle craze of the 1880s and 1890s. Perhaps as many bicycles were bought for the thrill of a head-long rush down the nearest hill as for travel from one place to another. Analysis of the psychological effect of a fast ride was a popular topic in bicycle literature of the period.

The exhilaration of speed was not unknown, then, at the time when the automobile appeared. People who had enjoyed bicycles and fast horses took to automobiling immediately: "The chief cause for the modern automobile is its speed," wrote one motorist in *The Horseless Age*, March 12, 1902. He assumed that most people shared his feelings: "There are few people who want a slow automobile after having ridden in a moderately fast one." There were few indeed who were unaffected by the experience, but some were upset by the force of their feelings. Was there a risk of mental derangement from the powerful emotions excited by a fast automobile ride? Some thought so; certainly there were disturbing signs of it in the behavior of many young "scorchers." Like any other intoxicant or narcotic, the euphoria of high speed was carefully examined for harmful side effects.

The appearance of cars was naturally modified to reflect their ability to go fast. While brute power was symbolized quite early in the front-engine hood, a satisfactory expression of speed potential took longer to evolve. The proper combination of abstract lines and forms helped: a long, low car looked faster than a lumpish one, and sweeping fenders also served the purpose.

The best way to express speed, however, was to make the car look more aerodynamic. Aerodynamics as such were not a matter of concern before the twentieth century, because nothing went fast enough to make wind resistance much of a problem, but through the analogy of hydrodynamics people were aware of some of its basic principles. For centuries men had been modifying boats to reduce drag, and the importance of smoothly graduated shapes and integrated details was well known.

Streamlining was seen on racing cars in the first years of the new century, most notably in this country on electric racers built by Baker and steam ones made by White and Stanley, but not much effort was made on passenger cars until around 1910, the

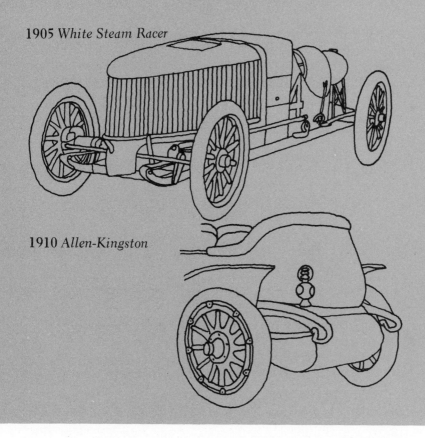

1905 *White Steam Racer*

1910 *Allen-Kingston*

year of the torpedo body. The tonneau on the 1910 Allen-Kingston torpedo body ("gunboat body" according to its makers) was carefully tapered and rounded off according to the best hydrodynamic principles. In boat design the shape of the stern is as important as the bow, but on cars like the Allen-Kingston the airflow was disturbed so much on its way back that the rear end in fact made no aerodynamic difference at all. Nevertheless, according to the principle of "you can believe anything if you try," many people claimed a noticeable reduction in dust eddies at the rear of such cars due to the shape.

Between 1910 and 1914 the cowl area of all cars evolved toward a smoothly tapered form. Other changes made in the teens in the streamlining spirit were the nearly universal removal of outside door handles and hinges and the adoption of raked windshields. In refining the shape of the body the analogy with

Toward an Aerodynamic Car **141**

boat design was explicitly made: in boasting of the redesigned 1914 models, a KisselKar ad in *The Horseless Age*, July 1, 1914, invited the reader to

OBSERVE THESE YACHT-LIKE LINES

Much has been said by car builders about yacht-like lines . . . here they are—sweeping, graceful, unbroken from the bow of the bonnet to "midships."

After the war, Americans seemed to lose interest in aerodynamics. "There are indications," reported *Motor Age* in November 1920, "that the streamline body is passing out. . . ." From the curves of the teens, the car of the '20s emerged with a body which frankly displayed its basic rectilinear forms. Windshields became upright again, body sides flattened, door handles and hinges reappeared, and body designers turned to other sources for inspiration. Judging by his tastes in automobiles, the average American motorist of 1925 was oblivious of aerodynamics.

Interest in streamlined cars continued in Europe, however. Economics may have had a part in this: while the American motorist could simply buy a car with a large engine if he wanted speed, this option was open to very few Europeans due to high gasoline prices and heavy taxes based on engine size. The only way to make an underpowered car go fast was through reduced wind resistance. Streamlining could also cut fuel consumption significantly.

An early experiment in passenger car streamlining was the Rumpler, made shortly after the war by a German aircraft firm. Though this car was never put into production, it combines in a remarkable way the essentials of what people in the next two decades would conceive to be "the car of the future." In its basic form, the Rumpler is round and blunt in the nose and long and tapered at the rear—the classic teardrop shape, seen in nature on fish and copied by man on Zeppelins and airplanes. A closed version of this car, which in theory might have been an even better aerodynamic shape, was also constructed.

The other "dream car" feature of the Rumpler, besides its basic form, was the placement of the passengers in the wide forward part of the car and the engine in the tapered tail. The rear

1921 *Rumpler*

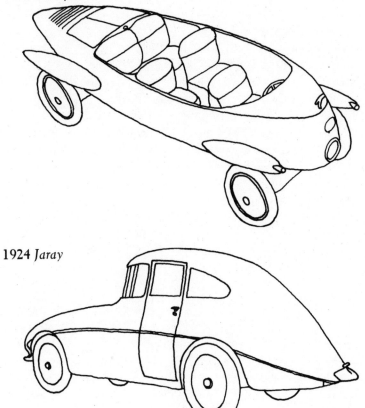

1924 *Jaray*

engine was a natural complement to the shape, because the narrow rear section was too small for passengers and too awkward for luggage space. It was perfect for the engine, though: not only was it just the right size, but it also allowed excellent accessibility.

A slightly more conventional approach to streamlining was taken by Jaray in France, who built several aerodynamic bodies on existing chassis for test purposes. Except for their scale, his cars all looked much the same. The illustration here shows one that was built in 1924. By widening the body past the wheels, the fenders and the runningboards disappear, giving the car a dramatically simple appearance. The flow of air is smoothly carried up the sloping hood, around the narrow superstructure, and down the carefully tapered tail.

Toward an Aerodynamic Car **143**

Aesthetic considerations were conspicuously absent in Jaray's reports on his streamlined cars. Air drag and the effects on performance and gas mileage were his main topics. Jaray himself must have thought his cars beautiful, or he would not have taken such care to design the graceful window line or include the gently curved molding on the side, but it is clear that few others shared his feelings. While admitting that practical advantages might be derived from such a body, *Motor Age*, December 18, 1924, gave the opinion that "it does not seem that there is any necessity for such measures in America," implying that Americans would rather pay more for gas than drive a car which looked like Jaray's.

Numerous attempts to break the land speed record in the late '20s gave publicity to streamlined racing cars. One of the most beautiful of these was the Stutz Black Hawk, built to break the record in 1928. In its general proportions the Stutz resembled a conventional open-wheeled racing car, but its shape was far more refined. The chassis and wheels were enclosed in smooth teardrop-shaped bodywork. To reduce drag the radiator was moved from the front to the sides of the hood, following aircraft practice. Unlike most earlier streamlined cars, the Stutz was generally considered to be beautiful, and pictures of the car were widely printed in newspapers and magazines. Unfortunately, however, the car was not aerodynamically sound: it had low drag but was unstable, and in a record attempt in 1928 it crashed, killing its driver and designer Frank Lockhart.

As sales figures spiraled downward following the crash of 1929, automakers turned to body design as a way out of their difficulties. Budgets were slim, and for a given investment, a new and successful body could improve sales far more than engineering changes. But there were high risks in such a course: if the new body turned out to

1928 *Stutz Black Hawk*

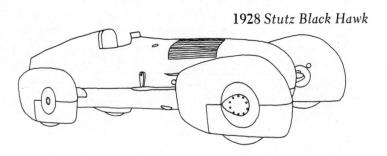

be unpopular it would mean extinction for any but the largest manufacturers.

In 1929 and 1930 many articles on body design were written in the "down with the old, up with the new" revolutionary spirit. Typical was one entitled "Verve of Automobile's Purpose Should Show in Body Design," which appeared in *Automotive Industries*, May 23, 1929. The shape of a conventional car was contrasted with that of a fish to show how its sharp corners and upright profile "seemingly obstruct its speed." The article concluded that "motor cars offer far greater possibilities for improvement in their appearance than their apparently stabilized design would indicate."

The Depression added force to these arguments, but the reception of the Pregnant Buick was still vivid in the minds of most automen, and it was left to Reo, a relatively small company, to introduce the first production car designed on the new aerodynamic theme. In the fall of 1930 the "Royale Eight," a deluxe model, was added to the regular line of Reo cars. Though conventional in its basic proportions, the spirit of the Reo design, as shown in a multitude of details, was radically different from other cars of that year. Where their lines were hard, its were soft, where they were square, it was rounded. The overall effect of its appearance was strikingly different.

The droopy, bulging front fenders of the Reo set the tone of the design. Their large radius curves make them look heavier than the usual type, an impression reinforced by the way the outer edges roll gently under rather than being finished with a sharp bead. The aerodynamic look is increased by the rounded grille, the long

1931 *Reo Royale Eight*

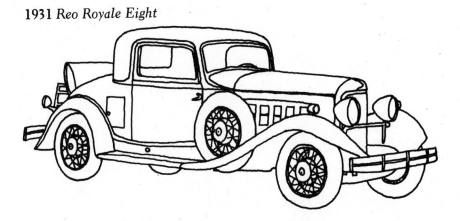

headlight shells, and the unusual rounded header above the slanted windshield. For more than a decade, most cars had had a visor or square "brow" over the windshield, and smoothing this area back into the roof gave the car a unique look.

Reaction to the Royale was almost unanimously favorable. Although its styling was "the most radical departure in lines that has been made in some time," according to *Automotive Industries*, September 27, 1930, car buyers were well prepared for a more streamlined car, and the Royale did not go too far in one step. "Sheer beauty of line . . . characterizes the Reo Royale Eight body," was the opinion of one admirer in the November 22, 1930, issue of *Automotive Industries*, while another wrote in the *SAE Journal*, January 1, 1931, that "the outstanding design of the year is undoubtedly the Reo Royale Eight."

People clearly wanted a streamlined looking car, and the Reo looked right. Had the Royale been presented purely as an aesthetic advance, however, it might not have been so quickly successful. Aesthetics disguised as practicality are more quickly saleable than if offered without rational apology. Not only was the Reo a fine looking car, but wind tunnel tests had shown that the improved aerodynamics of the new body reduced the power required to go 80 mph by 12 percent. Quasi-technical articles showing wind tunnel models, test apparatus, and graphs, were published widely, providing a perfect excuse for the conservative who secretly liked the looks of the car but did not want to be thought radical by his friends. "Looks a bit extreme, for me," he could say, "but it saves me money on gas."

The popularity of the Reo's appearance gave a strong impetus to the streamlining movement. The Reo showed that car buyers were not as conservative as previously believed. Though by earlier standards the car was advanced, almost radical, few unfavorable comments were heard on its appearance, and sales, by 1931 standards, were good. Radical design seemed to be the way to sell cars in the Depression, though (memories persisting) automakers were reluctant to believe it so soon.

The next car in the new generation of streamlined designs was the 1932 Graham Eight. Its styling was as far advanced beyond the Reo

1932 *Graham Eight*

as the latter had been ahead of its own immediate predecessors. It gave a similar general impression, of roundedness and aerodynamic form, but this was combined with a simplicity in detail which the Reo lacked.

Most of the style innovations centered around the fenders and the front end. The front fenders curved forward over the wheels like a breaking wave, reaching nearly as low as the bumper. Behind the wheels, the sides of both front and rear fenders were carried down to cover the chassis. The panels thus formed were called fender skirts.

Almost as original as the fenders was the treatment of the grille, which solved a problem which had plagued designers for several decades. With a traditional upright radiator, the area between the radiator and the bumper had been unavoidably unattractive. Spring horns, frame cross members, and shock absorber mounts, plus the inevitable coating of road dirt, made this part of a car a real mess. On the Graham this problem was solved by sloping the grille forward at the bottom and blending it into a splash pan, so that most of the awkward area was covered up. The smoothness of the 1932 Graham front end contrasts sharply with the looks of the previous model.

Automakers watched carefully for the public's reaction to the Graham. On February 13, 1932, *Automotive Industries* reported:

> Should the new Graham model be preeminently successful this year we believe that the speed with which rear-engined and fully streamlined cars come on the market will be accelerated by many months.

Toward an Aerodynamic Car   **147**

1932 Graham Eight

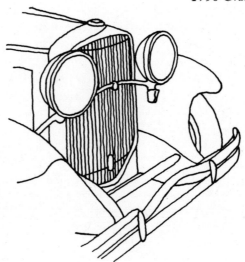

1930 Graham Eight

As sales figures were compiled it soon became clear that the Graham had received the same wide approval given to the Reo the year before. Twice in a row, radical new models had been successful. Again, *Automotive Industries*, June 11, 1932, reported:

> The automobiles with the most striking bodies have done better this year relatively than have the more conservatively designed vehicles. . . . When these now-successful body lines first came out, we heard them criticized plenty by rival manufacturers. . . . But they went over.

Regardless of the evidence, it was still hard for veteran motor executives to believe that the public appetite for radical design went very deep. Thirty years of experience had shown the opposite. But, in 1932, it was hard not to feel desperate. From over 4 million in 1929, total sales had fallen to around 2.7 million in 1930, 1.9 million in 1931, all the way down to less than 1.1 million in 1932. Economic catastrophe on this scale had never occurred before, and went far to convince people that what they had learned in the previous thirty years might no longer be valid.

The Depression brought a loud clamor from the press for advanced design. Build tomorrow's car today, the logic went, and the demand for it will soon revive the economy.

> . . . designers have recently been debating whether or not the fully streamlined car must come by gradual stages or in one or two big jumps from current practice. Six months ago, we were definitely of the former school of thought. Today— six months of looking at a lot of different "teardrop" designs and beginning to get the emotional feel of their functional harmonies—we begin to lean toward the one big jump idea . . .

reported *Automotive Industries* on December 26, 1931. Since many articles implied that revolutionary cars were imminent, motorists looked forward to the 1933 models with high anticipation.

As it turned out, 1933 was a year in which body designers consolidated their gains without going much beyond what had been done before. The easiest way to describe the average 1933 car is to say that it looked like the 1932 Graham: grille, fenders, and windshield were copied exactly by many manufacturers, and even such details as the headlight shape and the hood louvres were widely imitated. Apparently the general feeling was that it was a safer bet to copy a sure winner than to try to improve on it. While in 1932 the Graham was clearly the outstanding car of the year, in 1933 it was lost in the crowd. No one could disagree with the Graham ads in *Motor* in January 1933, which labeled it "The Most Imitated Car on the Road."

In 1933 automakers took advantage of the only proven low-risk method of improving auto appearance—by reducing the overall height, both apparent and real. This was partly accomplished by changes in tires and wheels. In 1933 the industry adopted "super-balloon" or "doughnut" tires, which were another step in the same direction as "balloon" tires had been in 1924. Much thicker in profile, and built for lower inflation pressures, "doughnut" tires reduced wheel size by two or three inches and generally gave slightly less rolling diameter than their predecessors. As before, thicker tires looked good to the average motorist. On July 2, 1932, *Automotive Industries* reported that, "Sales de-

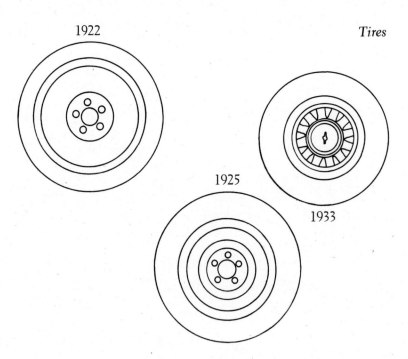

1922

Tires

1925

1933

1922 *Studebaker*

partment is interested in the appearance value of the new tires—in the beauty . . . and . . . the appearance of comfort which they give."

Adoption of the new tires effectively ended the quarter-century long question of whether wood-spoked, wire or disc wheels looked best. Each type had had its turn, and in 1933, wheels with stamped steel spokes were in the ascendant. But with tires encroaching from the outside, and hubcaps growing out from the center, not much of the wheel could be seen any more. In the end it did not matter which type of wheel was used, since it was out of sight anyway.

For the most part, however, height reductions in the new cars were made simply by lowering the roof down closer to the passengers. While this improved the appearance, many people were outraged by the lack of headroom and bad visibility in the new cars. In *Automotive Industries*, April 8, 1933, one relatively moderate critic wrote, "I do not advocate going back to the high chariots of past years, but I do say that the present vogue is outlandish. . . ." A stronger protest was printed in the *New Yorker*, November 12, 1932:

> We think motor car designers have been gradually going crazy. . . . The tendency today is to make a car that is more like a diving-bell than a pleasure vehicle . . . the whole car is built so low to the ground that we wonder why it is not infested with moles. The only way to get through the doors is by crawling through on one's hands and knees.

Gradually the interior of the automobile was becoming more closely tailored to the shape of its passengers. The time when people thought a car should provide room for the "aigrettes of the women and the silk or opera hats of the men" had long passed. By degrees, the roof had dropped to the point where, in 1933, the minimum standard suggested was "to be able to sit in the driver's seat with an ordinary felt hat on and have at least two inches clearance over the hat," according to a report in *Automotive Industries*, April 8, 1933. On many 1933 models this was not possible, however, and owners were forced to remove their hats before driving.

A handful of "Silver Arrow" show cars made by Pierce-Arrow were the only cars of 1933 which approached what motorists had been led to expect in the way of radical new bodies. On these cars the headlights were built into the fenders—nothing new for Pierce-Arrow, who had had this feature since 1914—but the fenders themselves blended into the body sides, which definitely was new. The rear part of the fenders disappeared into the very wide body, as did the runningboards. Radical streamlining was carried through to the rear in full fender skirts, which concealed the back wheels, and in a long, tapering rear body section.

The Silver Arrows drew a lot of comment from crowds at the 1933 shows. Most people liked the rear end design, but the front end and wide body were generally thought to be unattractive. With this reaction in mind, Pierce-Arrow stylists drew up plans for a limited-

1933 Pierce Arrow Silver Arrow (show version)

1934 Pierce Arrow Silver Arrow (production version)

production Silver Arrow for 1934, which combined a conventional front with a sloping back similar to the 1933 car.

By 1933 streamlining was no longer a new idea, and conservative voices, which had mostly been drowned out by rallying calls for novelty in the previous two years, began to be heard again. In *Automotive Industries*, January 28, 1933, one engineer interviewed at the New York Show said bluntly, "The streamlined form is essentially ugly. You can't get away from that, and I don't think you

Toward an Aerodynamic Car **153**

can ever get the public to like it." The same people who muttered about bad visibility and reduced headroom felt that automakers had gone too far in streamlining.

In the press, however, conservatives were still overwhelmingly outnumbered. Indications that advanced designs were continuing to sell better than conventional ones also pushed manufacturers toward a progressive point of view. On January 28, 1933, *Automotive Industries* noted:

> There is a strong feeling of change, mobility, and a general movement toward a new era of creative design. Consciously or unconsciously the movement seems to be pointing to some final streamline form. . . .

Cars with an overall blimp-shape were reported to be "inevitable" in one article after another. It was only a matter of time, it was said, before all cars would be shaped like huge teardrops—the time being variously estimated as the next year, five years off, or ten years off.

Predictions that revolutionary cars were about to appear were not, in fact, far from the truth, though the time it would take the new types to supersede existing designs was wildly underestimated. Two new cars, the Stout Scarab and the Dymaxion of Buckminster Fuller, were in preparation, and by the end of 1933 a Dymaxion prototype had been built. Both of them incorporated the essential "dream car" features seen on the Rumpler in 1921: a teardrop shape and a rear-mounted engine. The Dymaxion was the more radical of

Stout Scarab

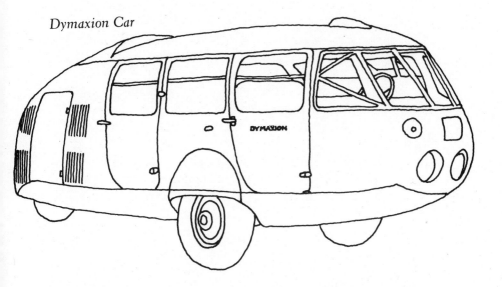

Dymaxion Car

the two, with three wheels (the rear one for steering) and a scissor-like double frame. Difficulties in financing prevented either of these vehicles from going into production, however, so the "teardrop type of car" was never put to the test of public acceptance.

Envious of the success of Reo and Graham with advanced body designs, and spurred on by the optimism and enthusiasm of the streamlining advocates, Chrysler decided to throw its mammoth corporate energies into producing a radical new model for 1934. The

1934 DeSoto Airflow

result was the Airflow, produced in two slightly different versions by Chrysler and DeSoto. As a product of the speculation of the preceding years, and as a pattern for trends to follow, the Airflow was the most significant car of the '30s.

Rarely had a major manufacturer set out to design a new car so little encumbered by the traditions of past practice. According to publicity release in *Motor*, January 1934, the aim was "to produce a motor car designed definitely from the ground up for today's motoring needs and conditions." The originality of the car itself bears this out. In order, the Chrysler statement describes the design goals as (1) improved weight distribution for ride; (2) streamlining; (3) structural strength; (4) better mounting of bumpers; and (5) more room inside.

The overall proportions of the Airflow contrasted with those of every other car on the road. Relative to the wheel positions, the passengers had been moved 20 inches forward, which in turn had pushed the engine out between the front wheels and the radiator still farther forward. The most immediate benefit of this change was that rear-seat passengers sat ahead of the rear wheels rather than over them.

The discomfort of the usual position had long been recognized. In 1908 Packard had introduced a special design which according to *The Horseless Age*, March 4, 1908, was "claimed to provide . . . comfortable riding qualities. In this new design the passengers are midway between the front and rear axles. . . ." Using a traditional front end, with the radiator over the axle, the rear seat could be moved ahead of the wheels only by making the

1908 Packard

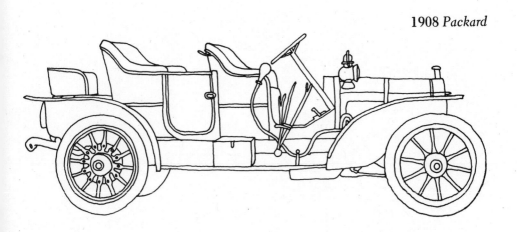

wheelbase inordinately long or by sacrificing rear-seat legroom. The latter course was taken on many close-coupled sedans in the early '20s, but this was an unsatisfactory compromise. By 1929 the proportions of the Stutz sedan were almost universal. Except for the addition of a slanted windshield with a rounded header and a slightly more rounded rear-body shape, the silhouette of a typical 1934 car differed little from the Stutz. Compared with this, the nose-heavy profile of the Airflow was a striking contrast.

The Airflow was nose-heavy in fact as well as appearance. Instead of the 40 percent/60 percent front-rear weight distribution of the usual car, the Airflow had 55 percent—well over half—of its weight on the front wheels. This allowed softer springs to be used at the rear, which reduced pitching and made the ride more comfortable. Even more important, it gave the Airflow more predictable handling on curves and better directional stability.

Another innovation on the Airflow was its construction: the body was used as a stressed member, which in combination with the frame gave forty times the torsional rigidity of the previous model. The body and windshield were ten inches wider, which substantially improved shoulder room and visibility, and a new type of seat was used.

Following the theoretical ideal of a blunt nose and a sweeping tail, the Airflow was clearly designed for low wind resistance, and appearances were borne out by a Chrysler report that nearly fifty models were tested in wind tunnels before the final form was chosen. But was the aerodynamic shape really beautiful? It seemed that many people liked a streamlined back: the rear view of cars such as the Pierce-Arrow Silver Arrow had been widely admired. On the Airflow coupes even the spare tire was put inside the car so nothing interrupted the flow of air at the back. Some other features like the steeply raked vee windshield and the full rear fender skirts had met with approval on earlier cars.

The front end was the problem. In a roundabout way this was even admitted by its designers. According to *Automotive Industries*, June 23, 1934, a report read to the SAE mentioned that:

> It was at first intended to make the radiator narrower, but it was found that not enough cooling capacity could be obtained in that way. The wide front was then adopted and the lower hood gives much greater visibility. . . .

The final design was more practical, perhaps, but the short hood and the broad front, in which headlights, grille, and fenders were blended in a heavy cascade of metal, were the exact opposite of what people had shown that they liked on earlier cars. Still, so much had been written about the need for a blunt nose for streamlining that maybe it would be accepted anyway.

At the time of its introduction the Airflow drew polite comments from the press, but most writers admitted to an initial dislike of the car. A typical article in *Motor*, January 1934, ran:

> At first glance, these cars will look strange to most people, but the writer finds that after you have looked at them for two or three days you become accustomed to them and sooner or later you begin to admire them. Finally you are quite likely to come around to the viewpoint that these cars look right and that conventional cars look strange. The writer, for one, believes that these cars will be a great hit.

The *Scientific American*, in February 1934, remarked in a similar vein that the "streamlined car may, in a very short time, be quite

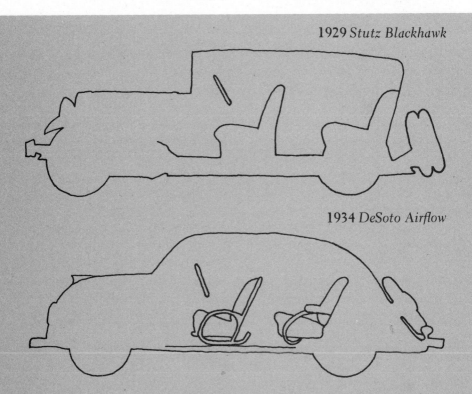

1929 *Stutz Blackhawk*

1934 *DeSoto Airflow*

as pleasing to the eye" as a conventional car, indicating that at the time of writing it was not. In any case, few people viewed the Airflow without forming a strong opinion about it: either they liked it or they detested it. "(T)he startling appearance of these cars," reported *Automotive Industries*, January 27, 1934, "has everybody talking. . . . We have yet to find anybody who is indifferent."

Like the Reo and Graham before it, the Airflow served the rest of the industry as an indicator of public taste. Rival automakers watched anxiously for the first sales figures to come in, meanwhile reviewing their own engineering capabilities to see how quickly they could bring out a similar car should the Airflow prove successful. Stakes were high this time. The Reo and Graham could be imitated relatively easily, by changes in the grille, fenders, and other superficial features, but one could not copy the Airflow without designing a completely new car—a very expensive and time-consuming project.

Initial sales indicated that, yet again, radical design was the way to sell cars. While declines in the production of some other cars were noted in the spring of 1934, sales of the Airflow seemed to be off to a strong start. On April 21, 1934, *Automotive Indus-*

1934-5-6 *Chrysler Airflow*

tries reported that a "backlog of orders for the current Airflow indicates public acceptance of the first approach to streamline form in automobile bodies." In May, production and shipments of the Airflow DeSoto totaled 3,141 units, an increase of 77 percent over DeSoto sales in May of the previous year, according to *Automotive Industries*, June 16, 1934.

Early published figures, however, were for production and orders, rather than for actual sales, and by the summer of 1934 the true story of Airflow sales began to come out. To the dismay of its makers and dealers, and to the relief of its competitors, sales of the Airflow appeared to be following the lead of the Pregnant Buick rather than the Reo or Graham. It had a few buyers, lured on perhaps by its unquestioned engineering excellence, or maybe even because they honestly liked its appearance. Most people did not: for them it had a rhinocerine ungainliness which automatically consigned it to the outer darkness of motordom.

As expected, dissatisfaction with its appearance centered around the front. The Airflow had the lumbering, stupid look of some early touring cars, such as the 1906 Grout shown in Chapter 2. It was similarly criticized, as looking clumsy and out of balance. The round blandness of the front also robbed it of the distinctive "expression" formed on most cars by the relations of hood, fenders, and lights. It had some of the same grotesque anonymity as a human face covered by a nylon stocking.

While auto sales in general rose 27.2 percent in 1934 over 1933, the Airflow prevented DeSoto and Chrysler from sharing the returning prosperity. Not only did DeSoto slip relative to other makes—from eleventh to fourteenth place—but its sales fell an appalling 47 percent. Improved sales of conventional models offset some of the losses on the Chrysler Airflow, allowing Chrysler to maintain tenth place in 1934 in spite of a 9 percent decline in volume (figures taken from *Motor*, January 1935).

While nothing could be done to change the basic shape of the Airflow, its poor reception prompted Chrysler stylists to rush through what small improvements they were able to make by '35. The rear end was unchanged; except for a trivial rearrangement of the cowl louvres, neither were the sides. The hood and grille, however, were entirely new. Instead of following the arc of the fenders, the hood was carried out to a point. Replacing the formless sieve used in '34, the new grille was "v-shaped and sloping from top to bottom . . . materially improving the appearance of these cars," according to *Automotive Industries*, December 29, 1934. A few sharp angles reduced the apparent weight of the design, and the longer hood gave the 1935 Airflow a "proud" look absent in the original. Sales momentum was not so easily built up, however, and though Airflow production staggered on until the end of 1937 (1936 for DeSoto), the total sales of the model were only 22,239.

Returning prosperity and the dismal fortunes of the Airflow dampened the enthusiasm of the streamlining advocates. No longer could they assume that aerodynamic cars would be received sympathetically by the public. Before 1934 the issue had been unclear: it seemed that buyers preferred advanced design, but the choice they were given was relatively limited.

The Reo and Graham were striking when they appeared, but few of their novelties were actually contrary to previous standards of beauty. The Airflow, by contrast, was not only a much larger jump beyond its predecessors, but features such as its proportions and blunt nose had long been unpopular. The question had been whether functional design, through its honesty and simplicity, would be thought beautiful even if it broke completely with earlier traditions. The answer, by the summer of 1934, was recognized to be an emphatic no.

The impetus toward a better form that was created by four years of unusual originality and boldness was not quickly lost, though its pace was reduced from a headlong rush to a more measured progress. The most significant cars of the period, the 1931 Reo Royale, the 1932 Graham Eight, and the 1934 Chrysler and DeSoto Airflows, had irreversibly changed the form of the automobile.

Used car prices around 1935 give an idea of how much these cars had altered public tastes: even the most beautiful examples of traditional bodywork depreciated in a startling way during these years. Part of the reason, of course, was that a Packard V12 or Duesenberg was too expensive for most people to run in the Depression, but part also was certainly due to the fact that, in 1935, cars built before 1932 looked more outdated than their age would indicate. Whether the rounded forms of the mid '30s were truly more beautiful was still a matter of debate, but they unquestionably looked more modern than the earlier square body shapes.

Beautiful or not, the new look had come to stay. Unlike most of the whimsical variations of the '20s, the innovators of the '30s had brought some genuine improvements to automobile design: such things as forward mounting of the radiator and engine, wider bodies, and larger fenders and aprons to cover the chassis were features which could not be discarded after a year or two, because their utility recommended them as well as their beauty.

The Graham and the Airflow set standards which designers of later cars would find hard to ignore. The Graham set an aesthetic standard by showing that a car could be beautiful just by having a pleasing and original basic form, without the assistance of special trim or decoration. The Airflow set a standard for practicality: it showed how drastically an apparently stabilized and satisfactory design could be improved. Compared with the earlier type, the Airflow configuration was superior in ride, directional stability, aerodynamics, passenger room, and luggage space—almost every one of the standards of utility used in judging a car.

From an engineering standpoint the proportions of the Airflow, with the passengers between the axles and the engine far forward, were clearly better than the usual arrangement. As Chrysler with the Airflow and others earlier had found, however, the big problem was the seemingly inconquerable dislike people had for the appearance of a radiator or grille mounted ahead of the front axle. When radiators were moved back to the axle in 1905 and 1906 the

1909 White Steamer

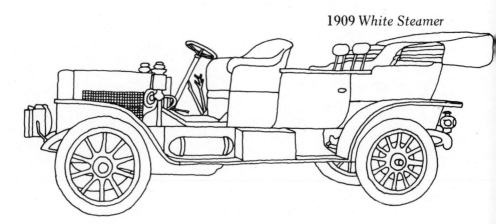

aesthetic improvement was loudly praised. The makers of the White steam car and a handful of others held out for a while, but by 1910 a radiator position either over or behind the axle was universal.

No one dared to tamper with this arrangement until 1919, when several cars, including the original Essex, appeared with radiators set slightly ahead of the axle. Public reaction was strongly against the change: "This is detrimental to the cars in looks," commented *Motor Age*, January 30, 1919, ". . . the effect is clumsy." Practical advantages notwithstanding, the radiators on these cars were soon moved back again.

There they remained during the '20s and early '30s. Meanwhile, however, rising highway speeds and average horsepower were exposing the limitations of conventional weight distribution and chassis design. The last straw was the introduction of mushy "superballoon" or "doughnut" tires in 1932–1933. The public loved these tires for their appearance and comfort, but they made conventionally designed cars dangerously unstable on straight roads and evil-handling on curves.

To meet the crisis many makes introduced independent front suspension in 1934. Though independent suspension has an advanced flavor the systems used were actually rather primitive in intent: through camber changes they were designed to reduce the grip of the front tires in turns, thus lessening the oversteer. As a stopgap measure to improve handling they worked well, and they also improved the ride, but the basic problems caused by bad weight distribution remained. Automakers recognized that some-

1925 *Miller Junior Eight*

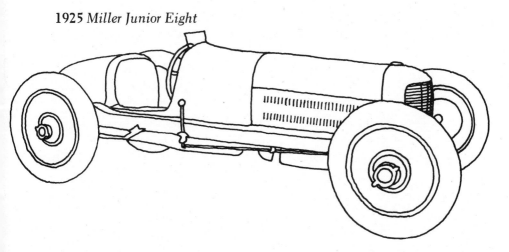

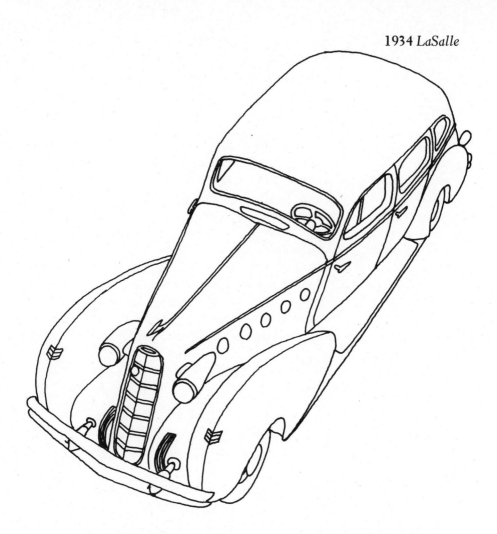

how the public must be made to accept a forward-mounted radiator.

By the separation of the grille from the radiator core inside, as on the DuPont Speedster, Cord L29, and earlier racing cars, the key to success had already been prepared. A grille allowed the front body to be shaped in ways which could be inefficient or prohibitively expensive for a radiator. In 1934 LaSalle took advantage of this by having a long hood which tapered to a very tall and narrow grille in front. Even though the grille was well ahead of the wheels it avoided a heavy, clumsy look by being so slim. A

1934 *LaSalle*

radiator built no wider than the grille on the LaSalle would not have had enough cooling capacity, but the separation in function allowed a large enough radiator to be used inside without spoiling the appearance.

The LaSalle made it look easy to reverse aesthetic preferences which had been strongly held for thirty years. It was the most widely praised new car of 1934, and its front end was the most popular feature. In January 1934, *Motor* characterized it as "distinguished" and noted that "the LaSalle looks about 20 inches longer than its wheelbase suggests." The January 20, 1934, issue of *Automotive Industries* agreed: "The LaSalle front end is graceful, most interesting, and reminiscent of Indianapolis racers." It was the most widely copied car of the year. One year later, on January 5, 1935, *Automotive Industries* said, "Automobile styles this year appear once again to have been influenced profoundly by LaSalle, as was the case some years back when the car was first put on the market."

The Airflow had demonstrated the practical benefits of a forward-mounted engine, and the LaSalle showed that a car with these proportions could be handsome. Gradually other makers followed. In the next several years, engines and bodies inched forward on the chassis. Though this was unquestionably a functional advance, few cars managed to evolve as gracefully as the LaSalle. For example, the 1935 Ford, on which the engine and body were moved forward 8½ inches, looked clumsy compared with the previous model, but its proportions made it look more modern. In the showroom, modernity is at least as successful as beauty, and the 1935 Ford sold well.

The unhappy career of the Airflow was not one which automakers wished to emulate with their own productions, and worthy features of that car were adopted only in the most roundabout way by other makers in 1935. Even though its smooth "aerodynamic" back appeared on the 1935 Pontiac and others, and its full rear fender skirts were also copied, a similar general appearance was carefully avoided. Or it was until the introduction of the 1936 models, when the unbelievable happened: the wraps were swept off the new cars, and there it was—another Airflow, hiding behind the nameplate of Lincoln Zephyr.

In their basic engineering the two cars were closely similar. Radical proportions, which concentrated weight on the front wheels

1935 *Pontiac*

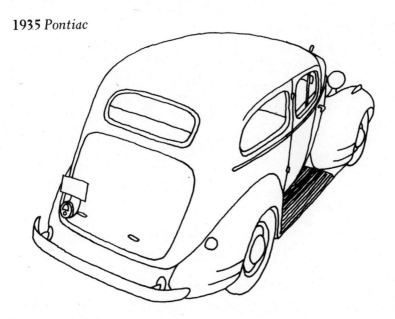

and placed the passengers between the axles, were used on both, which inevitably resulted in a similarity of profile, with a short hood in front and a long sweeping tail. Some original features of the Airflow were carried further on the Zephyr: the body truss of the former was refined into a unit construction on the latter, and the Zephyr body grew even wider than its model—so wide that the runningboards were squeezed into narrow strips.

The most marked difference between the cars was in the execution of their styling. While the basic forms were similar, the

1936 *Lincoln Zephyr*

1936 *Lincoln Zephyr*

Zephyr was by far the more graceful. The Zephyr had a relatively flat hood which came to a vee-front like the bow of a boat. The angularity of the hood and grille and the trough between the fenders and hood relieved the front of the heaviness which people disliked in the Airflow. Clean design was carried through in details: the head-lights were faired into the fenders, the hood louvres were simple, and the gently curving sides were free of ornamentation other than a simple molding at the belt line. At the rear, the fenders and the top swept in from the sides, forming a delicately tapered tail which minimized the width and bulk of the car.

The Zephyr was widely praised in the press for its style, and with a V12 engine, excellent passenger and luggage space, and a reasonable price, its sales prospects seemed good. The public, however, was not so easily tricked. Too many people could still recognize the Airflow lurking inside the new sheet metal of the Zephyr, and even after two years of acquaintance with the Airflow, most people still thought its wide, nose-heavy proportions ugly. Though not Airflow-like, sales of the Zephyr were not particularly good.

Cars with unorthodox mechanical configurations have often been the basis for unusual body designs, and the front wheel drive Cord of 1936, designed by Gordon Buehrig, was no exception. Like earlier front-drive cars it had the advantage of low overall height, and in

1936 *Cord*

many ways it carried the theme of streamlining further than ever. Teardrop-shaped fenders, a sharply raked vee-windshield, and a smooth rear end had been seen in less dramatic form on other cars, but the Cord also had concealed door hinges, flush mounted taillights, and headlights which folded out of sight into the fenders. Even the rear license plate was enclosed. Other unusual points were the omission of runningboards and the use of a boxlike hood girdled by horizontal grille-louvres.

1937 *Studebaker*

The appearance of the Cord was very popular. Most magazines shared the opinion of *Arts and Decoration* in November 1936, that it was "a triumph of integrated design," and according to an informal poll of visitors at the 1936 New York Auto Show it was one of the most admired cars on exhibit. Rival manufacturers seized on details such as the horizontal grille-louvres for inclusion of their 1937 models. In the next year, Studebaker and others had grilles which carried around into horizontal hood louvres without a break.

By the standards of 1931 the average car of 1936 had progressed a long way toward a fully aerodynamic form, but not everybody was happy with the change. On April 25, 1936, *Automotive Industries* reported that:

> Within the past year, the voices of authority have been raised in soft, but articulate, protest against the present trend in the appearance of passenger cars.

Walter Dorwin Teague, a noted industrial designer, was asked what kind of car he drove:

"Oh," he said, "a 1934 Ford," which didn't seem to interest anybody much until he added, "You know, that was the last decent exterior design of an American car . . ." Several other designers . . . were inclined to agree with the speaker.

As well as disliking the general form of many cars, according to *Automotive Industries*, December 14, 1935 Teague was also critical of the use of chrome moldings, "now hung on our cars like beads on a Zulu chief."

Such criticisms did not cause much concern in Detroit. Ugly or not, the new cars made older cars look dated, and because of this they sold well. The bulbous forms of the new look did cause one problem, however, which disturbed automakers considerably: they tended to erase many of the visual indicators of price, on which much of the appeal of middle-priced and luxury cars is based. In November 1936, *Arts and Decoration* remarked that "the Pierce-Arrow at ten thousand dollars looked like the Chevrolet at seven hundred and fifty, bigger, but not quite as up-to-date. . . ."

"To the eye of the average automobile owner," noted *Automotive Industries*, November 11, 1933, "the sight of considerable body overhang in the rear is not beautiful." Nor had it ever seemed so. In the earliest days of the small runabout, the chassis ended at the axle on each end, just like a buggy. When front engines came in, for a brief period the engine hung forward over the front axle and the tonneau stuck out the back, but soon the problems of a long wheelbase, such as poor maneuverability and structural weakness, were found to be exaggerated, and the axles resumed their former positions near the ends of the car.

In most respects, having the axles at the ends of the car was a good thing. A long wheelbase minimized pitching, and at a time when all cars were decidedly tail-heavy and their suspensions were primitive, it provided enough directional stability to keep them from being excessively dangerous. It also looked good: there was something satisfying about having a wheel at each corner, and the long stretch of the wheelbase gave a rangy and elegant effect.

One problem unsolved by this construction, however, was luggage space. Except for a few small pockets and lockers, the average touring car had no place at all specifically designed for

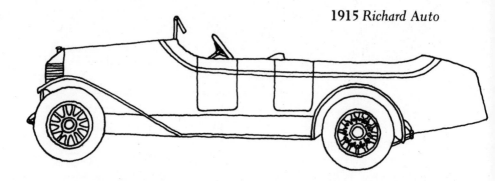

storage. If full passenger capacity was to be used, baggage had to be roped on to the runningboards and fenders, where it was exposed to rain, mud, and dust. What was needed was an accessible, adequately large, enclosed compartment designed for luggage, which would not encroach on passenger space or lessen the maneuverability of the car.

Some thought was given to the problem in the teens, but the suggested solutions were aesthetically unacceptable. On January 23, 1915, an advertisement appeared in *Automobile Topics* for the Richard Auto, which had a "Chemineau Body," featuring an extended trunk at the rear with room for the top, spare tires, and "full equipment of tourists' baggage" in fully enclosed compartments. Nothing further was heard of the Richard Auto, but the idea of the extended trunk was revived in less extreme form on the 1917 Pathfinder. The Pathfinder had a rounded, protuberant rear end which resembled the back of some early torpedo bodies. The extension was not nearly as long as the one on the Richard Auto and

1917 *Pathfinder*

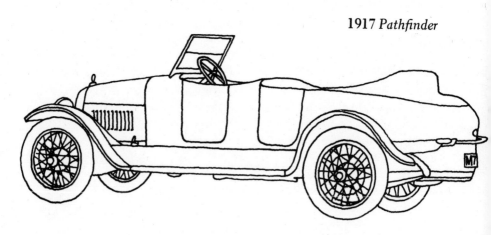

was designed to enclose only the top and spare tires, though some luggage could be fitted in when the top was up. It fulfilled its functional requirements, but most people thought it was ugly, and it had no imitators.

By the early '20s a makeshift solution to the problem had appeared in the form of the rear-mounted luggage rack. This made luggage easier to tie on and less likely to fall off, but, on arriving at his destination, the traveler was still confronted by a filth-encrusted suitcase. On some cars, such as the 1923 Buick shown in Chapter 3, the rack carried a factory-mounted wooden trunk, which was large enough for suitcases and also improved the car's appearance. Unfortunately such a trunk did not look so attractive on full-length sedans, and with the decline of the close-coupled sedan in the late '20s its use was confined mostly to large luxury cars.

On the new cars of the '30s the body was enlarged to cover many parts which were previously exposed: larger grilles and aprons covered the front of the frame, fender skirts covered the sides, and rear body panels were drawn down to cover the gas tank and rear part of the frame. The luggage rack and spare tire suddenly stood out as crude obstructions to the flow of air sweeping over the new forms. A way had to be found to enclose both tire and luggage inside the car without offending the buyer's concepts of beauty.

The 1934 Buick is a good example of a car with styling in transition from the square forms of the '20s to the rounded look of the late '30s. Its long headlights, deep fenders, and rounded roof

1934 *Buick*,

show its affiliation with the streamlined school, but its designers were reluctant to forego the traditional elegance of sidemounted spares or the convenience of a luggage rack. They compromised: the side mounts were not hidden, but the tires were enclosed in metal covers; a luggage rack was included, but by moving the rear of the body forward slightly, space was also made for a built-in metal trunk without making the rear end extend too far out. In 1935 outside racks were nearly extinct and the spare tire was moved inside on most cars, and by 1937 built-in metal trunks like that on the Buick were widely used.

With greater use of built-in trunks the rear overhang of the average car was gradually increasing, but even compared with these the long extended trunk of the Cadillac 60 Special looked startling when the car was introduced in 1938. Not only did it stretch farther out beyond the wheels than any earlier design, but the trunk was, for the first time, fully integrated into the rest of the design. On many cars a built-in trunk was optional, and looked it: neither the curves nor the moldings on the body sides carried into the trunk. The hood, body, and trunk of the 60S, on the other hand, were brought together by the reintroduction of the "pregnant" bulge which killed the Silver Anniversary Buick in 1929: the curve of the top edge of the hood was carried back as a bulge along the window sills and back to the trunk. Use of the bulge made it seem as if the top, not the trunk, were the part added on last, which gave more emphasis on horizontal lines than the old style of added-on trunk.

In spite of its significance in the evolution of functional design, the extended trunk was not the feature of the 60S singled out by the press at its introduction. That honor was given to its enormous

1938 *Cadillac 60S*

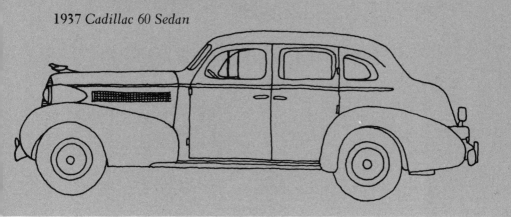

window area, as one might expect at a time when vision from the average car was about the same as from a tank with its periscope shot away. Compared with the previous model, the windshield of the 60S was enlarged 27 percent and the windows from 32 to 53 percent. Elegantly rimmed with narrow strips of chrome, the windows also gave the 60S an airy look which contrasted favorably with other cars. Other notable features were the omission of runningboards and reduced overall height.

In the design of the 60S, Cadillac stylists seem to have felt that the tradition of gentle curves and bulbous forms, begun by Reo in 1931, had run its course in 1938. Alongside other 1938 cars the 60S looks very rectilinear: the tops of the fenders are almost straight lines, which drop abruptly at the back; the roof is flatter than any seen since the arrival of the all-steel top in 1935 and 1936; and the window frames are decisively squared off. While the trend toward integration of forms is continued in the 60S, the inspiration of the teardrop definitely is not.

As engineers in the late '30s demanded that engines and radiators be moved ever closer to the actual front of the car, body designers returned to the problem that plagued the Airflow, that of an unwieldy, bulky look in the front end. Tapering the hood inward to a tall and narrow grille, as on the 1934 LaSalle and its imitators, helped the appearance, but as the grille grew narrower (and more graceful) it also caused cooling problems.

1938 *Lincoln Zephyr*

An original solution to the problem appeared on the 1938 Lincoln Zephyr. Cooling air was taken in through twin grilles in the aprons between the hood and fenders, and the front of the hood was closed to form a solid vee-front. This was a further step in separating the outer appearance of the automobile from its internal functions (the air goes in to cool the engine, not the wheels as it appears to on the Zephyr) but it was successful in eliminating the appearance of heaviness. Even though the enlarged valances gave the new car a more bulky front end than its predecessor, the new grille design made it appear lighter.

On August 27, 1938, *Automotive Industries* reported on a test in which an audience was shown car pictures, two or three at a time, and asked which they felt was best looking. All but a few of the cars shown were production 1938 models; the exceptions were radical

1938 *Graham*

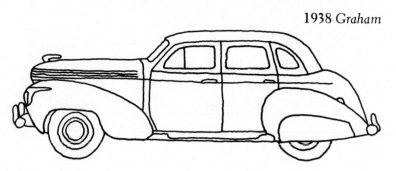

European show cars. In the press, the Cadillac 60S, the Zephyr, and the racy new Graham drew the most praise. The 60S was not separated in the test from other Cadillacs, putting it at a disadvantage, but early odds would have favored one of the other two cars to take top honors. Which would it be? The votes were counted, and the winner was . . . Packard!

It was not even close: not only did Packard draw more than twice as many votes as any other car, but it led in every sex, age, and income group. Though the styling of the Packard was entirely conventional, it was done in good taste and had no objectionable features. It also had the virtue of strong continuity with previous models (the grille shape was an elongated version of the Packard radiator of 1904), which was something no other car had to nearly the same extent. Its overwhelming popularity amply supported the conclusions of the article: that the public likes cars which are "abreast of current style but not a minute ahead of it." Nor do they like cars which "lag behind the procession in looks," but, curiously, they did not include the Packard in this category. "Despite its preservation of its traditional radiator lines, Packard received almost no mentions as being 'not advanced.' "

In the fern-grown swamps of earliest time the fins on small swimming creatures evolved into flippers and then into feet. Though millions of generations separated each stage, one can see from the fossilized remains that the process was orderly: new limbs sprouted

1938 *Packard Eight*

and grew while old ones withered and dropped off, and the forms changed to adapt to altered circumstances.

In the late '30s the progressive evolution of body design followed the Darwinian model more closely than ever before. Its course was predicted confidently and accurately years before the actual developments occurred. In 1931, in a discussion at an SAE meeting reported in the *SAE Journal*, January 7, 1931, L. Clayton Hill described future front-end styling:

> I think lamps are going to disappear as individual units mounted out in front of the car; they will be built into the car. We shall gradually lead the public up to this by incorporating lamps in the radiator, then in the bonnet, and, finally, the fenders into the hood and lamps. Almost before we are aware of it the whole front end of the car will be made as one streamline unit.

By small annual steps the front-end elements of most cars began to melt together: in November 1936, an article in the *SAE Journal* noted that bodies "are clearly in a transient stage toward a more complete yet practical streamlined form." The 1937 Oldsmobile, for example, has wider, more bulbous fenders than ever: the "catwalk" or valance between fenders and hood is a few inches lower than the fenders themselves, but the pod-shaped headlights are still attached by stalks to the sides of the hood. On the succeeding model the headlights begin to sink into the fenders, which are enlarged to swallow up the catwalk and part of the grille.

In 1939 the example of the 1938 Zephyr was widely copied, and the formerly vertical emphasis began to change to a horizontal one. The 1939 Studebaker combines Zephyr-like apron grilles with a low, vestigial hood-front grille, and has headlights flush-mounted in the fenders. An evolutionary resting-point came with the horizontal-bar type grille shown on the 1941 Pontiac. The grille had finally become decorative sculpture inside a cavity, rather than a porous body panel, and the way was open for the strange and fantastic creations of the '50s.

The course of evolution in the shape of the rear part of the body was less easy to predict in the early '30s, though it was clear that it would change as drastically as the front. The inspiration—of aerodynamics and related simplification of forms—was the same. It

1937 *Oldsmobile Eight*

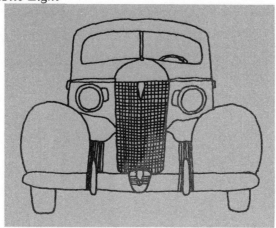

1938 *Oldsmobile*

1939 *Studebaker*

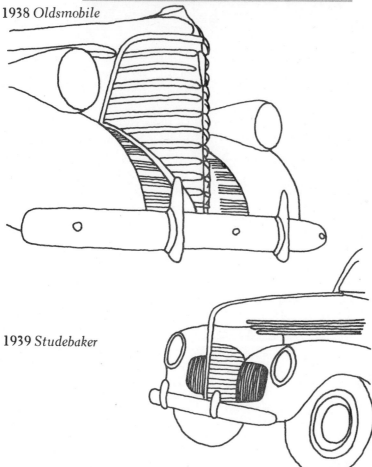

was thought that low drag depended as much on the shape and smoothness of the back of the body as it did on the front, so the same attention was given to parts which might interrupt the air flow.

The first step beyond the old tucked-under style was the "beavertail back" shown on the 1934 Buick, in which the body panels swept down and toward the rear to cover the gas tank and rear part of the frame. The rear slope became more gradual as the passenger compartment moved forward, and in the late '30s a rounded back, as shown on the 1940 Ford, came into vogue.

1934 *Buick*

1940 *Ford Deluxe* V8

Bodies with rear trunks followed a separate line of development. In the middle and late '30s one could order many cars with either a smooth back or a trunk on an otherwise similar body. Around 1940 the two types began to merge. The 1940 Chevrolet is typical of the G.M. approach. Though the car was said to be inspired by the Cadillac 60S, its contours are much more rounded, closer to the streamlined type. Chrysler-made cars used a sloping back with a squared-off lower section which only suggests an extended trunk.

As late as 1940 it was unclear what the rear treatment of future cars would look like. Numerically, variations of the extended trunk seemed to be gaining ground, but one of the most popular styles of 1940 was G.M.'s new "torpedo" or "streamliner"

1940 *Chevrolet Master 85*

body shown on the 1941 Oldsmobile, which was very long and tapered, much like the Airflow coupe. One could almost say it was exactly like the Airflow coupe, as a comparison of their profiles shows. In seven years, "freakish" proportions had become the norm.

Fenders and body sides also evolved toward simpler, more aerodynamic shapes. Completely smooth sides like Jaray's experimental cars in the '20s were obviously the answer, from the standpoint of streamlining and passenger space, but the change from the narrow, pre-1930 type of body to the enveloping Jaray type was too drastic to be made quickly.

Every year after about 1933 fenders were gradually made larger and the main part of the body was widened. The Airflow

1941 *Oldsmobile Club Sedan*

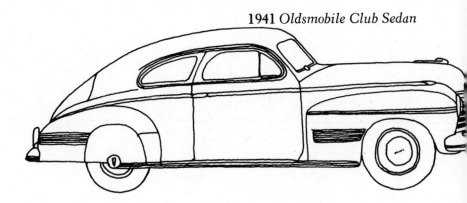

1941 *Oldsmobile/DeSoto Airflow*

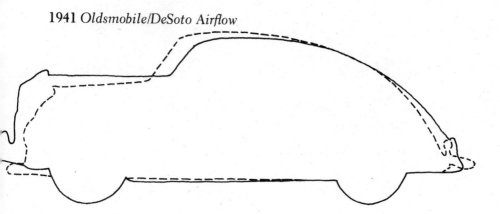

body was 10 inches wider than the model it replaced, but as in so many other things on the Airflow, this was a larger step than the public could accept. Body width on the average car only caught up with the Airflow around 1938, and this was only in the passenger compartment—the hood was still much narrower. The 1938 Dodge was typical for that year. The extra width finally allowed three people to be seated in front, and to make this easier, many 1938 models moved the shift lever from the floor to the steering column.

1938 *Dodge*

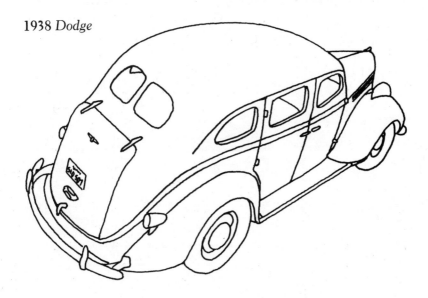

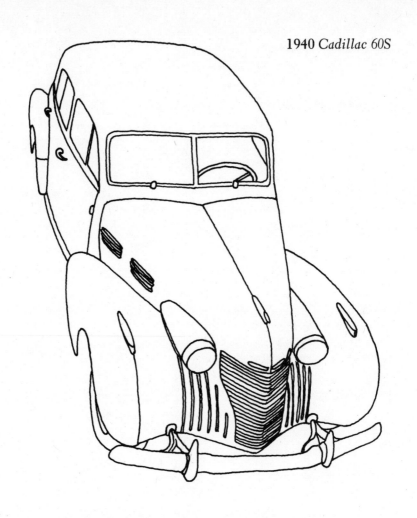

1940 *Cadillac 60S*

1942 *Packard*

1942 *Buick*

By 1940 bodies were only a few inches from the edges of the car, and runningboards were optional on many models. Though distinctly separate in the front view from the hood, the front fenders almost blended into the body sides at the rear. On two 1942 models they actually did: the Packard Clipper had fenders faired into the sides, while the Buick extended them all the way to the rear, effectively making the body sides part of the fenders. Whichever way it was to happen—by the body swallowing the fenders or vice versa—it was clear that on future cars their shapes were going to merge in one enveloping form.

In the late '30s cars had become more streamlined and functional, but also more depressingly sensible. Where were the rakish, utterly impractical expressions of wealth and power that had flourished a few years earlier—the Duesenberg J, the Stutz DV32, and others which had made men's pulses race? They had withered in the chill of the Depression, leaving only the hardiest family cars behind.

A car which carried on some of their flavor was the Lincoln Continental, introduced in the fall of 1939 as a five or six-passenger, two-door cabriolet. At 62 inches, the Continental was conspicuously lower than its contemporaries, which ranged in height between about 65 and 72 inches. The hood of the Continental was seven inches longer and three inches lower than other Lincoln models, and the passenger compartment was compressed into a

Toward an Aerodynamic Car 185

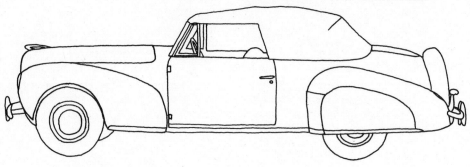

relatively short length: though this made the rear-seat legroom cramped it gave the car long-nosed, close-coupled proportions which recalled the elegance of luxury cars built a decade earlier. Executed in unfaltering good taste, its styling created a sensation at its introduction.

The Continental was different from its contemporaries not only in its styling but in its personality. It was not easily categorized: though it could carry as many people as some sedans, it was far too exotic to be considered a mere family car. Its convertible top, rakish proportions, and V12 engine gave it sporting associations, but it was not a sports car either, certainly not in the European tradition of the Mercedes and not even in the American sense of the Stutz roadsters of the late '20s. These cars were made for driving at high speeds and shared some features with race cars; the Continental, on the other hand, was too large, heavy, and dignified ever to be driven like a real sports car. Nor was it simply a luxury car. Though it was refined, expensive looking, and well finished, it was smaller and less ponderous than luxury cars were expected to be.

Mercedes 500K

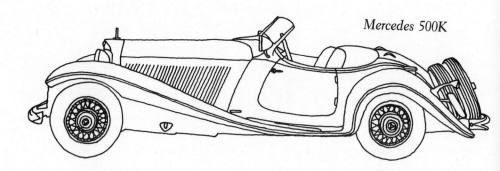

Though it included influences from each of these types, the Continental was no more of a compromise than they were: the family car was designed primarily for utility, the sports car for performance, and the luxury car for comfort and ostentation; on the Continental, other considerations were subordinated to style. It was a stylist's car: like the brass-adorned touring car of 1903 or the enormous V16 Cadillac roadster of 1930, the Continental functioned primarily as an ornament for the owner and only secondarily as transportation.

Whether or not the general public was ever much excited about streamlined cars is hard to determine, but it does not matter much anyway. What is important is that the clamor for them in the press pushed automakers into making a start in that direction with such cars as the Graham Eight and the Airflow, and once begun, there was no turning back. If the Depression had not made motor executives jittery, perhaps the change might have been delayed, but as it was they had little choice.

Regardless of how it began, the streamlining theme of the '30s caused the automobile to evolve rapidly toward a more functional form. Due to changes in the body, the car of 1940 could carry three people in the front instead of two, and had an enclosed space at the rear for luggage instead of a primitive exposed rack. Stylists had persuaded the public to accept the aesthetics of new proportions which would give better ride and handling. Following the basic evolutionary tendency to cover up the mechanism, begun with the earliest horseless carriages, during the '30s the front and rear of the frame, the radiator, the gas tank, and other parts disappeared underneath the body. Aerodynamics were also improved, though not as drastically as some people had hoped: the smoother shapes did not help gas mileage or performance very much, but they did reduce wind buffeting on the highway.

Compared with other decades, body changes in the '30s were quite closely allied with functional requirements, but there were a few backward steps nonetheless. The most obvious one was the problem of visibility from inside. Hoods became higher than ever, windows lower, and roof pillars thicker. In 1937, coincidentally with a traffic fatality figure which easily surpassed every previous mark and would stand as a record for many years afterward, cars were introduced which were harder to see out of than any ever made before. Following the example of the Cadillac 60S, most manufacturers began to enlarge window area in 1939 and 1940, but they still had a long way to go.

Another retrograde step was in accessibility. In 1930 removal of the hood exposed the top and sides of the engine, and just about everything could be easily reached. In 1940 the hood panel was reduced to a small hatch above the huge fenders, and many parts were harder to work on. Part of the blame for this problem can be put on the aesthetic preference people had for a narrow hood, but most of it was due to the blending together of front-end elements into a single form. Unification of the front end was an inevitable and generally beneficial development, so the accessibility problem probably could not have been avoided entirely.

5
Dream Cars and Nightmares

The mechanized wonders of World War II amazed even the blasé American public. In response to the wartime need U.S. factories spawned all manner of ingenious vehicles capable of rolling, swimming, creeping, or flying—amphibious trucks, airplanes which could fly at nearly the speed of sound, and much else besides.

It was a new machine age, and after witnessing such quick development in the military field, many people expected similar advances in vehicles for civilian use. Automobiles suddenly began to seem like rather a primitive form of transportation. Instead of starting up the Ford and driving off to work in the morning, it would be more fitting to step into a quietly whirring helicopter and whizz at incredible speed to a private heliport on the office roof. Helicopter travel was a popular fantasy in the postwar era: compact, powerful helicopters were often portrayed as successors to the automobile.

It was clear, however, that the automobile would be around for a while longer. But it was not enough that it merely carry on the prewar automotive tradition. In the new era, an automobile had to be something more than what it was before. It had to share in some of the excitement of the jet age, and take on the flavor of the fantasy world of helicopters and airplanes. Drivers did not want to be reminded of driving a car; they wanted to imagine themselves as pilots instead (from James Thurber's "The Secret Life of Walter Mitty"):

"Rev her up to 8,500! We're going through!" The pounding of the cylinders increased: ta-pocketa-pocketa-pocketa-POCKETA-POCKETA. The Commander stared at the ice forming on the pilot window. He walked over and twisted a row of complicated dials. . . .

In 1945 one magazine after another tantalized its readers with "inside" stories on fabulous new vehicles ("even now being prepared for production in Detroit"). An April 1945, *Mechanix Illustrated* interview with George Walker (later to become chief stylist at Ford) carried illustrations of the new cars. None of them looked much like an automobile. Most had concealed wheels front and rear, flat sides, and bumpers which combined with the grille in front and wrapped around to the sides. The general effect was of a flattened, inverted bathtub. All of them had increased glass area, sometimes carried to the extreme of an aircraft-style full plexiglas canopy over the passenger compartment. *Mechanix Illustrated* confidently predicted such cars would appear no more than 18 months after the armistice.

After a buildup like this, the first postwar cars were pretty disappointing. Automakers simply dragged old dies out of storage and set them to work. There was a serious shortage of materials, and when production resumed in the spring of 1946 it was only a trickle. Though hawked as '46 models, the cars were no more than very thinly disguised '42s.

For a while, at least, there was no incentive for automakers to come up with anything new. After a four-year fast, the car-buying hunger of America was at an all-time high. The newest cars on the road were four years old, and the average age was far greater.

1945 dream car

1946 *Frazer*

All of this combined to make a seller's market: there were long waiting lists for every kind of car, and buyers were happy with anything they could get.

The first true postwar car was the Kaiser-Frazer, made by a company whose postwar formation exempted it from the 1942-model hangover of other makers. It was designed by Howard ("Dutch") Darrin, formerly of the noted custom body firm of Hibbard and Darrin. It was received enthusiastically by the press and was awarded "Grands Prix d'Honneur" in concours d'elegance at Monte Carlo and Cannes.

The Kaiser and Frazer shared a body shell which was the evolutionary endpoint of several prewar styling trends. The fenders, for example, had disappeared into the flat sides, though from the front and rear they could still be distinguished from the hood and rear deck. The wide passenger compartment was by now almost squarely between the axles, for optimum riding comfort, and the extended trunk was raised and enlarged, giving it greater capacity and a visual equivalence with the hood in front.

Another new car to appear in 1946 was the 1947 Studebaker, which had a completely restyled body by industrial designer Raymond Loewy. Though its basic shape was no more advanced than the Kaiser-Frazer, it had a much more radical flavor. The most spectacular model in the new line was the two-door coupe, which was not only half a foot lower than most other cars, but also had the vast increase of window area predicted for postwar cars in the *Mechanix Illustrated* article. The windshield and rear window had fully twice the area of the previous model, which was largely

Dream Cars and Nightmares **191**

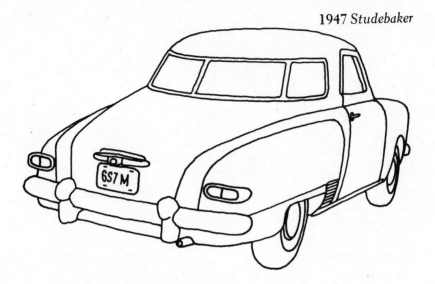

achieved by wrapping the rear window around the sides of the rear-seat passengers to give a bizarre "greenhouse effect."

It was hard to say exactly what the Studebaker looked like, but it certainly did not look like an ordinary automobile, and in 1946 that was a point in its favor. While moving one of the new cars into a Chicago hotel for its introduction ceremonies work-men were trampled by an excited throng of onlookers, and finally a police guard had to be called out to keep back the crowds. The Studebaker was an exciting step toward the postwar dream car motorists had imagined during the war years.

Even more of the features *Mechanix Illustrated* had pre-dicted for postwar cars appeared on the 1948 Hudson. It was strikingly low and broad, and had the lowest center of gravity of any U.S. passenger car. Hudson called its construction the "step-down" type because the floors were dropped below the level of the door sills. The concealed rear wheels, smooth sides, and slowly descending ridge in the side panels give it a look of com-fortable heaviness. As on the *Mechanix Illustrated* dream cars, the overriders on the front bumper are prominent in the front-end design, and the molding on the lower part of the side suggests a side bumper. With a bubble top and enclosed front wheels the Hudson would come close to the visions of 1945.

1948 *Hudson*

Sharing the Hudson's low, heavy, slightly bloated appearance were new models from Packard, Lincoln, and Mercury. The substantial look appealed to buyers, and at first brought favorable comments from the press—the Hudson had "sparkling styling of an advanced character," according to *Automotive Industries*, December 15, 1947—but some thought the effect was overstated: "If we persist in making a fetish of fat contours," Virgil Exner, future head of Chrysler styling, wrote in *Automotive Industries*, December 1, 1948:

> . . . the character and distinction which in the past have differentiated one make of car from another will disappear. . . . Dignity would be overwhelmed by ponderous, massive Hollywood concepts which have taken root in the field of automobile design. . . .

1948 *Packard Custom Eight*

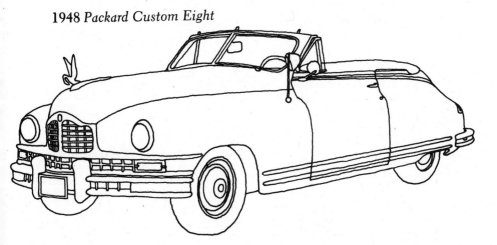

Whatever the initial response, the appeal of this body shape did not last very long, and when the bodies of these cars lived out their natural life span of about three years of production they were replaced by new designs which had very little resemblance to them.

Most automakers assumed that, whatever weird shapes the body of the postwar car was contorted into, underneath would be a conventional chassis of ordinary dimensions. An exception was the Tucker, which was scheduled for 1948 but never reached production. The Tucker had a rear-mounted six-cylinder engine, disc brakes, and other mechanical innovations under a body which combined jet-age features like a centrally mounted headlight which turned with the front wheels with a conventional fastback shape. A prototype had enclosed front wheels, but these were not retained on the final model.

The Tucker was one of many cars announced by newly formed small firms after the war. The Bobbi-Kar, the Airway, and the three-wheeled Davis were to compete in the economy car field with the postwar Crosley, which had been invigorated by a new 26-hp engine which weighed only 59 pounds. Willys introduced a slightly more civilized version of the Jeep, called the Jeepster, and made plans to produce the Willys Aero, a small conventional sedan. In the sports car field were the Del Mar and the Kurtis, both Californian creations.

1948 *Tucker*

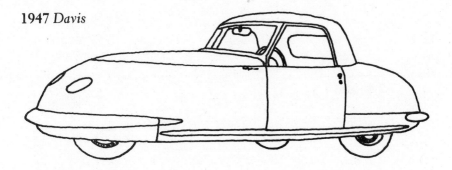

1947 *Davis*

These small firms gambled on the possibility that the postwar market would shift away from cars of ordinary size and design. They worried large automakers because, due to the seller's market, postwar buyers eagerly took anything, and it was hard to tell what their real preferences were. If a new firm set up production of a good economy car and then, when the market became competitive again, sales of the small car continued strongly at the expense of the big cars, established automakers would be at a disadvantage until they could develop a similar car of their own.

Hedging their bet on the usual type of big sedan, several large firms did development work on small cars. In the late '40s rumors were thick around Detroit: as late as July 15, 1949, *Automotive Industries* reported that "trade circles continue to buzz about light car developments in the offing." As production caught up with demand, however, it became clear that a small car was not what American buyers wanted. Much relieved, General Motors shelved their small car designs, and Ford sent theirs over to a European branch of the company.

The car which the majority of motorists dreamed of in the postwar era was not radical in size or engineering. It was basically the same thing they had always wanted: big and garish, with some distinctive style feature to set it apart from older cars. In 1949 the styling motif of the year was the hardtop convertible, a pillarless coupe body in which the visual bulk of the top is minimized to give an open "convertible look." Buick-claimed to have been the first with this type of body on their 1949 Riviera model. The tapered rear quarters of the Buick made it the best looking of the hardtops made in 1949,

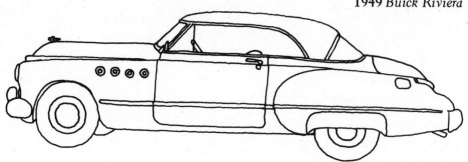

but Chrysler, who also showed a hardtop in this year, loudly disputed Buick's claim to have been first with the style. The Kaiser Virginian and Frazer Manhattan also had hardtops in 1949.

Actually, neither Buick nor Chrysler nor any other postwar maker was first with the hardtop: the principal feature (and most difficult engineering problem of the body) was the elimination of the side pillars for the top, and this was shared by the infamous "touring sedan" body type in the teens. These early cars looked long, low, and airy next to conventional sedans, just as the hardtops of 1949 did, but like them also the early cars were drafty, leaky, and filled with an orchestra of rattles and squeaks.

The new style was an immediate hit. Production lagged way behind demand in 1949, when hardtops made up only one-fifth of one percent of total sales, but in 1950 that figure shot up to 8.85 percent, according to *Automotive Industries*, March 15, 1951. At

1918 *Premier Limousine-Sedan*

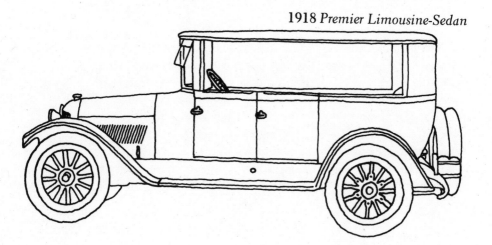

least some of its success seems to have been at the expense of the standard convertible, which from a level of around 5 percent of the total in 1947 and 1948 dropped to slightly over 3 percent in 1950.

By the early '50s family resemblances among cars of one corporation had come into sharp focus. By then, styling chiefs had had a chance to view the offerings of their competitors and form a coherent philosophy of styling development to guide the progress of all divisions. Aberrations were gradually weeded out so that by 1951 or 1952 there was a distinct "Chrysler look," "Ford look," or "G.M. look." Differences within the family such as between Plymouth and Chrysler, or between Ford and Lincoln, became more a matter of size and trim detail than of more basic dissimilarities.

Chrysler Corporation was betting on comfort and sensible conservatism. Compared with Ford and Chevrolet, the 1951 Plymouth had changed relatively little from the prewar model. To be sure, it had undergone the standard transformations of the period: it had a squared-off rear deck instead of the prewar fastback, it had more glass area and was fractionally lower; but it carried on so much of the flavor of earlier styling that annual changes were not easy to identify. It had more headroom than its competitors, but to do this it was higher, and looked it. It was also nine inches shorter than its competitors, which made it look dowdier still. Dodge, DeSoto, and Chrysler were progressively enlarged versions of the Plymouth, with different grilles and side moldings. Buyers apparently thought they looked dull; as the years went by, Chrysler cars dropped down on the sales charts by steady increments.

1951 Plymouth

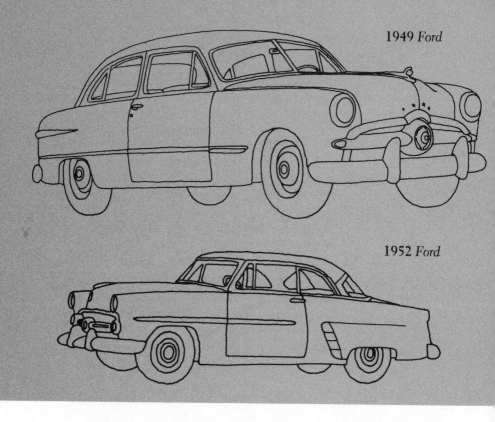

1949 *Ford*

1952 *Ford*

The Ford Motor Company placed its hopes on a crisp look with straight lines and square corners. In 1952 the original postwar Ford, already square-looking next to its competitors, was replaced by a new car which was even more so. Angular, forward-leaning bodies also appeared in that year on Lincolns and Mercurys. In sales the Ford was successful, but the Lincoln and Mercury were less so. The styling approach which worked for Ford in the low-priced field seemed less satisfactory in the medium and high-priced fields.

In the postwar period G.M. stylists seemed to have a magic touch. Low-priced Chevrolet and high-priced Cadillac were always popular, but it was in the middle range where G.M. cars were strongest. Every year middle-priced Buick threatened to take third place in sales away from low-priced Plymouth, and Oldsmobile was also very strong. What did Buick and Oldsmobile have, for which so many people were willing to pay so much money?

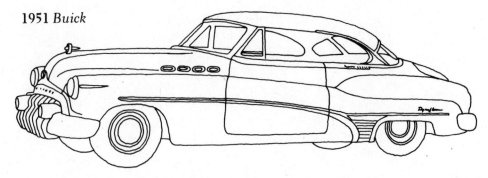

1951 *Buick*

It is easier first to enumerate what they did not have. Certainly they were not beautiful, in the conventional sense: they did not have grace, symmetry, or balance. No visual theme connected the front end with the back, and their styling motifs were disconnected. The Ford policy of clean design was obviously not used here. Nor was the Chrysler policy of sensible proportions. While the owner was given an ever-wider seat, which he did not really need, the roof was being lowered onto his skull. Externally, in length and width, the cars were monstrous: sometimes they were so big that owners had to rebuild their garages.

G.M. cars were impractical and unbeautiful, but people flocked to buy them because the cars gratified their emotional needs. The difference between the approach to styling at G.M. and elsewhere was that, ever since the early '30s, G.M. styling reflected a deeper understanding of the relationship between a man and his car, which is quite unlike his relationship with most other objects.

The naive designer of an automobile body imagines its future owner standing in his driveway admiring its sweeping lines, as he would admire a piece of sculpture. Certainly this relationship will exist some of the time, but a moment later the separation of car from owner vanishes as he takes the wheel. In an instant, the car is no longer a separate object but rather an extension of the owner, and in this transformation, the standards of appearance by which he judges the car change drastically. Purity of line, symmetry and balance are no longer as important as the symbolic features of the car. The driver has merged himself with the car to become a modern centaur, and the appearance of the car is his own appearance.

The car becomes an emotional outlet. At one time or another, most drivers use their cars to express feelings of aggression. The automobile satisfies this urge in a variety of ways: its engine multiplies the driver's physical power several hundred-fold, enabling him to rush down the highway like an enraged bull, threatening the world with his strength; its imposing immensity gives him confidence to bully other cars in traffic; and by the magnificence of its appearance he can awe his neighbors with his wealth and status. It is also, indirectly, a means of sexual expression, though the manifestations of this are ambiguous and often contradictory. The car is simultaneously an extension of the owner and a separate object. A long hood, for example, is a natural phallic symbol, but at the same time, psychologists have found that the automobile often symbolizes the mother: within its rounded body it encloses its passenger in womb-like comfort. This symbolism is carried to an extreme on pink Cadillacs with air conditioning.

To the owner, then, the automobile is both a separate object and an extension of his person. If it were only the former, conventional aesthetic standards might be enough for the stylist. The car which wins a gold medal from a panel of artists might also win the widest popularity for styling. Past practice had shown, however, that such distinctions are unrelated to public acceptance. To be successful on the marketplace, the styling of a car must include symbolic expression, perhaps an even more important consideration than ordinary aesthetics.

In the early '50s G.M. cars, particularly Buick, Oldsmobile, and Cadillac, fairly dripped with symbolic expression. Like an aborigine donning a horned and lurid ceremonial mask, the hen-pecked

1950 Buick Series 40

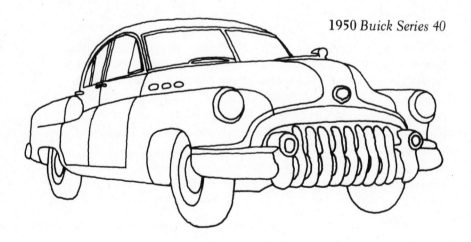

husband of suburbia happily climbed behind the wheel of his new 1950 Buick and set out to terrorize the populace. Few cars have had a more fearsome physiognomy: under a thick chromium lip its enormous mouth seems to stretch the metal skin above it in an effort to gape wider. Inside the mouth is a row of gleaming, carnivorous-looking fangs. Transformed from insignificance, the driver of such a car luxuriates in his disguise.

Combined with its purgatorial monster elements, the front end of the 1950 Buick had parts which suggested a battering ram. Many people instinctively think of a car in this role, and the Buick's heavy bumper guards topped by mallet-like cylinders seem designed to transmit force from the car to another object. In theory, at least, bumpers are defensive in function, but the ones on the Buick seem to be intended for offensive use.

The battering ram concept of an automobile extends to other parts of its appearance. All G.M. cars were made to look heavy, to a point verging on ponderousness. Part of this appearance was conveyed by the sheer size of the cars, but most of the effect was given through visual means. Large radius curves, for example, look heavier than square corners: a mound of sand looks heavier than a box of the same volume. The 1950 Buick is a mound of car, especially when compared with a squared-off car like the 1952 Ford. Its maximum width is low on the sides, and the upper part of the body is heaped heavily onto the fenders. All transitions between shapes are softly rounded. Another way of giving a heavy look is to conceal the wheels: on the Buick the cutouts are fairly low, but not to the point where the car would look too ungainly.

A heavy object makes a better ram than a light one, and the Buick looks splendidly suited for this purpose. It appealed to people not only as a way of subconsciously threatening the world, but also for instinctively felt safety reasons. Driving a heavy enough car, people thought, one could smash through any accident without being hurt much. There is a small measure of logic in this, but weight also tends to make a car harder to stop and maneuver, making an accident more likely, and on some objects, such as bridge abutments, even two tons of automobile produce little effect.

The appearance of heaviness is also attractive in other ways. For example, it appeals to the buyer's sense of value: "Ya get a lotta car for the money." Most people have a feeling that a big car, purely on the basis of its size, will be more comfortable. Part of this is logical: with an unsophisticated suspension, heavy cars tend to ride more smoothly than light ones, and since luxury cars have almost always been large, by the reverse logic large cars might generally be expected to be luxurious. Part also is instinctive: one naturally imagines a big fat car to be soft and pillowy inside—perhaps a manifestation of the automobile's symbolic maternity. Lastly, it is deeply ingrained in the American mind that "bigger is better": "Babbitt respected bigness in anything; in mountains, jewels, muscles, wealth or words," wrote Sinclair Lewis in 1922, and Americans had not changed much since. If the car in a man's driveway was bigger than his neighbor's he had a slight edge in the neighborhood hierarchy.

Size is only one of the features of G.M. cars specifically included for the purpose of impressing the neighbors. Another is dazzle and glitter: ever since the Stone Ages men have prized reflective objects such as polished stones and metal jewelry. Instinct says that a car which is ablaze with chrome trim must have been more expensive than a plain one, even though rational enquiry shows that in the total price of a car the cost of a few extra strips of bright metal is negligible. Knowing this, G.M. stylists have been liberal with their use of reflective trim. Ever since the early '30s G.M. cars have had more chrome than most others; the trend reached a temporary peak around 1942, eased off slightly in the first all-new postwar designs, and then resumed with a vengeance in the sort of metallic encrustations shown on the 1951 Oldsmobile.

G.M. stylists also recognized the automotive function of ostentatious display in the way they planned the increments of annual

1951 *Oldsmobile*

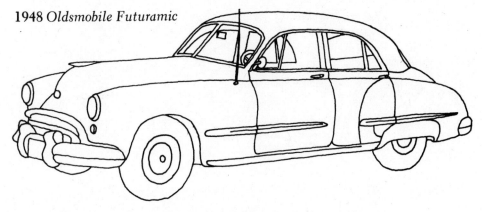

1948 *Oldsmobile Futuramic*

changes. The path of evolution from one model to the next is always painstakingly spelled out. A good example is the first postwar product of G.M. Styling, the 1948 "Futuramic" Oldsmobile. Several evolutionary trends were in progress at that time, such as the merging of fenders into sides, increase of glass area, enlargement of bumpers, and reduction of overall height, to name just a few.

In each of these things the new Oldsmobile was an advance over its predecessor, but the changes not made in the new body are as significant as those which were. The rear fender was not eliminated, for example: why do in one step what can be done in three or four? In noting that the fenders on the 1948 Oldsmobile were smaller and more closely aligned with the sides than on the 1947 model, the Olds owner was assured that progress was being made without being dizzied by radical and disturbing changes. Likewise the windows were not enlarged so much that they could not be enlarged again in the next year or two; the car was made lower, but only by a slight increment, and so on. In this pell-mell world, the buyer of an Oldsmobile could always be secure in knowing that his car looked precisely one year newer than last year's model, and would look only one year older than next year's.

Car buyers soon develop a feel for the direction of evolution, which gives them increased sensitivity to small annual changes. Curiously, it seems enough that this year's car is measurably "newer" than last year's. Changes beyond this minimum are excess: a car three years ahead of its time is not likely to have such success. The Kaiser had flat sides in 1946, for example, but in the early '50s G.M. stylists were still at work merging the rear fenders into the sides of

Dream Cars and Nightmares 203

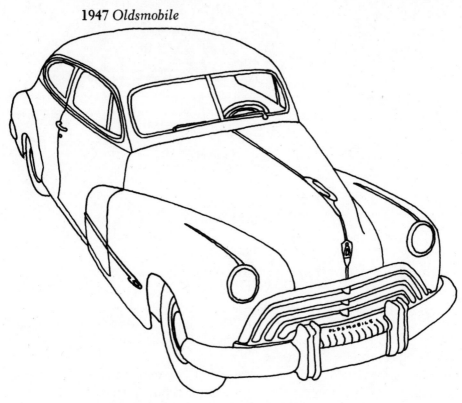

their cars, and every change they made was thought by buyers to have a modern look.

For middle and high-priced cars a reliable means of identification that stayed the same from year to year was almost a necessity. Why spend a lot of money on a Cadillac, if no one could tell what it was unless he got close enough to read the nameplate? Before World War II the best known example of such an identifying feature was Packard's radiator shape, which was retained in recognizable form from 1904 onwards.

Before the war, Pontiac, with its "Silver Streaks" of chrome running up the hood and down the back, was the only G.M. car with such a feature. In the postwar period trademarks were invented for other G.M. cars. Cadillac's first tail fins, for example, sprouted in 1948 as taillight bumps in the top of the rear fender. Opinion was divided on their aesthetic value: Tom McCahill, of *Mechanix Illustrated* (February 1949), did not like them: "Nothing in design since

1953 *Packard*

1948 *Cadillac*

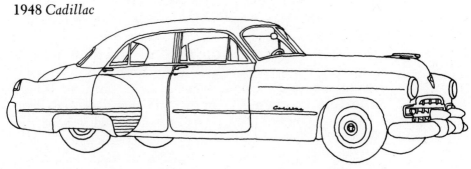

the New Look has created so much comment. 'They're different,' they say. Painting your nose red will make you look different, too, but who wants to do it!" Pretty or not, they served well to identify Cadillacs, and if you owned a Cadillac, you certainly wanted no one to be in doubt about what kind of car you had.

Buick came out with not one but two obvious trademarks. The first was the "sweep-spear molding" which curved downward from the top of the front wheel arch to meet the rocker panel (bottom of body) just in front of the rear wheel. "Ventiports" were the other identifying feature. Ostensibly these were holes to let out hot air from under the hood, but in this their efficacy was questionable. Like the Cadillac tail fins they were the butt of many jokes—they were said to be "portholes" for miniature stowaways in the fender, and the name stuck. But Buick owners loved them: they carried some of the connotations of power given by exposed exhausts in the '20s and '30s and, useful or not, they were something you could only have by owning a Buick.

Most of these symbolic design features are quite separate from conventional beauty and some run contrary to it. But in an unex-

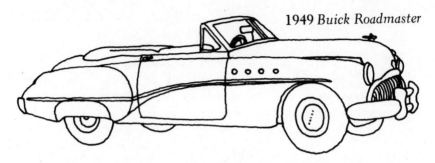

pectedly literal sort of way they provided the answer to postwar dream car aspirations. The 1950 Buick *was* a dream car, in that it blended perfectly with its owner's daydreams. More closely than any automobiles before them, the G.M. cars of the early '50s were tailored to a fantasy world, with all of its bizarre inconsistencies and unsettling reflections of the unconscious mind. In his hours behind the wheel the owner of such a car could muse pleasurably, imagining pedestrians running for cover at the approach of the Terror of the Highways or neighbors enviously calculating how much he had been able to spend on his car. In many subtle ways, the car pampered him and flattered his ego. A few people felt that such cars insulted their standards of good taste, but they were not numerous enough to worry G.M.

Flattery of the Walter Mitty type of owner was also evident in postwar Studebakers, though not to the same degree as in G.M. designs. The huge rear "greenhouse" introduced on the coupes in 1947 gave an unmistakable flavor of an aircraft canopy. The high point of airplane imitation was reached in 1950 with the "propeller-nose" model which had a round torpedo-shaped hood terminating in a chrome "cowling" with a small propeller-like decoration inside. Large numbers of would-be jet pilots flocked to Studebaker showrooms, and sales, already on the upswing from the original postwar car, reached a peak in 1950.

After 1950, however, sales dropped badly, and the decision was made to produce a completely new body, to be designed by Raymond Loewy. To put the company back on a sound footing something special was needed, and Studebaker gambled on advanced styling. The centerpiece of the radical new line, which

1950 *Studebaker*

appeared in 1953, was the two-door hardtop. It had a bold, lean look which instantly set it apart from all other cars on the road. At 56 inches, it was the lowest American production car, and it looked even lower because most of the reduction had been made in the body proper (thus lowering the belt line) rather than in the top. The body sides had a crease sweeping from the front fender into the door, but no chrome trim. The grille, bumpers, hubcaps, and other details were simple and tasteful.

The Studebaker's dramatic proportions and restrained styling gave it a kinship with the Italian school of design exemplified by the 1947 Fiat by Pinin Farina. This connection was played up by Studebaker in its advertising in *Motor Age*, February 1953: "This is the first American car with a real European flair. . . . New smartness and Continental distinction. . . ." Everyone agreed that the cars marked a new departure in U.S. car styling: *Automotive Industries* commented, on February 1, 1953, that they

1953 *Studebaker*

"break as sharply with American contemporary design as did their predecessors immediately after World War II." Press comments were mostly highly favorable and Studebaker received awards for design excellence from many independent institutions such as the Museum of Modern Art in New York, which rated it one of the world's ten most beautiful automobiles.

To an auto manufacturer, such praise is welcome but not essential. What really matters is public acceptance, as measured in sales. At the outset this was in some doubt. In March 1954, *Motor Trend*, quoting its '53 report, remarked that "whether or not the radically styled Studebaker will meet with public approval is hard to determine. . . ." As the months passed, it became clear that the new car was not very popular. Though Studebaker sales were improved over 1952, the overall market was so good in 1953 that, in the first 10 months of the year, Studebaker's market share dropped to 2.88 percent from 3.81 percent the year before, according to the August 1953 issue of *Motor Age*.

Such sharp disagreement between the opinions of design experts and those of the general public inspired many efforts to explain away the car's poor sales record. Thousands of potential buyers were lost, it was claimed, due to early production difficulties; this certainly contributed to the 34 percent drop in market penetration for the first five months compared with the year before, but even after production problems were overcome, sales were not very good. Another argument was that while the coupe was attractive, the sedans made on the same theme were not, and

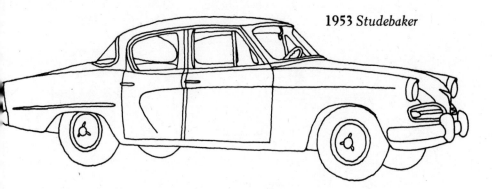

the popularity of the coupe was not enough to offset exceptionally poor sales of the sedans.

The fact is, the general public did not much like either of them. Due to its sharply sloping hood and rear deck, the car was occasionally called the "double-ended" Studebaker. The final judgment came from James Nance, president of what was then Studebaker-Packard, at the announcement in 1955 of a much-altered version of the car. In December 1955, *Motor Trend* reported:

> Speaking of Loewy-designed Studebakers of the recent past . . . Nance says, "You either liked it or you disliked it. It was a highly individualistic car."
>
> Speaking of the new sedan models, he says, "We feel that we have taken them out of the *fringe* market and put them squarely back in the *middle* of the market." Both quotes are obvious references to the former, controversial European look.

Handsome or not, the Studebaker of '53 was short on the kind of fantasy elements which made its predecessor successful. More than simple good looks were needed to sell cars.

From time to time movements have begun in the automotive world which, while not threatening to Detroit in terms of sheer sales volume, have served nevertheless to make motorists less satisfied with the standard Detroit products. In the early postwar period there were several of these, two originating in Southern California and one in the Northeast.

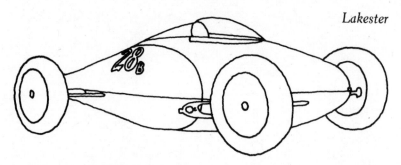

From California, there emerged a new breed of car called a hot rod. All elements of the hot rod had been seen before, though never in this combination. The hot rod was originally a racing car: some of the first cars to which the name was applied were designed for speed record attempts on the dry lakes, and used Ford or Mercury flathead V8 engines and teardrop bodies made from airplane belly tanks.

Top speed has always been an unmanageable sort of thing to test, however, so hot rodders soon turned their attention to a form of racing so simple and safe that it could be and always had been done everywhere: the standing start acceleration run. Drag racing started on a wide scale with the installation of the first stop lights, and it is only surprising that it took so long to become institutionalized. The first hot rodders ran acceleration runs like speed runs on the salt flats: cars were timed separately over the distance. With the adoption of the two-by-two, tournament style elimination and the quarter-mile distance the drag race format was complete.

The term "hot rod" has never been closely defined, and cannot be: every hot rod is different, and they range from slightly modified road cars to all-out drag racing cars. By the early '50s, however, the term usually brought to mind the following assemblage of junkyard-found pieces: a frame from an early Ford, perhaps a Model A, laden with a much modified V8 engine and cut-down Model T roadster body. The engine, nakedly exposed, was chrome plated wherever possible, and the body was painted a violent color like red or orange. The whole vehicle was cleaned and polished to an utterly impractical degree.

The ostensible purpose of a hot rod is to run in drag races, but it soon became clear that its function as a personal adornment

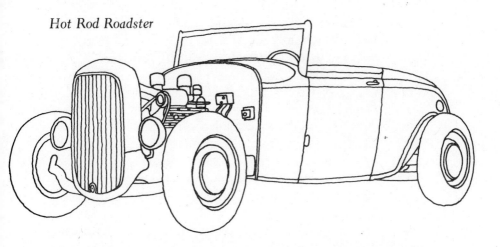

Hot Rod Roadster

was equally important. What better display of power and masculinity could there be than a drive down Sunset Strip in a gleaming hot rod? Just listening to the big V8 grunting through its huge chrome-plated exhaust pipes was enough to convince most people that the car was fast enough to make its driver black out from G-forces, and if there were any doubters, they could be shown impressive tire marks at the will of the driver.

The closest progenitors of the hot rod were the cut-down Ford speedsters made in the teens. Like the postwar hot rod, they traced their genealogy through the junkyard: to the basic chassis (well used) were added speed equipment, wire wheels, and a sporty roadster body. They were also usually personal creations of the owner. The principal difference was in the overall design aim. The early Ford specials were imitations of such cars as the Mercer Raceabout, a fast, well-balanced combination sports/racing car; the hot rod, on the other hand, was patterned only after itself—it was made to accelerate fast in a straight line for a quarter mile, period. The hot rod is inseparable from the drag race. Its unsuita-

Ford speedster

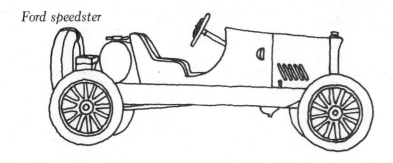

bility for anything else seems almost intentional: steering, suspension, brakes, and streamlining were pointedly ignored by the hot rodder and were barely adequate for ordinary road use.

Also of Californian origin was the custom car, which here should perhaps be referred to as the Kustom Kar to distinguish it from the products of special body makers during the '20s and '30s. The "custom" begins life as a standard American passenger car, but its appearance is "customized" or modified according to the tastes of its owner. This, of course, can be done on a small scale, by removing or altering pieces of trim, or very extensively, to the point where the appearance of the original body is completely disguised.

By 1952 or 1953 an extensive vocabulary of customizing motifs had been developed. One had to start with an "in" car, and this was determined by a combination of basic body shape, availability at a low price, and straight-line performance in stock form. A popular car for the purpose was the 1949–51 Ford. The first change was to "nose" the hood (remove the ornament and fill in the holes) and strip off all the standard chrome trim lines. Sometimes these were replaced by trim in other patterns, sometimes omitted entirely.

Then the headlights and taillights were "frenched" by blending in the surrounds with the body; the rear wheels were covered by skirts; the car was lowered, either just in the rear or all around; the grille was reworked with parts from other cars; a "Continental Kit" (outside spare on extended shelf) was added to the rear; and the wheels were covered by the gaudiest possible hubcaps, the best of which had "spinners" which flashed in the sun as the wheel turned.

Custom Car (1951 Mercury)

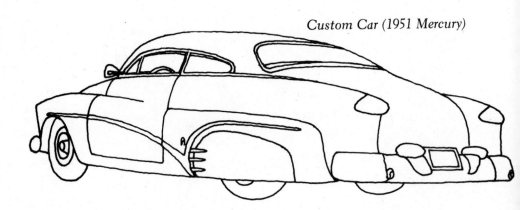

Creations of custom car kings such as George Barris went even farther than this. Barris' cars were often "chopped" and "channeled" by removing horizontal sections from the top pillars and body to make the car lower. The appearance of length was given by "eyebrows" projecting forward over the headlights and backwards over the taillights, and on some cars the rear fenders were actually extended a foot or more.

The sports car movement began shortly after the war in the Northeast but, like all things automotive, it soon spread to California as well. Two British cars spear-headed the movement: the MG TC, which was first imported in 1946, and the Jaguar XK120, which followed three years later. Like the hot rod or custom, these cars appealed to people because they were different from ordinary passenger cars.

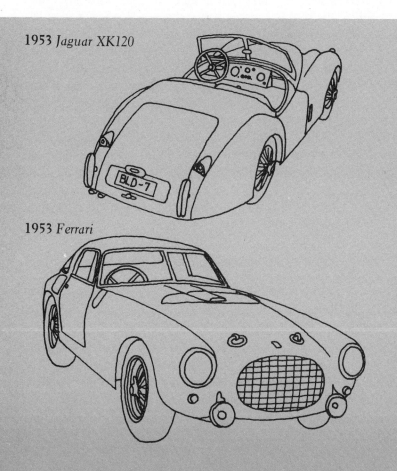

1953 *Jaguar XK120*

1953 *Ferrari*

Just as the customizer's dream car was often something he had seen only in pictures, the ideal of the sports car buff was an extremely rare and expensive Italian car like a Ferrari or Maserati. Its chassis was directly derived from pure racing practice, and the car itself could be used either for racing or for road driving. The coupe or roadster body had room for only two passengers. Essential visual features of the car were wire wheels and an assortment of air scoops.

Common to all of these movements was an anti-Detroit feeling. In their various ways, hot rodders, customizers, and sports car enthusiasts all thought conventional American cars were dull. The flowering of all these groups in the early '50s marked the end of the postwar honeymoon Detroit had had with the public. Unrestrained praise of American automakers had gone out of fashion; in its stead were a variety of heated criticisms. Detroit had not produced the car these people had dreamed of, so they had either bought from abroad or created their own.

Detroit made amiable efforts to satisfy its critics. The hot rodders were the easiest to please. The acid test of a hot rod was how fast it could go: a slow hot rod was nothing, regardless of how it looked. In 1949 Cadillac introduced a high compression 160 hp. V8, and the horsepower race was on. G.M., Chrysler, and (belatedly) Ford vied annually for the reputation of the year's fastest stock cars, trying to satisfy what an ad in *The Horseless Age*, August 1, 1917 termed "The Motorist's Ambition":

> Isn't it the ambition of every motorist to feel that his grip on the wheel makes him master of the road? He doesn't want to race, but isn't it a joy to know that when Bill Smith tries to pass him he can let 'er out and give Smith the Ha Ha?

In the next decade the horsepower of Detroit's most powerful car was to rise from 160 to 400. The hot rodder could no longer be sure of winning stoplight drags with ordinary looking sedans, and, what was worse, the people who mattered knew this. The hot rod's image of invincible power was tarnished.

The customizers were also not hard to please. Essentially they accepted the concept of a big ostentatious car, but within these limits they wanted more variety. Detroit responded by offering an ever-greater choice of colors, trim patterns, and other appearance options. Many motifs of the customizers were adopted:

the forward-leaning headlight brows on the '53 Studebaker came from customizing practice, as did the Continental Kit on the '52 Nash.

In the creation of stylist's dream cars for display at auto shows, Detroit set up a pattern of interest arousal and subsequent satisfaction that paralleled custom car activity. Few customizers were original: the few who were furnished an ideal for the masses who were not. The average teen-age customizer got his inspiration from magazine pictures or chance exposure to a fancy or unusual custom car. By transposing a few details from it to his own car, he carried over in his imagination much of the excitement of the original.

Detroit dream cars were the ultimate in customs. They were in the same vein as the fancy customs made elsewhere, only more so: they were lower, gaudier, more expensive-looking, and were all over hung with custom gimmicks like scoops, hidden lights, tail fins, invisible door-closing mechanisms, and so forth. A good Detroit dream car would steal the show from almost any custom.

The customizer had to do his own work to imitate top custom cars, but if he wanted a car with the flavor of a Detroit dream car all he had to do was wait for a year or two and then buy the appropriate Detroit product. The relation between show car and production car was particularly organized and rational at G.M. Starting in 1950, G.M. held annual auto shows around the country which they called "Motoramas." Along with new production models, dream cars were displayed which prefigured future motifs of G.M. passenger car styling. The LeSabre, shown at the 1951 Motorama, was a composite of G.M. themes such as the Buick spear and Cadillac tail fins. To satisfy the custom crowd it had a novel and complex grille and air scoops in the rear fenders. It also had a wraparound windshield, which came out on the larger production G.M. cars in 1954. G.M. show cars came of age in 1953, when they were given divisional identities and the same styling

LeSabre

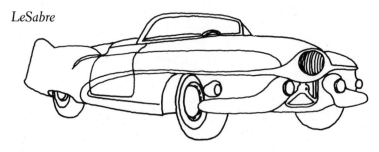

(slightly exaggerated) that would follow on regular cars two or three years later.

The hobby of customizing continued, of course, in spite of Detroit's pre-emptive efforts, but it lost its anti-Detroit bias. Stylists who worked on the dream cars were brought into the fold. They were thought of as just another breed of customizer, and their creations were regarded alongside those of George Barris and Ed ("Big Daddy") Roth as fashionplates of customizing trends.

Compared with the hot rodders and customizers, the sports car set was hard to please. For one thing, they bought their sports cars partly because of the snob appeal of their foreign origin. A retaliatory Detroit sports car would be unavoidably American. For another thing, the conditions which had encouraged mechanical sophistication in Europe, such as widespread interest in racing, no speed limits, high gasoline prices, and taxes based on engine size, were absent here, thus giving U.S. manufacturers neither the incentive nor the knowledge to imitate the foreigners in this respect. Thus at the outset, any realistic U.S. sports car design would lack some of the important items on which sports car snob appeal was based.

What was left? Well, there was styling. By way of Farina, some sports car items such as air scoops on the hood made their way onto Nash and other cars. Then a wire wheel craze began. In 1953 you could buy anything from hubcaps stamped with a wire wheel pattern to an all-out set of real wire wheels. The best of the real kind were those on the Buick Skylark, introduced in August 1952. But the public was not fooled; such cars were still a far cry from real sports cars.

Buick Skylark

1951 *Nash Healey*

Chevrolet Corvette prototype

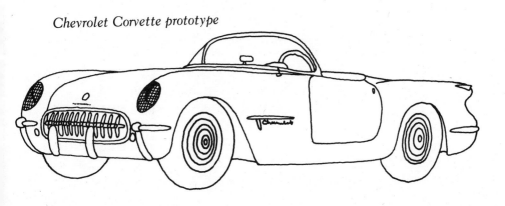

The only way to cater to the sports car cult was to make a two-seater roadster. The first postwar effort of this sort by a major manufacturer was the Nash Healey, introduced in the U.S. in early 1951. It was not strictly American: the chassis was built by Healey in England, and the styling was by Farina; the six-cylinder engine and drive train from a Nash Ambassador were the only American components.

At the Motorama in 1953 Chevrolet introduced the Corvette, G.M.'s conception of a sports car. The Corvette was an extremely low two-seater which combined European sports car motifs like wire-mesh covered headlights and a simple, relatively narrow grille with G.M. Motorama favorites like projectile-taillights and a wraparound windshield. Anticipating only a small production, G.M. pioneered the use of fiberglass body panels (which were cheaper in the expected numbers). By the publicity given to this advanced construction, some attention was diverted from the Corvette's unexciting mechanical specifications.

The Thunderbird, Ford's entry into the sports car field, was announced in the spring of 1954, and production began that summer. The extra year taken to develop the Thunderbird was evident in better planning of its image than the Corvette had had. In a clumsy sort of way, the Corvette had been aimed at real sports car owners of the "in" group—no one else would have endured the Corvette's primitive roadster top—yet in so many ways it was obviously not a sports car in the European sense. Its automatic transmission and complete lack of mechanical innovation were drawbacks too great for sophisticated Jaguar and Porsche owners to swallow.

Ford did not even call the Thunderbird a sports car: it was a "personal car," which was something quite different. Ford recognized the difficulty of appealing to the sports car set and the meager financial rewards of attempting it. Instead, they made a car which attracted owners of American cars who wanted something small and sporty but who were reluctant to forego the comforts of an American sedan. The Thunderbird was perfect. It had handsome styling which, except for the hood air scoop, was purely Ford in origin, with characteristic straight lines and large round taillights (a Ford trademark since 1952). Its well-designed folding top and roll-up windows kept its passengers warm and dry,

1955 Ford Thunderbird

and a removable hardtop was available which made it even more comfortable. Its V8 engine gave it good acceleration and its soft springs and slow steering made most American drivers feel right at home.

In every field for which it was intended, the Thunderbird was a complete success. From the time it went on sale it outsold the Corvette several times over. On the U.S. automobile market its prestige was unmatched, and its similarity in body styling to the regular line of Ford passenger cars radiated some of its glamour onto them. In this respect, Ford took better advantage of the Thunderbird than Chevrolet did of the Corvette: the Corvette had few links with regular Chevrolets, in either styling or promotional emphasis. The Thunderbird also drew praise from independent judges of aesthetics: it was given awards and otherwise singled out for special recognition for its styling. The only roles in which it did not distinguish itself were ones for which it was explicitly not intended—as a racing car or serious sports car. Few Jaguars were traded in for Thunderbirds, and at the sight of one, the sports car buff raised his already-lifted nose still higher. Ford did not care; the car served its intended purposes well.

The years passed, and G.M. cars, ever more bulbous and ornate, sold better and better. Buick moved into third place in overall sales, dislodging Plymouth, and chrome-laden Oldsmobile was more popular than ever. After a while, rival automakers began to recognize a pattern in G.M.'s success: it seemed that the bigger and more ostentatious a car was, the better its sales would be.

Decisions were made at Ford and Chrysler to outdo G.M. at its own game. A new generation of fantasy-vehicles was on its way. "Already we have seen a horsepower race," reported an article in *Motor Trend*, March 1954. "Next will be a styling race."

The first entries had already been introduced: for 1954, G.M.'s larger cars, Oldsmobile, Buick, and Cadillac, had an entirely new body. At a fraction over 60 inches high, it was about three inches lower than the previous model, and newness was conveyed by the wraparound windshield and flatter roof and belt lines. A bewildering variety of loud two-tone color combinations were offered. Trademarks such as Cadillac fins and Buick spear and portholes were emphasized more than ever, and recognition was given to customizers in the hooded headlights and (on Cadillac) combination bumperette/dual exhaust outlets. Summing up the impression given by the new Cadillac, *Motor Trend* remarked in March 1954, "These cars may have the outlines of a landing barge, but it's the one the admiral rides in."

In 1955 retaliatory efforts from other makers hit the market. The cars from the Chrysler Corp. were the most changed. Gone were the stodgy, "sensible" cars of the recent past; the 1955 line, designed by new chief stylist Virgil Exner, looked modern and flashy. The Plymouth was typical of the new "Forward Look" Chrysler cars: it was as long, low, and wide as anything in its field, and when seen from the side, the forward slant of the body at the headlights and backward slant at the taillights made it seem to stretch even longer. It had all the modern features, such as a

1955 *Plymouth*

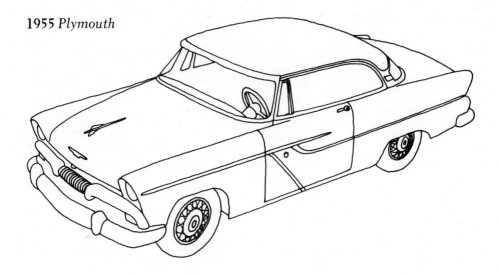

wraparound windshield, dazzling chrome side trim, and a vast array of two-tone color combinations.

Most automakers produced new bodies in 1955, and they all followed the same pattern. They were uniformly longer, lower, and wider than before, and looked it; they had wraparound windshields, jagged chrome decorations on the side, and the most conspicuous possible hubcap design. Color schemes seemed to be inspired by tropical birds and jungle flowers—cars painted red, orange, pink, white, or yellow were much in evidence. The gaudy effects were mostly due to the color and deluxe trim, however; in their basic body lines, the '55 cars were as clean as in any previous year.

The first serious attempt by other manufacturers to match G.M., to make cars larger, lower, heavier-looking, and gaudier, was an unqualified success. The market share of Chrysler, which had made the most drastic changes, had the most improvement, with their four lines (Plymouth, Dodge, DeSoto, and Chrysler) moving up an average of one place each on the sales ladder. Better yet, it seemed that new styling policies at Ford and Chrysler expanded the whole auto market rather than simply reapportioning shares in it. Over 7.9 million cars were sold in 1955, surpassing comfortably the previous all-time record.

Dream Cars and Nightmares **221**

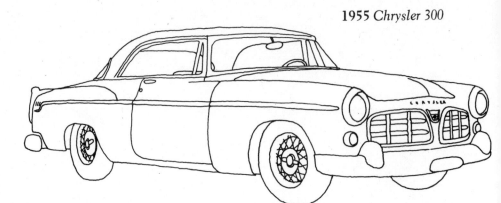

In September of 1955, the editors of *Motor Trend* selected what they considered the best styled cars of 1955. In the top three choices, the first two were predictable. The first was the Chrysler 300 hardtop, a good example of the Chrysler Corp. "Forward Look." Second place was given to the Ford Thunderbird, which as a sporty two-seater had an obvious appeal. In third place was the Chevrolet Nomad . . . a station wagon! In winning a beauty contest, this body style had finally come of age.

Station wagons recognizable as such appeared in significant numbers in the early '20s. Most of the early ones were made by special body manufacturers to fit on standard chassis, especially Fords. Only a few companies, like Star from 1923 on, offered them as a standard body choice. Most of the early ones were used as second cars on estates and farms, and the demand for them was small. Only in the late '30s did the concept of a station wagon as a practical family car become widely accepted. By 1941 most low-priced makes and some medium-priced ones offered station wagons, but the demand for them was still very limited.

When auto production resumed in 1946, the demand for station wagons was more than 50 percent greater than it had been before the war. The station wagon outgrew its role as an estate car and was discovered to be well suited to the needs of a suburban family with many children. Gradually it became the symbol of comfortable domesticity. Ads showed station wagons laden with indecently healthy young families, with tents, sleeping bags, and the family dog, driving through picturesque scenery in the sum-

1922 *Ford Station wagon*

1942 *Pontiac station wagon*

mertime. Station wagon sales climbed steadily, from 0.7 percent of the total in 1940 to 2.2 percent in 1947 and 2.6 percent in 1948, according to *Automotive Industries*, March 15, 1950.

In spite of its rapidly increasing sales the station wagon was still far from perfected. In the late '40s much of the body was still being made from wood. Besides being expensive, this construction was not as resistant to weather as steel body panels protected by modern auto paint. The varnish tended to peel and crack, which in turn made the wood unattractive. Other problems were rain leaks, rattles, and drafts. The large interior space was hard to heat adequately in the winter. Last but not least, the station wagon was always the "plain sister" of the body styles. Station wagons always looked a bit like trucks.

Progress in utility was made in the early '50s by the adoption of the all-steel body. Chrysler had them in 1949, Fisher Body made the change in 1950 for General Motors bodies, and Ford switched over in 1952. With the steel body the problems of leaks and drafts were reduced, though the new cars had, if anything, more rattles and road noise than the old wooden type. For a while, nothing was done about the appearance. Some of the new steel bodies were painted one solid color or a two-tone arrangement divided at the belt line, but many were finished in a simulated wood pattern to look just the way they had before.

In 1954 G.M. showed interest in station wagon styling by showing a dream wagon called the Nomad. It was made on the compact Corvette chassis, and was designed to be a combination between a sports car and a station wagon. It drew an enormous amount of interest, which led to rumors that a production sports wagon on the Corvette chassis was in preparation. The production Nomad appeared in 1955, but on the standard Chevrolet chassis. It was no sports car, but it had all the utility of any other wagon in a body of decidedly handsome appearance. Its principal styling innovations were the steep forward rake of the roof pillars, and the use of a thick pillar behind the door and relatively thin ones farther back. The rear pillars were chromed, not painted, to accentuate the difference. The roof gave the same greenhouse effect as the 1947 Studebaker coupe.

In 1955 station wagon sales climbed to around 9 percent of the total sales. With a steel body it had reached an acceptable level of comfort and durability, and finally, in the Nomad, it had received the attention it deserved from the styling department. It retained the principal quality that had favored it from the

1955 Chevrolet Nomad

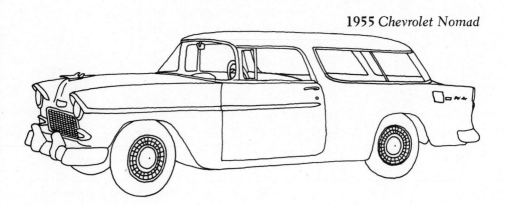

beginning—unequalled practicality, in its space for passengers and baggage and in its ease of carrying awkward objects. In functional design it was a step ahead of conventional sedans, but its still-humdrum image kept it from replacing them as the standard type of car in use.

In the postwar period Cadillac rose to a dominant position in the luxury car field. After 1950 one could almost say that it was the only American car left with an untarnished reputation for quality, comfort, and the high price that goes with them. Former competitors had dropped by the roadside. The Depression caused a blight in the luxury car field from which it never recovered. Lost in that dark age were Peerless, Marmon, and Pierce-Arrow, names which were famous for luxury cars back to the earliest days, plus Duesenberg, DuPont, Cord, Stutz, and others. Packard survived only by making a smaller, cheaper model, and thereby sacrificed the prestige of its name. The Lincoln Continental was dropped in 1948. Ordinary Lincolns and Chryslers were not in the same class.

The situation was particularly galling to Ford, the second largest automaker. Ford did not resent the profit G.M. made on the Cadillac as much as the prestige that the car had. "The Standard of the World," Cadillac called itself, and the glow of popular admiration surrounding the car helped other G.M. divisions as well.

In retaliation, Ford made plans to revive the Continental. The new version would be the most elegant, most carefully constructed car made in America—and the most expensive. Its high price would limit ownership to a select few. Even at $10,000 apiece Ford did not expect much financial profit from the car, but if the reputation for making the finest car in America could be wrested from Cadillac the effort would be worthwhile.

The new Continental was planned for introduction as a 1956 model. All through 1955 rumors circulated about it, and the company carefully leaked just enough information to keep them going. Walt Woron, writing in the May 1955 issue of *Motor Trend*, remarked, "Never can I recall so much interest abounding in the release of a single new automobile." An editorial comment in the same issue was: "There will be no sales problem for this limited production gem."

At the auto shows in 1955 Cadillac exhibited a dream car called the Eldorado Brougham, a low, four-door hardtop with no vent windows (built with the assumption that air conditioning would be standard). Rumors about the new Continental caused such a stir that Cadillac decided to build a production version of the show car to compete with it. The Eldorado Brougham was to be built to the same high standards and sold at a comparable price. The Continental was not to be allowed to take the reputation of America's top luxury car by default.

Though the cars were similar in many other ways, it was clear from the remarks of company officials that their styling themes would be quite different. The theme of the Continental was labeled "modern formal." According to the April 1955 issue of *Motor Trend*, a Continental Division spokesman described the car as a "functional, enduring design emphasizing an air of distinction and elegant simplicity." The show version of the Eldorado Brougham, on the other hand, was a far cry from "elegant simplicity." It featured a blinding stainless steel roof and quadruple headlights, as well as the usual Cadillac trademarks like fins and two huge, chrome-plated "Dagmars" or bullets in the grille. In the December 1955 issue of *Motor Trend*, Cadillac sales manager James Roche indicated that the flavor of the production version would be the same: "Roche feels that the Brougham is strictly modern, not just 'modern formal' and left unsaid the implication that the two cars do not directly compete." Certainly they would appeal to buyers of different tastes, but both sought the admiration and awe of the general public, and to this extent they would indeed meet head-on.

The first thing most people commented on when the Continental Mark II was introduced was its thematic similarity to the original Continental design. Compared with other 1956 cars, it had an unusually long hood, a short passenger compartment, and short rear deck. This rearward bias of the passenger compartment recalled not only the earlier Continental but also the classic silhouette of the '20s and early '30s. An unusual feature of the original car was its externally mounted spare tire, and this was echoed in the '56 version by an upright spare-tire shape stamped

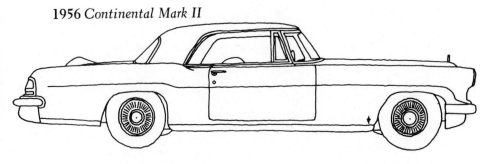

in the deck lid. Another detail which brought to mind the earlier car was the squarish blind quarter panel on the top; the postwar trend had constantly been toward lighter and more open roofs, and beside them the Continental roof gave an impression of privacy and formality.

In other details the styling of the Continental followed conservative contemporary trends. At the rear, the exhaust exited through bumper guards at each side of the car. In front, the headlights were countersunk into the fenders so that, from the side, no rim was visible; this was a common customizing motif. Everywhere there was evidence of restraint: the grille was a simple shape with mesh inside; the hubcaps were plain by 1956 standards; and there was no chrome trim on the sides except for a single strip along the rocker panel. For members of the press and public who had been railing against the garishness and bad taste of Detroit cars, the Continental was a direct reply. Few could find anything to criticize on the point of good taste.

In response to the elaborate pre-introduction buildup, many orders came in from people who had never even seen pictures of the car. When it was introduced, *Time* reported on October 10, 1955: "All told, 2,100 orders have come in. Production will be limited to about 4,000 cars annually, less than expected demand." As soon as it reached the showrooms, however, it became evident that few people were much excited about "modern formal" styling. Most of the pre-introduction orders evaporated, and registrations for the first ten months of 1956 were only 1,338, or comparable to the number of Chevrolets made before the morning coffee break on a good day (figures taken from *Automotive News* as reported in *Motor Trend*, March 1957).

"The revival of the American classic has had rough sledding this year. Sales have been disappointing," said *Motor Trend* in September 1956. Production crawled on until mid-1957, when it was suspended after a total output of 3,012 units.

Large sales had not, of course, been the purpose of creating the Continental Mark II, but its fate in the marketplace signaled a failure in other areas as well. To take the title of "Standard of the World" away from Cadillac the Continental had to approach the public's conception of the ultimate in styling as well as in other things, and this it did not do. There were some who thought it was the most beautiful car since the war, but the general public regarded it with apathy. "Some say that the Continental styling was too 'old fashioned,'" commented *Motor Trend* in October 1957 after the car's demise. People seemed to think that a car costing $10,000 should show it a bit more obviously than the Continental did.

Since Cadillac's plans to produce the Eldorado Brougham were only given final approval when it was seen how much publicity the Continental was receiving, it was far from ready when the Continental appeared in the showrooms in the fall of 1955. Sales figures and other indicators soon showed that Cadillac's prestige position was not in serious jeopardy, and the Eldorado Brougham project lost momentum. A few were eventually sold in 1957, but it was never really in production, even on the small scale of the Continental.

Sales of 1956 models were reasonably good by pre-1955 standards, but they did not come up to expectations, and Detroit wondered why. Car magazines gave one answer: this letter to *Motor Trend* in June 1955 was typical of reader's comments:

1957 Cadillac Eldorado Brougham

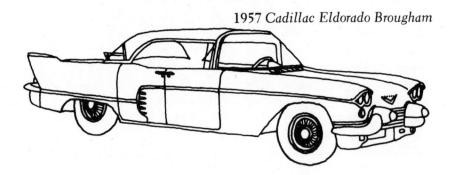

As an average American auto fan, I would like to express my opinion of the '55 American cars. To put it bluntly, with few exceptions . . . they are pregnant, 4-wheeled, chromed-up barges. . . .

Another wrote to *Motor Trend* in September 1955:

I think modern styling with the cut-up lines and/or the paint and chrome haphazardly slapped on must make the real artist lay awake at night.

These opinions were expressed in most of the reader's letters and (in somewhat diluted form) in many magazine editorials. A few individual cars were praised for their styling but remarks on the general trend of Detroit design were almost always derogatory.

Compared with sales figures, printed criticisms were not taken too seriously in Detroit. And in 1956, the gap between the public's stated opinions and its buying habits was wider than ever. A few cars with simple and conservative styling, such as the Thunderbird and Chevrolet Nomad, had sold well, but the weight of numbers was overwhelmingly on the side of the "pregnant chromed-up barges." Buick and Oldsmobile held third and fifth places, respectively, in the 1956 sales race, and on the other side of the coin, the restrained and tasteful Continental was rejected. In spite of all the criticisms, it seemed that most motorists really did want larger, gaudier, more resplendent cars every year, and in Detroit, approval was given to plans for '57, '58, and '59 cars that would make the '56 models look plain by comparison.

1955 had been the big year for new bodies, and in the usual three-year cycle entirely new cars would not be introduced until 1958. But the styling race was in its most frantic stage, and many automakers, such as Ford, Mercury, and all the Chrysler divisions, took the drastic step of bringing out completely new designs after only two years. Along with the regularly scheduled new Oldsmobiles, Buicks, and Cadillacs, this made 1957 another banner year for styling changes.

As in 1955, the most radical alterations were in Chrysler Corp. cars. In 1955 they drew level with the competition after

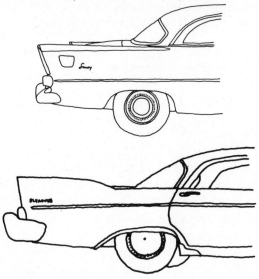

many years of lagging behind; in 1957 they rushed ahead. "Suddenly it's 1960!" was Plymouth's new slogan, and the contrast between the modest ridges on top of the '56 fenders and the huge tailfins soaring above the '57 would make one think that more than a year separated the two cars.

Tailfins were the most conspicuous feature of 1957 Chrysler cars. All models had them: Plymouth's were short and angular, and the ones on the other cars stretched up and back from somewhere around the back door. Chrysler's interest in wedge-shaped silhouettes started several years earlier in dream cars styled by Virgil Exner, and began to show in both the appearance of the '56 "Forward Look" cars and in their advertising emphasis. One ad in the November 1955 issue of *Motor Trend* asked:

> How is a Chrysler-built car similar to a jet fighter, a Gold Cup racing boat, and a bigtime race car? The answer to this riddle lies in the silhouette—namely the wedge-type profile.

A half-hearted attempt was made to persuade people that they were functional in helping directional stability, but few believed and few cared. Instinctively everyone knew why they were there—as a prop for the owner's fantasies. There was Walter Mitty, crouched behind the wheel of Miss America IV, the exhaust of its huge aircraft engine burbling through the water: ta-pocketa-pocketa. . . . The dream car as fantasy vehicle had come a long way since 1945. People were still driving cars, not airplanes or helicopters, but the appearance of the new models made it easy to imagine that they were something different.

The '57 Chrysler cars also exuded newness as few had ever done before. The public had long been told to expect tailfins on future cars, and here they were. There was no danger that anyone would mistake a '57 Plymouth for a '56. In other respects as well, the '57 Chrysler family was unquestionably newer: at 55 to 57 inches high, they were lower than their predecessors and almost all of their competitors, and the rake of the windshields and rear windows was made more acute, which vastly increased glass area and made the cars look more streamlined.

In decorative treatment the new line catered to all tastes. For customers who wanted restraint in detail the Chrysler was ideal, with a relatively simple grille and no chrome trim on the sides at all on some models. People who wanted a loud and flashy car at a relatively low price could buy a Dodge. It had a twotone paint treatment with the fins and lower body painted in one color and the middle area another; with popular colors like red and white or gold and white the effect was blinding. At the other end of the price scale was the luxury-class Imperial with chrome-ringed projectile-like taillights, a dummy spare-tire shape stamped in the trunk lid, and a gaudy "tiara band" running over the top. For buyers who measured the return on their investment in the number of spaceship motifs they included, these cars were hard to beat.

Ford tried. They matched Chrysler's accomplishment in bringing out a new body only two years after the previous redesign. The new car was 3½ to 4 inches lower than before, and most

1957 *Chrysler*

models were 3 inches longer, except for the swank Fairlane which stretched out 9 inches farther (mostly due to increased rear overhang). The new Ford had fins, of course—not impressive in height compared with Plymouth's but exaggerated to satisfactory proportions by the pattern of the side trim. With the deluxe gold inset in the side trim panel and dazzling hubcaps, the '57 Ford looked conspicuous in almost any company.

The only '57 car that could make the Ford look plain was the Mercury. It shared Ford's basic body, but alongside it even the flamboyant Ford looked restrained. Its grille was a frantic conglomeration of chrome bars and mesh, and its sides carried sculpturing to new levels of complexity. The upper part of the rear fenders had a concave groove which contained gold anodized metal, and at the rear were taillights shaped like pie sections. The top line "Turnpike Cruiser" had a reverse-slanted rear window which raised and lowered electrically.

1957 *Ford*

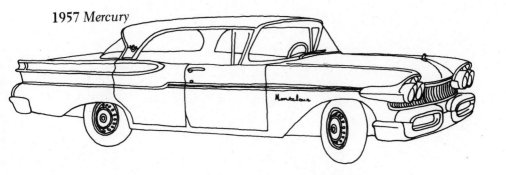

1957 *Mercury*

In 1957, for the first time in several decades, G.M. found itself out of step with the pace of contemporary styling. When the all-new 1957 Buick, Oldsmobile, and Cadillac made their debut, they already looked out of date. They were longer, lower, and wider than their predecessors, but the air of newness that they had always succeeded in conveying in the past eluded them this year. Certainly they were not as new-looking as the Chrysler line. Contributing to the dated look were the body sides with little sculpturing, relatively thick roof profiles, and no fins. Reporting on the Oldsmobile in December 1956, *Motor Trend* remarked: "Somehow we expected an outwardly more dramatic change in Oldsmobile appearance." And if these cars looked outdated, the case was even worse for Chevrolet and Pontiac, which only had a facelift on the '56 body.

Sales fortunes again seemed to favor the philosophy of excess. In one year, Chrysler's market share rose from 15.9 percent to 19.5 percent, boosting profits from $6 million to $103 million, according to *Time*, November 4, 1957. Ford outsold Chevrolet for the first time since the war, and with comparatively restrained cars, G.M. was the loser of the year.

1957 *Oldsmobile*

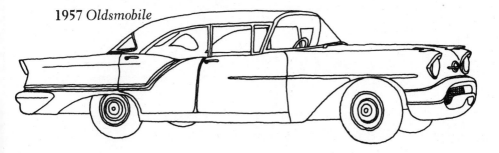

Thus the preliminary results, but there were also indications of growing discontent. Detroit's investment for new styling in '57 was comparable to that of '55, and it was expected that overall sales would be in the same range, but they were not: 6.1 million '57 cars were sold, making it a better year than '56 but nothing like '55. Public appetites for garish ornamentation had some limits. The '57 Mercury was not a success, and protests against the trend of Detroit design were growing louder. Sales of Rambler's smaller-than-standard car were growing faster than most others. Rambler ads compared their car favorably against the "huge, gas-guzzling dinosaurs" which cluttered other people's driveways. Sales of foreign cars grew to 3.5 percent of the total in '57, up 100 percent from '56.

Looking ahead to the 1958 model year, however, Detroit expressed its traditional optimism. On November 4, 1957, *Time* reported:

> "As the new cars go, so goes the new year." Exaggerated as that might be, the eagerness with which the public buys the new cars may well mean the difference between a good or a great year for U.S. business in 1958. . . . The automakers . . . (are) . . . hoping to sell at least 6,000,000 cars. . . .

Since neither 1956 or 1957 had come up to Detroit's hopes (in not equalling 1955, which had become the standard), automakers figured that potential buyers who had held off in these years might buy in 1958. But uncertainty lurked just below the surface, revealing itself in such things as Lincoln's schizoid phrase for their all-new 1958 body: "conservatively radical" (as reported in the June 1957 issue of *Motor Trend*). Final decisions of the '58s were made back in '56, however, and even if automakers had wanted to alter their '58 models in the fall of 1957 (and there was little indication that they did), the choice had long since passed out of their hands.

"As the new cars go, so goes the new year." After seeing the reception of the first-announced '58 car, the Edsel, businessmen across the country fervently hoped it would not be so.

1958 *Edsel*

The Edsel was a new car made by Ford which was planned for people who had been buying Oldsmobiles and Buicks. Into its formula its designers self-consciously put the ingredients of successful middle-priced cars. It was loaded with gimmicks such as push-button transmission selectors in the steering wheel hub; characterized as a car for the "young executive on his way up" with emphasis on middle-class suburbia; and publicized by a long series of "planted" rumors and blurry sneak photos. For the hot rodder, it had optional engines with impressive horsepower; and for the luxury-conscious, it had optional air conditioning.

The Edsel's basic body shell was shared with Ford and Mercury, but its external sheet metal was quite different. The most conspicuous appearance feature was an upright "horse collar" in the middle of the grille, which met a raised center area in the hood. In back the deck lid was depressed in the center, and terminated in two huge gull-wing shaped taillights. In the sides of the rear fenders were sculptured concave areas which were painted a different color from the rest of the body. Like almost all other '58 cars, the Edsel had four headlights in front.

The vertical grille combined with a hood bulge was a theme which had been considered by others before Edsel. In 1955 Packard had a dream car called the "Request" which had had a vertical grille of similar proportions to the Edsel's; in 1956 the Packard "Predictor" dream car had had a bumper mounted upright in the center. It was a logical retrograde styling motif which brought to mind the front-end appearance of many cars of the '30s, particularly the LaSalle. An article on styling in *Motor Trend* in April 1956 predicted that vertical grilles would become a common type in the next few years.

Dream Cars and Nightmares 235

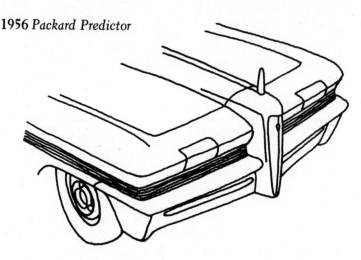

From the very beginning, the sales career of the Edsel was a catastrophe. It was introduced earlier than other 1958 cars with the hope of drawing extra attention to itself. This unfortunately exposed it to the competition of close-out sales of '57 models from other manufacturers, and it had a slow start. But even when conditions improved, no one seemed to want one. By trying to appeal to too many people, the Edsel appealed to no one. It was too small for luxury car buyers, too expensive for low-income buyers.

Most criticisms focused on the styling. However logical the vertical grille was, it just did not meet with prevailing tastes. The Edsel "looked like an Oldsmobile sucking a lemon," according to one common description. Its front-end appearance brought to mind many other analogies as well, mostly obscene. In other respects, its styling had the same failings as the '57 Mercury: it gave no dominant impression, as of weight (G.M. cars) or motion (Chrysler cars). It sat there, lumpish and square, under a thick crust of meaningless ornamentation, like an ugly woman with too much makeup. In not much more than two years the Edsel was hooted off the stage by a hostile public.

The other 1958 cars followed the trend toward ever-gaudier cars. G.M.'s policy of offering a car which was always slightly larger and more garish than its competitors was upset in 1957, when chrome-covered, befinned monsters from other makers made the

G.M. lineup look relatively subdued. Never in the recent past had owners of G.M. cars had to suffer such an indignity, and by 1958 an answer was ready for them. Chevrolet and Pontiac had a completely new body, which was longer, lower, and wider (by 8.7 inches, 4.5 inches, and 2.2 inches, respectively, on some Pontiac models). They were given generous helpings of luxury trim: all models had four headlights, and the top-line Chevy had no less than six taillights and three dummy air vents, one on each side and one in the roof.

Not to be outdone by either their competitors or their smaller stablemates, Buick and Oldsmobile made extensive changes in their year-old designs. The results were two of the most garish and ponderous-looking cars of all time. The Olds carried no less than 44 pounds of chrome trim, according to *Time*, May 12, 1958. A cluster of chrome spears swept back to the front door from the four headlights, and on the rear fender a rack of chrome lines filled the space above a massive projectile-shaped lump. Extra chrome was stuck on the hood, the roof, the rocker panels, and every other conceivable place without any apparent consideration for its place in the overall design. The car looked (and was) enormous: the front bumper alone appeared to weigh hundreds of pounds. The Buick carried a comparable tonnage of chrome, distributed slightly differently: a special feature was the grille, which consisted of 160 separate ¾-inch square chrome rods.

The big changes had come on most other cars in 1957, and for 1958 most of them made the standard changes of adopting four headlights and adding or altering ornamentation. The all-new Lincoln followed the prevailing trend: at 19 feet, 1 inch, it was the longest monster of all, and its immense flanks were hacked and gouged with random sculpturing. From the canted quadruple headlights to the reverse-slanted rear window the eye of the viewer was tortured with bizarre angles.

1958 *Oldsmobile*

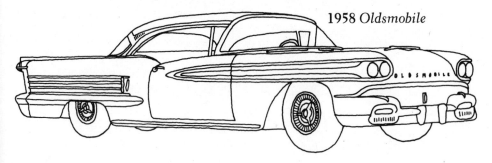

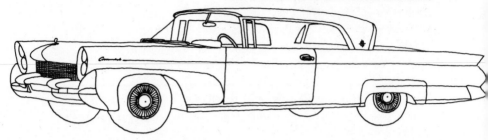

"It isn't pretty, but that's what the public wants." This had been the usual line of defense that industry spokesmen had used in the mid '50s to justify their products, and to the frustration of the vocal critics of Detroit styling, it seemed to fit the facts. But in 1958 buyers rebelled. The old approach to styling was suddenly no longer saleable. "Sales of all domestic makes are slow, to say the least," reported *Motor Trend* in February. "As the new cars go, so goes the new year"; and as 1958 new cars sales crawled toward a total of 4.3 million, the lowest figure since 1948, the country struggled through a major economic recession.

In March 1959, *Motor Trend* expressed the prevailing opinion on bad 1958 sales: "We believe that much of the reason for the poor sales of last year's cars can be laid at the doorstep of the stylists. . . ." Criticism of Detroit styling rose to a crescendo. George Romney, president of American Motors, was one of the most eloquent of the critics—his Rambler being immune from attack because of its smaller size and relatively sober design. "Does anyone recall," asked Romney, "a period when car design was subjected to as much lampooning in newspaper and magazine cartoons?" Carl Sundberg, an industrial designer, re-marked in *Motor Trend* for January 1959, that:

> . . . panning the American automobile has become a pas-time that threatens to replace baseball as a national sport. . . . There seems to be agreement . . . among de-signers that with a couple of exceptions, the year 1958 was one of the saddest years in the history of auto styling.

Almost everyone seemed to agree that the '58s were ugly. But some of the deductions made on this basis were questionable. In the same article, Sundberg argued that:

Only good design can succeed, because, believe it or not, most of the people, rich and poor, have much better taste than they are given credit for. They proved this when they refused to buy the 1958 models.

They had also refused to buy the Continental Mark II, however. Even more disturbing was their discrimination between various 1958 models: one of the cars which suffered least in the 1958 slump was the Oldsmobile, perhaps the most gruesome monster offered in that year.

Whether the '58 cars failed through sheer ugliness is open to debate, but it certainly can be said that their styling was poorly planned. The successful G.M. styling policies of the '30s, '40s, and early '50s showed that, to be successful over a period of several years, styling themes had to be evolved gradually. Something had to be kept in reserve so that, by a few changes, next year's car could always be made to look newer than this year's. It was always remembered that the basic body design would have to keep its appeal for three years, so no feature expected to have an ephemeral attraction would be included in its basic lines.

In 1957 and 1958 the frenzy of the Great Styling Race caused most automakers, including G.M., to forget the value of continuity. The 1957 Chrysler cars, for example, were made as low as their construction allowed, giving no room for further reductions. Even worse, the corporate identity was linked with tail fins, which were hard to develop further. They were already so high that raising them would seriously impair visibility, but lowering them would inevitably be regarded as a retrograde step. Because they lacked any real function they were doomed to a relatively brief popularity, but both through corporate policy and tooling investment Chrysler was committed to them for several years. For one year they were a sensation, but as early as the summer of '57 they were losing their appeal. In August 1957, *Motor Trend* predicted that: "radical fins . . . will gradually assume a decreased importance as many owners find them somewhat depressing after the newness wears off." The 1958 Chrysler cars were only too obviously the same as the '57s; minor trim changes made them look slightly different but not newer. By 1959 the fins had become an embarrassing sign of age.

Dream Cars and Nightmares   239

Like Chrysler, Ford went all-out on its 1957 Fords and Mercurys, leaving designers at a loss for changes to make for 1958.
The Mercury, already too elaborate for most people's tastes, was
made more so for 1958, with the inevitable results. The Ford was
altered, but, in spite of its four headlights, it did not look newer.
Round target-style taillights, a Ford trademark since 1952, were
inexplicably dropped, and the car became an anonymous conglomeration of makeshift ideas.

Seeing that their '57 models were about to be upstaged, Buick
and Oldsmobile became panicky when planning for '58, disre-
garding principles which had successfully guided their policies in
the past. The 1958 models had less family resemblance to the '57s
than the (all-new) '57s had had with the '56s. This did not harm
Olds as much as Buick: Buick even omitted the traditional portholes, and abysmal sales seemed to indicate that many people
could not find the right showroom without them.

The other problem with G.M. cars was similar to what Ford
and Chrysler faced. In their own ways, the 1958 Olds and Buick
were the ultimate—even G.M. could not build a car with more
mass and glitter. What could one do for an encore? Either the car
could be facelifted, and be in danger of becoming nondescript
like the Ford, or it could be restyled at vast expense. G.M. took
the latter course, and fell into another trap: after two major

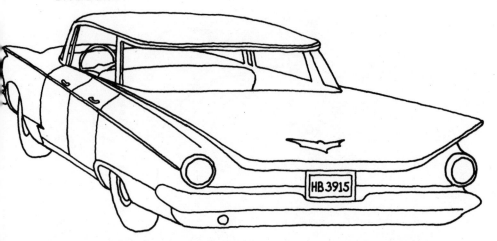

changes in two years, Buick (in particular) seemed to have lost its identity. People no longer saw it as the same car they used to admire so much, and the days when it could hold third place in sales seemed gone forever.

The 1958 cars sold badly partly because they did not look sufficiently newer than the '57s. Cars can only look newer if they are evolving in some direction perceived by the general public; e.g., cars have become lower by steady increments, so an exceptionally low car is immediately recognized as a very new one. By 1958 many evolutionary trends had run their course: for the time being, the cars were as low as the public would tolerate, glass area was nearing its limit, and overall size was as large as most people wanted.

Another trend even more disturbing to automakers was that styling itself, in the Detroit sense, seemed to be losing its influence. The automobile as fantasy-vehicle seemed to be on its way out. Temporarily, at least, motorists seemed to want cars which looked like cars again, not jet planes or Gold Cup racers. The only cars to sell well in 1958 were ones which, by postwar Detroit standards, were not styled at all—the imported economy cars like Volkswagen, English Ford, Fiat, and Volvo. The body of the Volkswagen, for example, designed in the '30s in the aerodynamic spirit of the Lincoln Zephyr, was almost universally thought to be ugly, yet this was the import which had the best sales.

The years following 1958 were a time of feverish back-tracking for most automakers. Ornate and fanciful decoration was out of favor, as was excessive emphasis on size and weight. As quickly as possible, the layers of chrome and sculpturing that had been planned in 1956 for eager buyers in 1959 had to be sheared off. Simplicity was the goal, and there was no time to lose.

The 1959 offerings could not be changed overnight, however, and in the hangover that followed the orgy of 1958, some cars appeared which were fully as ornate as their forebears. The 1959 Cadillac earned a place in the gallery with the 1958 Buick and Oldsmobile as a monument to excess. In front it had an enormous bejeweled grille surmounted by heavy-lidded quadruple head-lights, and in the rear, towering, jagged-shaped fins carried dual "moon rocket" style taillights. Cadillac was not the only 1959 car to embarrass its manufacturer: there were several other makes which carried the progressive uglification of 1957–1958 one step farther.

1959 Cadillac

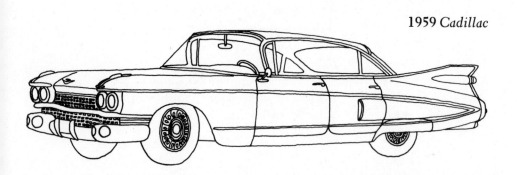

For the most part, however, G.M. and Ford reacted quickly to the crisis. On an absolute scale, their 1959 offerings could not be called sober; but by 1958 standards, they appeared to be so. In March 1959, *Motor Trend* commented:

> This year has seen more improvement in car styling than any year since 1955. . . . This movement is spearheaded by cars like the Pontiac and Buick. They are cleaner, more functional in design. . . .

In 1960 another big step was taken toward restrained styling. Ford introduced a new body with a single horizontal chrome molding running along the belt line. Wraparound windshields were replaced on some cars by a simpler design with backward-leaning windshield corner pillars. Bizarre two-tone paint arrangements had virtually disappeared.

For some reason, stylists at Chrysler Corp. did not seem to comprehend the change in public taste. The 1957 bodies, which for the most part had had a graceful appearance in their original form, were repeatedly facelifted and became more elaborate and gaudy every time. Being smaller than G.M. or Ford, Chrysler did not have the reserve capital needed to make large-scale emergency alterations in the way that was done, for example, on Buick and Oldsmobile in 1958 and 1959 and on Pontiac in 1959.

But in 1960, when the trend toward simplicity was well advanced among its competitors, Plymouth introduced an all-new body which ranked with the worst of the '58s for excessive and meaningless ornamentation. In front the headlights rested in huge "cat's-eye" panels, which wrapped around to the side and past the front wheels. On two-tone models this panel was painted differently from the rest of the car, giving it an awkward disjointed

1960 *Ford*

look. In the rear were fins that soared as high as the ones on the '57 car.

An interview with Chrysler-Imperial stylists by *Motor Trend* in September 1960 indicated that the ornate styling of Chrysler cars was not an accident caused by unavoidable long lead times but was an intentional policy. The stylists outlined their policy of "modern classicism" in styling, which was a far cry from the nominally similar approach used by designers of the Continental Mark II. The Chrysler stylists advocated functionalism in the form of a return to such things as old-fashioned separate headlights and radiator-like grilles. Their efforts materialized in the 1961 Imperial, which featured four 1930-style headlights mounted on stanchions in front of the fenders. At the rear, taillights hung on stalks from enormous and ungainly looking fins. This car seemed designed to wrest the title of the World's Most Grotesque Automobile from the numerous strong contenders of the late '50s.

1961 *Imperial*

Unlike the situation of the early '50s, critics of Detroit styling in the late '50s really meant what they said. For the time being, at least, the popularity of the wildly ornate automobile was over. Staggering on in the same old course, Chrysler paid dearly: from the peak year of 1957, when it held close to 20 percent of the market, it had slipped to under 12 percent by 1961.

In automobile design the decade of the '50s was an age of fantasy. The idea of the dream vehicle was evident in G.M. cars by 1950, and gradually found its way into other cars as the Great Styling Race gathered momentum. It was based on valid observations of the psychology of the car owner and driver, and up to a certain point it was highly successful.

But wherever fact and fantasy are mixed, the balance must be nicely calculated. The fact of an automobile is that it is a four-wheeled motorized vehicle made to carry passengers. The fantasy elements which suggest an airplane, spaceship, or road dragon which are added on later must not obscure the basic identity of the automobile, or else they will seem as if designed to deceive. The monsters of the late '50s were not only intended to look like spaceships or jet planes but they were intended to look less like automobiles. Wheels, for example, were often hidden or deemphasized in the overall design, which helped to strengthen the illusion that the car was made to hover or fly.

When the illusory elements became too insistent it was almost as if the automakers were asking motorists to accept the illusion as fact. What was it, a car or an airplane or a rocket ship? From being a gentle stimulant to pleasurable daydreams, the jet-pods, fins, and so forth began to seem like an affront to the motorist's intelligence, and he would no longer buy cars which had them.

6

The Specialty Car

Most American automobiles of the 1890s were conceived by their builders as an alternative to the horse and buggy, and were accordingly built with a similar carrying capacity, appearance, and general utilitarian flavor. The problems of making them run, steer, and survive on the rivers of mud and stony tracks they were driven on preoccupied their designers. The slogan given by one maker to his products—"Rigs That Run"—reveals an attitude many pioneer automakers had toward the automobile.

For the customer, however, mere transportation was only one of the many functions of the automobile. The sporting role of the automobile was certainly one of the first specialized uses of the machine, independently discovered by most of its owners once they were accustomed to its operation. Few owners could resist the urge to "give it a loose rein." "Made it up to Uncle George's in twenty-seven minutes," the owner could afterwards boast to his friends at the General Store. Many drivers of small runabouts habitually travelled at full tilt, clutching the tiller while the car leaped like a kangaroo over potholes and bumps. Such people were loudly but ineffectually criticized by *The Horseless Age* which claimed, probably rightly, that the short life of most runabouts was due more to hard driving than to deficiencies in design. In this way the sport and racing role of the automobile began in this country, and in the early years of the new century the type took on a distinctive form following the French pattern.

Most early automobiles were mainly used for specific trips from one place to another along known routes, but some owners took advantage of their car's agility in taking expeditions to previously inaccessible areas. Driving into the back country, many happy fishermen discovered well-stocked lakes and streams in places which could not easily be reached with a horse and buggy and were too far away to ride to comfortably on horseback. Since early roads were often as bad to drive on as anyplace else, a car that could take road use could usually take off-road use as well, but as roads improved, the off-road vehicle gradually became a specialized type.

Beyond one extreme of passenger car design is the pure racing car; beyond another is the truck. Shortly after the turn of the century motor trucks began to take over from horse-drawn vehicles, particularly in the city where traffic congestion and parking problems made horse-drawn wagons inconvenient. For ordinary driving, trucks had the same disadvantages then as they do now, but at some time every car owner has wished for the truck's load-carrying capacity. To provide some of the advantages of both, some early cars had rear bodies which could be removed to make

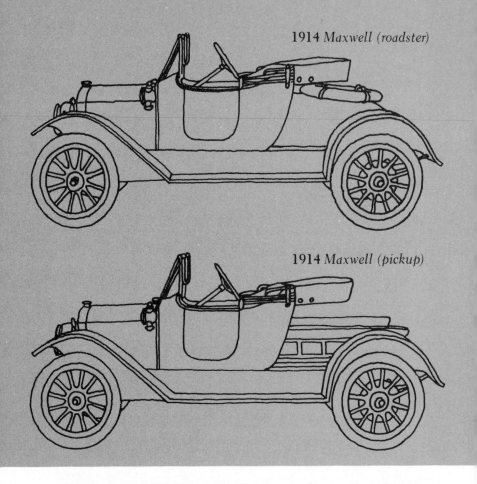

1914 *Maxwell (roadster)*

1914 *Maxwell (pickup)*

a flat deck. In 1914 Maxwell offered a roadster with a factory-made pickup truck back which could be mounted in place of the rear body when the occasion demanded.

The evolution of the standard car moved on, from the mid-engined runabout, usually built for just two passengers, to the 5 to 7-passenger touring car. But a wide variety of specialized types also flourished. In this category one would have to include special luxury cars, built primarily for prestige and only secondarily for practical conveyance. Specialized prestige cars differ only in degree from ordinary cars, since most cars are built with an eye to impressing the neighbors, but in cases like the limousine the distinction is pretty clear. A limousine like the 1906 Packard was half again as large as the usual car, was five times heavier, and cost ten

times as much. To have full effect, it had to be driven by a uniformed chauffeur. To be sure, it could carry passengers from
place to place, but for the money it was one-tenth transportation
and nine-tenths display.

Another specialized type occupied the other end of the
economic scale. This was the perennial bare-bones-of-
transportation vehicle, generally cramped, spartan, and feeble
compared with the ordinary car, and which made up for these
drawbacks (at least in theory) by lower cost and simpler construc-

1914 *Dudley Bug*

tion. The motor buggy, mentioned in Chapter 2, was one example of the type; another was the cyclecar, which enjoyed a similar but even shorter period of popularity in the early teens. By combining the small size and light weight of a motorcycle with the stability and seating comfort of an automobile, the designers of these vehicles hoped to create the perfect compromise; but flimsy construction, often unsafe design, public apathy, and competition from the Model T quickly sent the cyclecar into limbo.

The standard type of car, through its evolution from mid-engined runabout to touring car to sedan, ruled the vast domain of the automobile market, but a few remote areas were held by the specialty types. Cars made for sport, utility, prestige, or economy had periods of popularity or neglect, but rarely disappeared for long. American-made sports cars were absent briefly in the late '30s, and a firm line between cars and trucks left the utility field empty until the appearance of the factory-built station wagon in the '20s. As people's standards went up, the unchanging Model T descended to the bare-bones economy level, and with its demise this field was occupied only fitfully by the American Austin (subsequently the American Bantam) and the Crosley. Ornamental prestige cars were the hardiest of the lot, but even they, after the glorious period of the late '20s and early '30s, went into decline until the introduction of the Lincoln Continental in the fall of 1939.

1947 Crosley

In the '50s specialty cars regained a firm place in the American scene. The station wagon expanded the utility car field way beyond anything dreamed of before, and sports cars were introduced by major manufacturers. The public appetite for specialty cars grew far more rapidly than Detroit could satisfy it, and foreign sports and economy cars were brought in to fill the gap. Only the all-out prestige car seemed to be out of favor, as the Continental Mark II, which was about the only serious effort in this direction, met with little success.

In the '60s the specialty car underwent a transformation which almost caused it to outgrow its name. Before 1960 these cars occupied the fringes of the car market, catering to a few people who wanted a car for an unusual purpose. In the '60s, however, car buyers began to choose more specifically according to their needs, and the specialty car almost became the standard type. Evolution of the standard sedan slowed up as automakers shifted their attention toward an ever-wider range of sports, luxury, utility, and economy cars.

The first car to catch the full flavor of the modern specialty car era was the four-passenger Thunderbird, which replaced the earlier two-passenger car in 1958. At first glance, the new Thunderbird looked much like any other two-door hardtop, but there were many important differences. It was a luxury car that was smaller than a standard Ford sedan—this was something new. It was called a "personal car," like the original two-passenger version.

1958 *Thunderbird*

This made it exempt from many standards of judgment that would have applied if it had been considered just another hardtop. It was very impractical, for example: since it was very low the transmission hump was huge, making it impossible to seat six people, so it was made with four individual seats for four people. This arrangement made it exclusive, according to Ford publicity, and people loved it. It also had very little luggage space and was exceptionally hard to enter for rear seat passengers, but after all, it was a personal car, not a family car.

From the time the "toy tonneau" was tacked onto the "Gentleman's High Powered Runabout" there seems to have been an inverse ratio between rakishness and practicality. The mere fact of impracticality seems to give a car a more exclusive or sporting air, almost independent of its actual appearance. The toy tonneau seemed adequately practical because it was more so than the two-seater runabout, even though it could not compare with a real touring car. The four-passenger Thunderbird enjoyed the same relationship with the original two seater, and outsold its predecessor by a wide margin. It was made to be an ornament and served this purpose well.

Many of the loudest complaints made about Detroit cars in the late '50s were about their unnecessary size, weight, and power, their cost, their greed for gas, and their inability to fit into garages and parking places. Foreign cars were used as a standard of comparison beside which American cars came off badly, especially since the virtues of the imports were often wildly overrated and their shortcomings generally ignored. A clamor arose for Detroit-built small economy cars, and the Motor City obediently bestirred itself to produce them, even though by earlier standards such cars were considered a fringe item not worth the attention of American producers.

One smaller American car was already being produced in the late '50s—the Rambler American—and Rambler publicity influenced the movement toward smaller cars significantly. Except for showing by its success that buyers of small cars tended to care less about appearance than others did, however, the Rambler American merits little attention in a history of style, since it was just a revival of an earlier model which, even when new, was not notable for its appearance.

The first of the new-sized cars to appear with fresh styling was the Studebaker Lark in the fall of 1958. It was essentially an economy model Studebaker with most of the front and rear overhang chopped off. At 184½ inches, it was about two feet shorter than one of the low-priced three, but was almost that much longer than the Volkswagen. The intermediate size was chosen for several reasons. For Studebaker, one was that many parts of the car could be taken with little change from larger models. Also, a 160-inch car (Volkswagen sized) could not be built for as much less than a 180-inch car as one might expect, and even when building a small car the remnants of the traditional "more-car-for-the-money" Detroit attitude could be seen. It was then felt, perhaps correctly, that American motorists would not put up with the cramped interior dimensions in a domestic car that they would tolerate in an import. Calling the new cars small was not only inaccurate, but was also potentially offensive to the multitudes who held to the traditional American belief that "bigger-is-better"; the new cars were accordingly dubbed "compacts."

Amid much fanfare, compacts from the Big Three were introduced in the fall of 1959. Of these the Falcon was the most direct answer to the public's stated desires. Mechanically it was utterly conventional. Its body was a shrunken version of a big sedan's, with theoretical seating for six. Round bull's-eye taillights proclaimed it a Ford. Its simple styling drew loud praises. In November 1959, *Sports Cars Illustrated* described it as "the best looking Ford since the Thirties," and most people agreed.

1959 *Studebaker Lark*

In designing the Corvair, G.M. deviated from the conventional pattern of the Falcon. Like the Volkswagen, the Corvair had a rear-mounted, air-cooled engine and all-independent suspension. This allowed a flat floor and an exceptionally low body only 52 inches high. The lowness of the car allowed stylists to keep the height/length proportion reasonably close to that of a big car, thus avoiding the boxy, dowdy look so much feared in the design of a small car.

In execution the Corvair body was simple to the point of severity. A bulge in the side just below the belt line gave a welcome horizontal highlight, and the roof (similar to a design introduced on the big G.M. cars in 1959) combined style with good rear-seat headroom. But the front end, without the benefit of a grille, was blunt and square, and the car had an unmistakeably utilitarian air about it. "There is bound to be plenty of disagreement about this," said *Sports Cars Illustrated* in November 1959, "but we think the Corvair is the plain jane styling-wise among the Big Three's Little Three."

1960 *Corvair*

Plain or not, the Corvair was one of the few American cars in history to have a strong effect on the styling of European cars. To be sure, cars built by European subsidiaries of U.S. automakers have sometimes shared motifs of their large relatives in the U.S., but the influence of the Corvair went way beyond this. The roof design and the belt-line bulge that continued around the front and rear of the car were the two most imitated features. In the early sixties, Simca, Fiat, and Renault produced cars that were clearly inspired by the Corvair, and NSU built what was almost a verbatim copy, though in two-thirds scale.

Like G.M., Chrysler veered slightly away from dead-center conventionality when designing their compact Valiant. Virgil Exner, the father of the fin fad, was still head of Chrysler styling, and as a result the Valiant had rather flamboyant styling which contrasted sharply with the sobriety of the other compacts. With a long hood and short, sloping rear deck, the proportions of the Valiant were intended to recall the profile of prewar cars. Lumps over the front and rear wheels suggested separate fenders, and the central air scoop in front was more like a radiator than a conventional grille. A final retrograde motif was the spare tire shape stamped into the rear deck.

1962 NSU Prinz

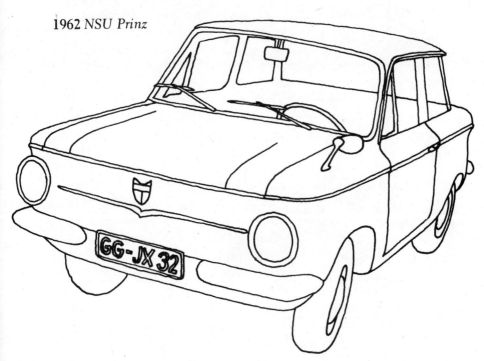

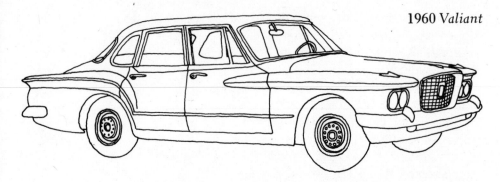

It was generally agreed that the Valiant's styling differed basically from the American idiom; if not American, what was it? European, of course. "Valiant has a distinctly European flair," said *Motor Trend* in December 1959. Some motifs were certainly closer to European practice than to American, such as the front air scoop and the strong emphasis on the wheels through trim and full-wheel cutouts; but the cluttered pretentiousness of the whole was closer in spirit to American styling of the '50s than to the clean lines favored in Europe.

If styling appeal is more a matter of quantity than quality, then the Valiant had more of it than the other compacts. Many liked·it. In April 1960, *Sports Cars Illustrated* commented that: "Few bystanders were indifferent to the Valiant's styling and those in favor far outnumbered those opposed." But the same report did say that a "significant criticism" was of the "loudness" of the design. In any case the Valiant did not look cheap, and to escape this it was perhaps worth looking a bit garish.

In sales the runaway winner among the Big Three compacts was the Falcon. It was the simplest in construction, the cheapest to buy (by a small margin), and the cheapest to run. In its performance, handling, and mechanical specifications there was nothing that could have made anybody's heart beat faster; but its appearance was attractive, and while not unusual or remarkable, it had proportions that would retain their appeal.

Compared with sales of the Falcon, the Valiant was not as successful as had been hoped, but the real loser was the Corvair. Rear engines, air cooling, and independent rear suspension were perhaps appealing to technically minded buyers, but there were few such people. The fact was that the Corvair's fancy specifications did not make it into a good car: it was noisy, not very reliable, and, until the rear suspension modifications of 1964 and 1965, ill-handling. Whether its appearance helped or hurt its popularity is hard to determine.

If motorists wanted an economy Ford or Chevrolet, presumably they would soon want an economy Dodge, Mercury, Buick, or Pontiac as well. Detroit responded quickly to the real or imagined need. In the spring of 1960 the Mercury Comet appeared—a restyled, slightly stretched version of the Falcon. For the 1961 model year Dodge introduced the Lancer—a Valiant with a different grille and trim. The trend continued. Soon there were smaller Buicks, Oldsmobiles, and Pontiacs, (the Special, F85, and Tempest), which were around 188 inches long (versus 180 inches for the Corvair, or 210 to 215 inches for a big sedan) and shared styling features with their large relatives—the Buick, for example, had small portholes, and the Pontiac had a split front grille.

Few people were much excited by the "senior compacts," as these cars were called, but the momentum Detroit had built up to produce cars of every size and variety was irreversible. G.M. was annoyed by the relative success of the Falcon compared with the Corvair, and in retaliation begat the Chevy II, a boxy, inoffensive, utterly conventional small sedan. Ford was upset by the introduction of the G.M. senior compacts in a market segment not covered by a Ford product; the result, introduced for 1962, was the Ford Fairlane. Chevrolet then found that it had no answer to the Fairlane—the Chevy II was smaller and the big Chevy was bigger—and it was losing sales to senior compacts from other G.M. divisions. After a seemly gestation period the Chevelle was born—another conventional, inoffensive sedan. Meanwhile the G.M. senior compacts had grown bigger . . . and so on. Alarums and excursions became a regular feature of the Detroit repertory.

1961 *Buick Special*

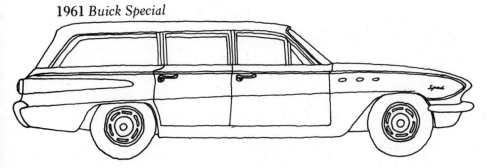

In the aftermath of the Great Styling Orgy of the late '50s there was a furious scramble among automakers to simplify the appearance of their cars. Piece by piece, the nonfunctional appendages added during the '50s shriveled up and dropped off. In 1960 Ford and Mercury abandoned the wraparound windshield, and in the next year were followed by just about everyone else. Fins shrank, and there was a return to one-color paint jobs. Side sculpturing several inches deep, which had been common, melted away, leaving the body sides with slight crease lines or no accents at all.

A handsome example of the new trend was the all-new Lincoln Continental introduced for 1961. From its predecessor, a nineteen-foot monster with sides creased and wrinkled like the hide of a rhinoceros, a greater change could hardly be imagined. The 1961 car was well over a foot shorter than before, and its square, severely simple lines recalled the Continental Mark II. Except for a straight chrome line running along the rocker panel at the bottom and a very thin trim line around the wheel openings, nothing interrupted its smooth sides. "The styling is one of the most distinctive in any domestic car," was *Motor Trend*'s opinion in April 1961, and many others agreed. Even after a year the car drew attention: reporting on the virtually unchanged '62 model, *Motor Trend* remarked in May of that year: "styling comments are not generally part of a road test but the Continental's lines are so unusually clean and attracted such universally favorable reaction, that they deserve mention. . . ."

Preference for simpler design was not unanimous, however—a change so complete from styling tastes shown in the '50s could not be made so fast. A negative opinion on the restrained styling of the new cars was given in the January 1961 issue of *Motor Trend:* "my pet gripe is body styling . . . Look at the new Lincoln styling. Different—but good? The new Olds and

1961 *Lincoln Continental*

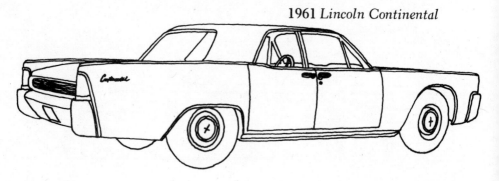

Chevy are particularly weak examples in the G.M. camp." Like the Lincoln, the 1961 Chevy was subdued and formal looking; the Olds was more elaborate but by former Oldsmobile standards it was positively naked of embellishment, except on the special "Starfire" model, which had a huge brushed aluminum side panel, red trim accents, and a flamboyant jet-exhaust motif. Among the cars which the *Motor Trend* writer liked was the 1961 Dodge, which carried on Chrysler's theme of automotive American Gothic.

Such opinions were an exception, however; that the large majority of buyers were on the side of simplicity was proven by the reception of the 1962 Plymouth and Dodge. These cars had been extensively restyled to include many of the Valiant's motifs: long hood, short deck (accentuated by a sharply raked windshield and relatively upright rear window), lumps on the sides to suggest old-fashioned fenders, and air scoops in front. At 202 inches, they were much shorter than before. Chrome accents were splashed on with a generous hand, and the overall effect was of bizarre proportions and illogical complexity.

Even before the introduction of the cars, Chrysler had an inkling that all was not well. In April 1962, *Motor Trend* reported:

> Back last September when Chrysler Corporation previewed its all-new Plymouths and Dodges to the press, enthusiasm was high. There was a difference about them that most everyone seemed to like. Their impact on Chrysler Corporation dealers, however, was exactly the opposite. And as usual, dealers seem better able than the press to sense which car is hot and which is not.

1962 *Dodge*

The Chrysler escaped the disfigurement that afflicted the rest of the Corporation's cars, and its cleaner lines brought it considerable success. But with the ball-and-chain of disastrous Plymouth and Dodge sales hanging on it, the Corporation's share of the market sank to a mere 8½ percent by the end of the 1962 model year. Quick action was needed, and out went chief stylist Virgil Exner, who was replaced by Elwood P. Engel, formerly an assistant to George Walker at Ford. Feverish restyling activity began. First priority was given to removal of objectionable features on the 1963 models, and a completely different car was planned for 1964.

From the time of its appearance in 1958 the four-passenger Thunderbird had been a runaway success. Even in the gloomy year of its introduction its sales were good, and in subsequent years even more people came to consider the Thunderbird an essential adornment to their driveways.

Curiously, however, the success of the car did not immediately provoke the flood of imitations from competitors that one would expect. Part of the problem of competing with it, perhaps, was in discovering what worthwhile things it offered. It was smaller than most standard sized cars, but weighed just as much, so that a huge and wasteful engine gave only leisurely acceleration. Interior seating was strictly limited to four, and was cramped at that; luggage space was almost nil; and in spite of its semi-sporting background, the Thunderbird in the early '60s was one of the worst handling cars sold in America.

What it offered was prestige, but the origins of this elusive quality were hard to find. Its styling helped some, but hardly seemed remarkable enough to take full credit for the car's success. It appealed to the surviving segment of the public which, deep down inside, really liked the 1958 Oldsmobile, but which nevertheless would not buy such a car again due to an awareness that ostentation on that scale was out of fashion. The original four-passenger Thunderbird body was continued with minor changes through 1960, and in 1961 a new body featured different contours but showed the same approach as before—1958-style rocketship motifs (slightly muted) combined with a few luxury/

retrograde details like wire wheels and fake landau irons on the roof.

One thing the Thunderbird did have was gadgets, probably more than were offered on any other car. It had all the standard items—power seats, power windows, power top, power radio antenna, air conditioning—as well as a swing-away steering wheel and a vast array of more-or-less redundant dials, warning lights, and dashboard switches. These flattered the intelligence of the driver and awed the passengers; they made the car seem much more complex (and therefore expensive) than it really was.

In the inarticulated dreams of thousands of people the Thunderbird owner was seen as a prince of suburbia, wealthy, distinguished, unmistakably successful. Through buying a Thunderbird, the new owner cloaked himself in these qualities, at least in his own eyes, and due to the wide currency of the Thunderbird image, in the eyes of many of his neighbors as well. The car itself was almost incidental to the image, but it did have enough to continue the illusion. From its two-passenger days and its smaller size the Thunderbird carried sporting associations; it was known to be expensive and thought to be more so than it was; and finally, the sumptuous upholstering and gadgets inside gave promise of luxury, perhaps more than the cramped accommodations actually provided.

By 1962 sales of the Thunderbird had grown to the point where even if other automakers had only a hazy idea of what they were after, they could no longer afford to let it go unchallenged. The first challenger was the Studebaker Hawk. Ever since the mid-'50s, the Hawk had been offered as a sporty high performance

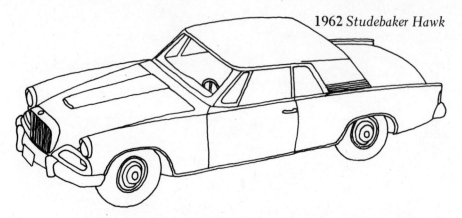

version of the Loewy Studebaker coupe introduced in 1953. It underwent various transformations—fins were added, then shorn, and so forth. Sales were generally poor. For 1962 Studebaker engaged Brooks Stevens Associates for assistance in restyling the nine-year-old body to suggest the flavor of the Thunderbird.

The result was not much more than a Loewy coupe with a large Thunderbird roof affixed, complete with "formal" blind rear quarters and square lines. A retrograde detail was the dummy radiator grafted onto the front of the hood. The car was introduced with much promotional noise and waving of hands, but after nine years of familiarity the public could recognize the old coupe under almost any disguise and few people were much excited by the change.

Before the 1962 model year was out the Hawk was joined by the radical Studebaker Avanti, introduced as an early '63 model in June 1962. The Avanti had a fiberglass body designed by Raymond Loewy on a Studebaker Lark chassis. Its body was highly unusual. To start with, it was a fastback coupe in the European GT tradition, but enlarged to American proportions. In itself this was an adventurous move: the fastback coupe shape had

1963 *Studebaker Avanti*

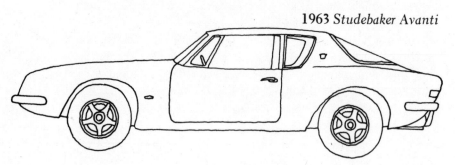

been developed and refined on small cars during the '50s, but on big cars it had rarely been used for fear of recalling the undesirable old-fashioned look of the "streamliner" fastback bodies of the late '30s and '40s.

The Avanti had other original styling features as well. For a long time, U.S. cars had had a much longer overhang over the rear wheels than in front. The Avanti changed this: its overhang was nearly the same at both ends, giving it by contrast the appearance of a very long hood and a truncated rear end. Strict symmetry had likewise been the rule in domestic syling, but the Avanti had just one bulge in the hood, on the left side in front of the driver. Again in the front end it broke all rules. Instead of the usual grille of chrome bars, the hood was carried down to a high bumper, with a low, wide airscoop built in below for the radiator intake. Another departure was the longitudinal curvature of the sides, suppressed in the area of the door for a wasp-waisted, "Coke bottle" shape.

It was generally agreed that the Avanti's styling was original, but not many people liked it. *Car and Driver* in January 1963 tried to justify it on grounds of practicality:

> Whatever you may feel about the lines and aesthetic appeal of the Avanti, it is a very sensible design with good aerodynamic properties. . . . The flush-fitting windows contribute a sizable drag reduction and help keep wind noise low. . . .

In many ways, it is clear that the Avanti was made to appeal to Thunderbird owners. It was a sports/luxury car, made smaller than a standard sedan, and had room for four people. The price began between four and five thousand dollars. The Avanti had a jet-plane-like instrument panel with some instruments placed above the windshield, a whimsical and impractical feature in the same vein as many Thunderbird gadgets.

There were also some differences from the Thunderbird, however, and these were perhaps more significant than the features they had in common. For one thing, exterior styling of the Thunderbird was geared to the least sophisticated segment of the public, the unrepentant 1958 Oldsmobile lovers. The Avanti was at the opposite end of the scale: it appealed to people whose tastes ran to Ghia-bodied Lancias and other such exotica. Also, it emphasized the sporting side of the sports/luxury combination. It had better-than-average handling, and was the first American car to offer modern disc brakes. A supercharger was available which enabled it to set records at Bonneville. The Thunderbird, on the other hand, was sporting only in dim and distant memory. It was actually a luxury car in thin disguise. The complacency with which Thunderbird owners accepted handling comparable to a 1935 Packard certainly indicated that they were not closely allied with the sports car set.

Eventually it was inevitable that G.M. would make an imitation Thunderbird. Following a careful study of the Thunderbird appeal, G.M. introduced the Buick Riviera for the 1963 model year. The Riviera was based on a shortened Buick chassis on which suspension changes had been made to give better handling and a huge engine added for extra acceleration. It went fast and handled well for a big car, enough to receive favorable mention in road tests.

Many points of the Riviera directly recall the Thunderbird. Its length of 208 inches was, like the Thunderbird, slightly less than a standard-sized sedan. Its interior seating was "personalized" by an enormous driveshaft hump in the center with console added, making it unambiguously a four-passenger car. It had gadgets in the Thunderbird tradition. A dashboard plaque was available which said

RIVIERA
Custom Built for
John Doe

1963 *Buick Riviera*

Buick's mechanical conscience, a buzzer which sounded if a pre-set speed was exceeded, was an option, as was a tilt-away steering wheel to ease entry and exit for portly owners.

The strongest appeal of the Riviera, however, was in its styling. No one could avoid noticing it, even though in most respects its appearance was restrained. It was a close-coupled hardtop with a square formal roof, like the Thunderbird and the earlier Continental Mark II, but from most angles the spaceship flavor of the Thunderbird was absent. The elegantly chiseled roof had a discreetly small rear window, set in from the sides as on a limousine, and rimmed with a narrow, flush-mounted chrome beading. The razor-edge motif was carried through to the fenders, where subtle creases and ridges took the place of chrome trim lines. Low on the sides, a large ridge like the rub rail of a motorboat overshadowed the bottom side panels, making the car look lower than it was. The side appearance was unified by a flowing belt line curve which swept up over the rear wheels. Only in front was restraint abandoned. Reasonably unified, the front end suggested battering rams, and carried on the spirit of the 1950 Buick.

The styling of the Riviera was extremely popular with almost everyone. Press comments on its appearance were unanimously favorable, though the grille was sometimes criticized. *Car and Driver*, October 1963, called it "The Most Impressive Car of the Year": "First of all, it's the best looking car of the whole crop. The front end is a little unsanitary, but everything else is gorgeous. . . ."

For 1963 Chevrolet introduced a new Corvette called the Sting Ray. Befitting its role as G.M.'s attention-getting production dream car, the Sting Ray had styling which was a departure from the conventions of U.S. or European cars. Like the Corvair, its appearance was unified by a ridge below the belt line which ran right around the car. Fender bulges for the front wheels protruded from the plunging hood. Front-end styling was unusual: in the ordinary sense there was no grille. The belt line ridge carried around to the front, forming a protruding lip into which folding headlights were built. Slender bumpers floated below the lip. All one usually saw behind the bumper was a dark cavity, though a mesh grille did lurk back in there somewhere. Like the first model

of the preceding Corvette series, the Sting Ray was cluttered with dummy air vents and unnecessary chrome, apparently designed to be removed on subsequent models for low-budget improvement in appearance.

Then there was the fastback roof, like the rest of the car different from what one would expect. From the windshield to the back of the windows there was nothing unusual. There was even a gill-like air extractor in each rear quarter, as on countless European sports cars. But behind that the roof not only swept down from the top but also in from the sides, terminating in a point like a boat-tailed speedster of the '20s. A solid divider in the middle of the rear window added to the bizarre effect.

With its new body and independent rear suspension the Sting Ray was newsworthy, but press comments were not unanimously favorable. The Sting Ray was, after all, loud, over-decorated, and for a sports car, overly large. But the public loved it. Its popularity was greater than even Chevrolet had expected. By January 1963 demand had so far outreached production that there was a delivery delay of three to four months, in spite of the first two-shift work day in the history of the Corvette plant.

For a while in the early '60s it almost seemed as if high style in the Detroit tradition was an obsolete concept. In 1956 the public gaped in admiration at a new taillight shape or fender contour. In 1961 it seemed as if no one gaped with much approval at anything any more. The meek shall inherit the earth: conventional, inoffensive sedans took an ever-wider share of the market. The Falcon was a success, and in Detroit committees, plans for the Chevy II, Ford Fairlane, and Chevelle were taking form. Chrysler was beginning to retreat from its garish styling policy, and even Buick and Oldsmobile, ordinarily the last defenders of automotive ostentation, were fairly plain. Again the hardy myth arose that car buyers, unless manipulated by admen and stylists, are a rational group, unaffected by the mere appearance of a car, who choose according to its practical virtues. In the early '60s, magazine writers congratulated the public for its apparent maturity.

Beneath the surface, however, not much had changed. The emotions which the 1950 Buick had been built to gratify still lurked in the motorist's subconscious. The 1958 Oldsmobile did not result from a G.M. stylist's diseased imagination but was a response, however ill-timed and badly executed, to a real need. In Detroit, few people doubted this, but still there was a problem. However unchanged the motorist was in his basic psyche, it was clear that he would not accept 1958-type styling motifs. Fins, massive grille bars, and lumpish side sculpturing would not sell in 1961. The problem was to find new motifs which would satisfy the owner's emotional needs without offending his post-1958 standards of good taste.

In finding a solution Pontiac led the way. A disastrous 1958 model underwent major surgery for 1959: the bumpers were straightened and made lighter in appearance, the side moldings were made simpler, and a distinctive new grille was introduced, consisting of two wide "nostrils" separated by a sheet metal extension of the hood. The wheels were moved closer to the edges of the car: this not only improved handling and appearance, but it

1959 *Pontiac*

also gave Pontiac a catchy advertising theme—"Wide Track"—which called attention to the car's size.

Pontiac styling was pretty outspoken, but for some reason it did not offend many people. Even with dual fins atop each rear fender and a bold grille, the '59 was praised for leading the way to cleaner, simpler forms. Improved sales pushed the market share from under 5 percent in 1958 to 6.33 percent in 1959, according to *Motor Trend*, February 1965. In the next couple of years the body shape became squarer and simpler, but it was never inconspicuous. Except for a temporary absence in 1960, the split grille remained as a loud proclamation of Pontiac's identity.

Stylists gradually found where ornamentation could be added without giving offense. For example, no one seemed to object to complex and flashy wheel covers. Bejewelled grilles, if reasonably organized, were acceptable, as were multiple taillights and fake rear grilles. In side decoration the unforgivable sin was haphazard and illogical arrangement; if all lines were horizontal, a considerable quantity of sculpturing and chrome trim could be added without exceeding the limits of public acceptance.

In pushing the buyer's tolerance for ostentation to the limit, Pontiac had to take risks. In 1962 came the biggest gamble: in the evolution of the split grille, the center divider grew into a projecting vertical "beak." In its favor was its aggressive, thrusting look and Freudian associations, but many people noted some resemblance to the despised horse-collar front of the Edsel. Again the gamble paid off: from 372,871 in 1961 sales jumped to 528,654 in 1962, or over 7.6 percent of the market . . . putting Pontiac solidly in third place in sales. Though aggressive advertising must be given part of the credit for Pontiac's success, the popularity of its styling was probably the most important reason.

1962 *Pontiac*

Pontiac stylists seemed blessed with infallibility. In 1962 a deluxe two-door hardtop called the Grand Prix was introduced, which featured a luxury interior and a few small exterior changes, notably a change in the grille to emphasize the center beak. Following a successful first year, the '63 Grand Prix was given extra attention by stylists. Contours front and rear were squared off, and the headlights were changed to a vertical arrangement. Most significant were the sides: free of trim except on the rocker panel, they had a subtle horizontal crease about half way down and a slight wasp-waist constriction at the doors which swelled out again in the rear quarters. This Coke-bottle or venturi shape was also used on the Avanti and the Buick Riviera, but due to the insistence of Pontiac advertising and the ubiquity of the cars themselves it came to be remembered as a Pontiac innovation. Along with the Riviera, the Grand Prix was one of the most admired cars of 1963. It achieved the elusive and self-contradictory ideal of successful luxury car styling, "conspicuous conservatism."

In the early '60s most manufacturers played a waiting game. It was clear that people would not buy cars styled in the idiom of the late '50s, and for lack of any clear indication of what they did want, most makers played it safe with innocuous looking cars and waited to see what the others would do. Pontiac was the first to break away from the pack. With a market share soaring over 8 percent in 1963 its success became obvious, and by 1964 competitors were busily working on their own ersatz-Pontiacs.

In 1965 the highways were swarming with imitation Pontiacs. Here, there, everywhere a Pontiac. Ford made one of the closest copies, with squared-off corners, almost flat sides with a crease part way down, and vertically stacked headlights. The intermediate-size Ford Fairlane and Mercury Comet also had

1963 *Pontiac Grand Prix*

marks of the Pontiac influence. Such brazen imitations of G.M. styling drew widespread comment, but since the cars were generally attractive there was not much serious protest. In October 1964, *Car and Driver* reported on the Ford Galaxie:

> The styling is so strikingly non-Fordish that if it weren't for the emblems, the 1965 Galaxie . . . could be described as "extravagantly anonymous" . . . .

In November of that year, *Motor Trend* concurred:

> It's a well-known fact that Ford's Product Planning Committee relies heavily on merchandising research to help executives evaluate new design trends and philosophies. So it's natural that current examples of . . . competitor's cars should lead them to amplify the slab sided look as the latest palatable expression of style.

Due to the time lag of design and tooling, the imitation-Pontiacs introduced in 1965 had only caught up with the 1963 Grand Prix. In the meantime, Pontiac stylists had pushed ahead with new ideas. On the '65 they amplified the Coke-bottle shape of the '63–'64 models by the addition of two features from the Riviera, the flowing belt line and the ridge ("skeg line") on the lower part of the sides. The skeg line exaggerated the bulge in the rear fenders by curving downward where the belt line curved up. The result was a car which followed the proven formula of seeming longer, lower, and wider than most, and which had an aggres-

1965 *Pontiac*

sive and luxurious look. To the frustration of Pontiac's competitors, who had long been trying to achieve the same thing, the
new car was unusual, expensive looking, and highly conspicuous
without losing its air of refinement and good taste.

The 1965 Pontiac was greeted with more enthusiasm than
ever. *Motor Trend*, February 1965, described it as:

> Long, low and sleek by anyone's standards. . . . Each year,
> Pontiac manages to come up with a design that looks even
> more exciting than last year's model—1965 is no exception.
> Quiet elegance is what we saw when we first looked at the
> Bonneville. . . .

To describe the styling as "quiet" was perhaps something of an
exaggeration. In March 1965, *Car and Driver* characterized it as
"flamboyantly good-looking, with great swooping curves and ero-
tic distribution of masses in its total configuration." In any case,
everyone agreed that it was handsome, and Pontiac sales rose.

G.M.'s competitors, having worked for two years to duplicate
the 1963 Pontiac, found upon the introduction of the 1965 models
that they were farther behind than ever. The Riviera's belt line
curve and wasp-waisted sides were widely adopted on G.M. cars
in 1965 and gained instant popularity. Chevrolet was one which
had them: "The Impala," rhapsodized *Car and Driver*, October
1964, "is an eloquent denial in metal of that hackneyed theory
about the intrinsic gaudiness of Detroit's cars." The Corvair,
which followed the same theme, elicited even more outspoken
praise from *Car and Driver*, "the Corvair is—in our opinion . . . the most beautiful car to appear in this country since
before World War II."

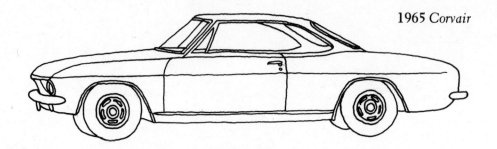

Just when they felt they could relax for a while, competitors were again plunged into desperate activity to imitate G.M.'s styling innovations. By 1966 Ford had managed to graft onto the rear quarters of their car a slight bulge, which by 1967 had grown into a full swelling shape as large as that on the '65 Chevy. Plymouth was not quite so quick to act: their '66 car was an excellent interpretation of the 1963 Pontiac, complete with split grille and vertically placed headlights, but it took them a year or two longer to catch up with the Coke-bottle shape.

Motor Age remarked:

> It is regrettable that hitherto when one manufacturer has secured an idea which proves popular, others are too prone to fall in line and copy, not realizing that not only does a copy always create a bad impression, but it has the effect of making what was an individual type a matter of common usage.

This particular comment was printed February 6, 1919, but the same general sentiment has been frequently expressed ever since the turn of the century without any visible effect on car designers. Imitation, though regrettable in other ways, has always been a popular way to make money without taking much risk. Apparently it is not true that a copy always makes a bad impression.

Though it lagged behind G.M. in the development of styling themes, Ford led the industry in its understanding of the irrational side of car ownership. Its masterpiece was the Thunderbird, a car which developed the American automotive tradition of ego-gratification to a ridiculous extreme. Ford's Product Planning

Committee worked full time to discover still more avenues into the motorist's subconscious. A central assumption behind this research was that only a minority of car buyers actually purchase a car for its practical merits. Price always influences the decision, but much depends on styling, image, and other things not directly related to its function as transportation.

Almost by accident, G.M. stumbled on a market for impractical cars with the Corvair Monza. The Monza was originally a special sporty version of the Corvair made for the auto shows. It was followed by a production Monza in 1961, which had bucket seats, tachometer, four-speed gearbox, and special trim. The Monza was quite successful, even though, as transportation, it was a very poor buy: rear seat room was desperately cramped, and luggage space was minimal. Like the "personal cars," the Thunderbird, Avanti, and Riviera, and sports cars like the Corvette, the Monza's emphasis on style and image at the expense of useful space placed it in the category of a specialty car, ostensibly for a small group of people who were willing to make such sacrifices. Yet sales exceeded expectations, and Chevrolet cheerfully made them by the thousands. Judging by the cautiousness of Corvair development and the lack of heavy promotional emphasis, however, the parent company seemed to feel that the market for such an obviously impractical car must be ephemeral and limited in size.

After careful study of the Monza phenomenon, Ford's researchers concluded otherwise. They were aware of the inverse proportion between sportiness and practicality that had inspired the creation of thousands of marginally habitable cars in the past.

1910 *American*

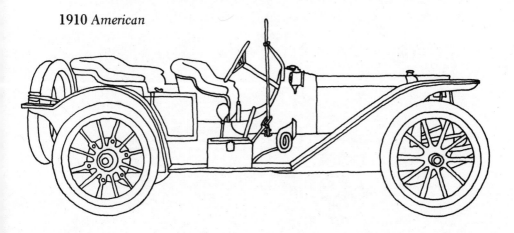

Impracticality was not an impediment to the Monza's success: rather it was one of the reasons for it. Low price was also important. All the car needed to appeal to a vast potential market was much more power (which for weight and cost reasons indicated a front engine) and louder, more conspicuous styling.

The result of Ford's enquiry into the Monza's success was the Mustang, introduced in April 1964. Mechanically there was nothing special about it: it was pieced together mostly from existing Fairlane components on a chassis about the same length as a compact. But its styling and image were blended in a unique combination which justified Ford's claim that it was truly a new type of car.

Its most notable styling feature was its overall shape. Instead of being in the middle of the car the Mustang's passenger "greenhouse" was set well toward the rear, making the hood nearly twice as long as the rear deck. The greenhouse was unusually short, which emphasized the difference. Though hailed as an original idea on the Mustang, these proportions were a perennial retrograde motif. In theory it should have been an appealing theme: a long hood has always had wide appeal, and it gave a slight resemblance to front-engined racing cars; but in spite of these advantages, such emphatic use as it had on the Mustang was still something of a gamble. The Continental Mark II and the Valiant, which had similar proportions, were not universally admired, and the public had loathed the long-hooded 1962 Plymouths and Dodges.

One thing certainly was true: the Mustang was styled for effect rather than for function. Its shape was cramped here, bulged there at the dictates of fashion, and had as little to do with functional requirements as the potbelly of a department store Santa Claus. In fact its engine was no longer than in any other car; the extra hood length was simply wasted space. At the rear,

1964 *Mustang*

the passenger compartment and trunk were crammed tightly together, leaving the rear seat fit only for legless children and the
trunk only large enough for a few small suitcases.

At the price of occasional garish touches, Ford stylists succeeded in making the Mustang stand out from other cars. The
shape was distinctive, and no one could miss the protruding air
scoop in front. The headlight "brows," fake air scoops in the
sides, dummy louvres, and decorative ridges had some of the
flavor of 1958, but in the intervening years stylists had learned to
apply them more tastefully. The loudness of Mustang styling drew
some criticism from the press. In May 1964, *Car and Driver*
reported:

> We can well understand Ford management's wish to give the
> Mustang a distinctive and possibly unique appearance, but
> the result strikes us as inexplicably amateurish. . . . Better
> preparation for future improvement could hardly be
> devised. . . .

Like the Thunderbird, the Mustang relied heavily on an
image created by its size, appearance, and promotion. Since it
was a unique type, one-sided comparisons could be made with
other cars: it was smaller and handier than most sedans; it was
more roomy than a sports car; with a six-cylinder engine it was
economical; and with a V8 it was quick. And, significantly, at a
base price of $2,368 f.o.b. Detroit it was remarkably cheap to buy.
There was nothing anywhere near it in price that was as sporty
and distinctive.

In Detroit some people laughed when Ford announced a
sales target of 250,000 Mustangs for the first twelve months of
production. A week after the Mustang's introduction Ford was the
only one still laughing. Showrooms swarmed with buyers, and
dealers sold the cars as fast as they could fill out order forms.
Everyone wanted a Mustang, from teenagers to businessmen to
retired couples. Mustang plants clattered overtime, and for a
short time in late summer the car held third place in sales behind
Chevrolet and the bigger Fords. It was one of the most successful
cars ever introduced: in 1965, its first full calendar year of production, more than half a million were sold.

Having only the more exotic Corvair Monza to meet the

Mustang challenge, G.M. was caught way off guard. Chrysler did a little better, in that it did at least build a car specifically to compete with the Mustang, but unfortunately the car itself was a disaster. Starting late, and with a small budget, Chrysler stylists grafted a huge fastback roof onto an otherwise standard Valiant and rushed it into production at about the same time as the Mustang. Called the Barracuda, the car was only too obviously a stopgap effort. Aesthetically, the new roof was not a success. In May 1964, *Car and Driver* tactfully remarked that, "the body shape seems a little thick toward the back—probably the result of the dual need for rear head room as well as visibility." Chrysler compounded the problem by stressing the car's practical features, such as the seven-foot-long storage area which could be made by folding the rear seats flat. The Mustang seemed sporty partly because it could scarcely carry people, much less awkward loads. Had Chrysler ignored the problems of headroom, visibility, and storage space and designed a low and rakish roof instead, the story might have been different, but as it was, sales of the Barracuda were less than 10 percent of the Mustang's.

If the Barracuda was a disaster, no apt word can be found to describe the Marlin, American Motors' effort to share some of the Mustang's success. The Marlin appeared almost a year after the Mustang. Like the Barracuda, it was not much more than an enormous fastback roof built onto an existing passenger car chassis. But if the Valiant was a poor starting point, the ponderous Rambler Classic was a lot worse. Seemingly to ensure disaster, AMC stylists added a bizarre black panel onto the center of the roof and rear body and drew a black border like a smear of mascara around the side windows. Sales were "scarcely enough to justify advertising expenditures, let alone tooling," according to

1965 *Barracuda*

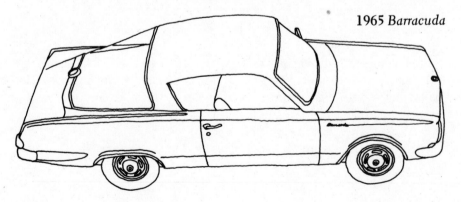

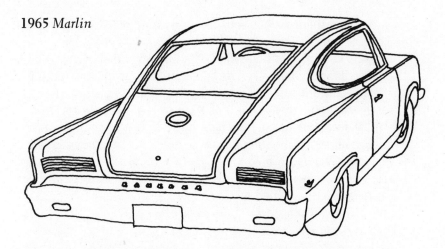

Motor Trend, May 1966, and the car was soon hooted into de-served oblivion.

Through most of the '50s and '60s G.M. styling led the indus-try, and rival manufacturers were frequently criticized for copy-ing G.M. themes as openly as they did. When the Mustang was introduced, however, G.M. had nothing to match it with, and in designing their own version they showed that they had as little conscience about borrowing ideas as anyone else. The 1967 Cam-aro, G.M.'s Mustang-car, was within a couple of inches of the Mustang in every dimension inside and out, and shared its salient styling features of long-hood, short-deck proportions. It also was based on existing chassis components, from Chevrolet's intermediate-sized Chevelle. Its price, option list, performance, and appointments were scarcely distinguishable from those of its competitor.

Though just as brazen, the designers of the Camaro were not as skillful in plagiarism as others had been of their own work. In spite of the Camaro's similarities to the Mustang, its styling was

1967 *Camaro*

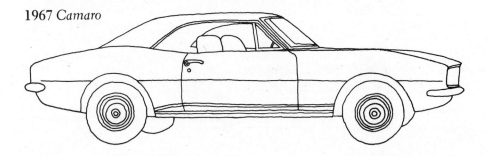

far more restrained. It looked like a streamlined, front-engined Corvair Monza, complete with a Coke-bottle shape that was emphasized by a peak in the rocker panel molding that reflected the dip in the belt line. The roof design was a smooth almost-fastback, and the grille was a simple mesh-filled horizontal opening. It sold moderately well, but was not as popular as the Mustang. It seems that many people missed in the Camaro the fake louvres, air scoops, emblems, and sculpturing they found on the Mustang. Wide stripes of bright paint around the nose and tail were still not enough to give its simple form the rich flavor that Mustang owners seemed to like.

In 1967 Mustang-type "ponycars" reached the height of their popularity: in that year they made up one-seventh of the total market. More cars constantly entered the field. Pontiac had their own version of the Camaro, called the Firebird. Mercury borrowed the basic Mustang body from Ford, enlarged it, covered it with ornate sculpturing and sold it under the name of Cougar to ex-Thunderbird or 1958 Oldsmobile owners who were anxious to buy a sporty car without experiencing cultural shock. Plymouth made a second try at the Barracuda, including such well-proven features as the G.M. flowing belt line. It was a great hit with the press ("Unquestionably the best-looking car out of Detroit in 1967," according to *Car and Driver*, December 1966), but was not so successful with the public, perhaps because it did not employ the long-hood/short-deck theme of all the others. Even American Motors, to efface the memory of the Marlin, introduced a long-hooded sporty car in 1968 called the Javelin, about which nothing was remarkable, except that it was at the same time widely admired for its styling and designed at American Motors, reflecting the leadership of new head stylist Dick Teague.

On the whole, the second-generation imitations of the Mustang were notably unoriginal. Except for the Barracuda, all had

1967 *Barracuda*

the same proportions, interior accommodations, and general appearance, and the Barracuda did not benefit from the difference. This pattern of imitation was a phenomenon typical of the '60s. One automaker, prodded on by loud public clamor, competition from abroad, or sometimes an inspired guess, would produce something slightly different from the average American car, and it would become popular. Often no one, not even the originator of the new idea, could truthfully say he knew exactly what it was in the new car that people liked, but it was clear that, on the balance, they liked the whole thing. Not wanting to risk mistaking the source of the new car's appeal, competitors would rush to their showrooms exact duplicates of the innovator's car. The appeal of the Mustang had something to do with its size, proportions, and the delicate balance between practicality and sportiness. Beyond this, no one could say for sure. Why take a chance with something different?

When the Riviera was introduced in 1963 it was expected to draw sales away from the Thunderbird. As it turned out, most of the people who bought it were lured away from ordinary middle and high-priced sedans rather than from the Thunderbird. The specialized role of the luxury/personal car seemed not to be so specialized after all. Thousands of people shrugged off the lack of rear seat comfort and luggage space in return for the style and prestige of the Riviera.

The success of the Riviera inspired Oldsmobile to produce their own version of a luxury/personal car. It would not do, however, simply to build an outright imitation of a Thunderbird or a Riviera; this type of car must have distinction. Olds decided to use front-wheel drive to set their car apart. This would allow them to seat six passengers in a car the height of a Riviera (53 inches), would give the car extra snob appeal, and (if their engineering development was successful) would provide practical benefits. Another essential feature, of course, was the right blend of styling which would draw attention but not be considered garish.

The result of Oldsmobile's efforts was the Toronado, introduced for the 1966 model year. Its styling was spectacular. Its long hood and fastback roof followed the European G.T. tradition, but

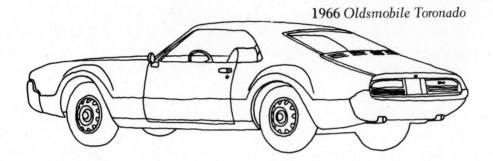

the expansion of these proportions to the size of a 2½-ton car
made quite a different effect. An immense overhang in front,
contrasting with the short overhang in the rear, gave symbolic
recognition of the front-drive system. The wheels were strongly
emphasized, not only by their own impressive design but also by
heavy circular bulges in the body above the wheel openings. Notable also was the complete absence of a conventional belt line: the
inward-leaning rear quarters of the top blended into the sides
without a break. As on several other G.M. cars, front quarter
windows were eliminated; a more efficient ventilating system was
expected to compensate for them on cars without air conditioning. A final touch was a folding headlight arrangement, which
gave the front end a clean appearance.

The Toronado's styling drew favorable comments. On a car
explicitly made for "conspicuous consumption," few people objected to such things as the wasted space forward of the front
wheels. In September 1965, *Motor Trend* gave it top honors:

> If we had to rate the 1966s according to styling interest, we'd
> do it this way . . . (1) *Oldsmobile's Toronado* takes the
> cake, of course. Its front drive and styling make it the most
> exciting 1966 car we've seen.

For a car which differed so markedly from the conventional U.S.
idiom, it was very popular.

As a general rule, however, real innovation has rarely paid off
in American car design, and this was proved yet again in 1966.
The Buick Riviera, which shared the Toronado's basic body shell,

was even more successful: one magazine after another raved over it. *Car Life*, November 1965, said:

> The vote for the handsomest car of 1966 surely must go to the Buick Riviera.

In August 1966, *Car and Driver* went even further:

> Certainly the Riviera GS is one of the most beautiful automobiles to reach the American market. Its fastback styling is the most successful effort of its kind on a car of such formidable dimensions.

The difference between the Toronado and the Riviera can be summarized by saying that the innovations on the former were carefully pruned off on the latter. The Riviera had a conventional drive train, instead of the Toronado's front drive. Buick stylists shifted the body back on the chassis, giving more overhang in the rear and less in front; they gave it a conventional G.M. sweeping belt line; they smoothed the roof down into a vestigial rear deck rather than chopping it off short; and they sheared off the Toronado's wheel arch bulges, though still leaving the wheels fully exposed. The result was a longer, sleeker version of the old Riviera, remarkable only for its use of a near-fastback roof line and an aggressive W-shaped front end (pointed in the center and at the sides). Its popularity was another triumph for conservatism.

A lot of the apparent diversity of automotive forms in the '60s was more in name than in fact. In 1959 a Chevrolet sedan was just that, while in 1967 it could be a Chevy II or a Chevelle as well. These permutations, however, did not really add anything new to the automotive scene, being little more than different sizes of the same type of car. But some of the new arrivals were really new,

1966 *Buick Riviera*

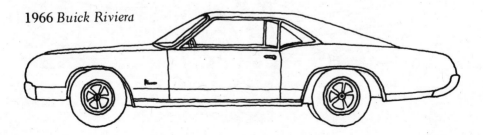

reflecting a novel combination of automotive functions or a suddenly expanded acceptance of an old form which made it into something different. The Mustang was a new blend of functions: it occupied a previously neglected part of the spectrum between family car and sports car, neglected because of its apparent unsuitability for either role. Though it kept hereditary resemblances, it had a distinct identity of its own.

An example of an old form in an expanded role was the four-wheel-drive car, of which the World War II Jeep was the earliest mass-produced example. After the war ended, the Jeep continued to be produced for a small civilian market. An effort to gain wider appeal for the car, by building a slightly more civilized body on the chassis and calling it the Jeepster, was not a success, and the Jeep descended to the automotive working class, being used for hauling and towing on the farm, plowing snow, and such tasks.

The maturation of the four-wheel-drive car and the station wagon were similar. Following changes in people's living habits and activities, these cars moved off the farm into a larger role in the automotive scene. For the four-wheel-drive car the change

Army Jeep

was not so much in form as it was a vast expansion of the car's uses. In the '50s and '60s outdoor activities such as camping, hunting, and fishing became more popular. Beaches and deserts became subject to motorized exploration. For all these things, a Jeep was the only suitable mode of transport.

There were a few changes made in the vehicle itself. Even to fulfill its recreational role successfully it had to be made more comfortable in ordinary driving, since most owners had to drive quite a long way on regular highways to reach an area where its off-the-road abilities could be used. With the original Jeep, owners accepted the noise, rough ride, and uncertain highway behavior as an unavoidable part of ownership, in much the same way that touring car owners in the early days had endured the hardships of an open car; but the International Harvester Scout and Ford Bronco, four-wheel-drive competitors of the Jeep introduced in the '60s, showed that these disadvantages could at least be reduced, if not eliminated.

The new thing about four-wheel-drive cars in the '60s was not the change in the vehicle itself, but the fact that for the first time they were considered cars, to be used in most cases like any other car. In 1950 the idea of using a Jeep for ordinary transportation was almost as preposterous as using a farm tractor, but by the late '60s it was not uncommon.

Another vehicle which came into wider use in the mid '60s was the bread-loaf or slab-nosed van. Credit for the domestication of this type must go to the Volkswagen Microbus, which was introduced into this country in the 1950s. Vigorously advertised as the perfect vehicle for a large family, a small school, or an owner who wants more space than an ordinary station wagon, it was modestly successful in the U.S. market.

1967 *Ford Bronco*

The strong point of a van is obvious: on a chassis of a given length, there is no shape which gives more interior room than the van's simple box. Having the engine under the rear floor, as on the Volkswagen, gives outstanding interior spaciousness, but makes loading from the rear difficult. The engine can alternatively be mounted in a box between the front seats. The main problems of the van are that the ride in the forward-mounted driver's seat is choppy and the height and blunt shape of the car make it unsteady and prone to crosswinds on the turnpike.

As the noncommercial use of vans grew, so did the number of makes in the field. Perhaps the most handsome of the group was the Chevrolet Sportvan, which had its engine mounted in front between the seats. Styling possibilities on a van are obviously limited, but by the shape of the windows, the design of the front end, and the creases on the sides the Sportvan achieved a clean and attractive appearance.

A third type of vehicle to be domesticated in the '60s was the pickup truck. As noted earlier in this chapter, pickup trucks ap-

1967 Chevrolet Sportvan

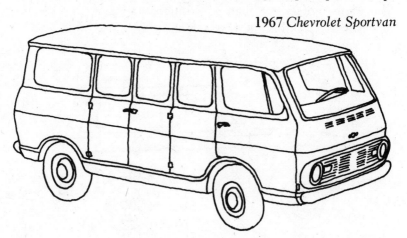

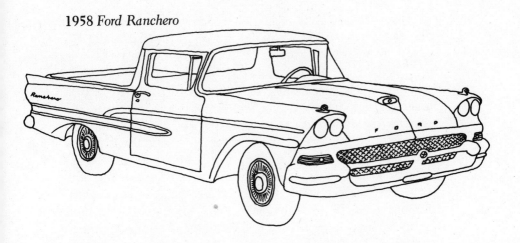

1958 *Ford Ranchero*

peared very early on, either in factory-built form or as homemade adaptations of passenger cars. In a few rural areas of the country the pickup truck became the accepted type of family vehicle, but in most areas it was regarded, like the Jeep, as something you drove only when on the job. In 1957 Ford helped the pickup truck take a few steps up the social ladder by coming out with the Ranchero, a pickup on a station wagon chassis which had the styling, comfort, and luxury features of a sedan. The movement continued with the Chevrolet El Camino (G.M.'s Ranchero), then with a pickup truck with front and back seats like a sedan's made by International Harvester, then with station wagons made on half-ton truck chassis, and so on. The line between trucks and cars, once so clearly drawn, was gradually erased by vehicles which had the utility of the former and the looks and luxury of the latter.

When animated by a promising new idea, Detroit sometimes swoons away in an almost involuntary fit of propagation, awaking to find the streets filled with a new breed of cars. This happened once with the original small car idea: the compacts alone were not enough, but were followed by the senior compacts, intermediates, and so on—Chevy IIs, Fairlanes, Chevelles, Comets—in a seemingly endless swarm. Ford's preparations for the Mustang planted the seed at Chrysler, and the Barracuda was born, followed by the

The Specialty Car 285

Cougar, Camaro, Firebird, Javelin, and Dodge Challenger. The Thunderbird begat the Avanti and Riviera, which begat the Toronado. In theory, at least, each of these types began life as a specialty car—for economy, sporting flavor, or prestige.

Automakers seemed unafraid of the contradiction implicit in the concept of exclusive cars for the millions, at least in the luxury/personal field pioneered by the Thunderbird. In 1967 Cadillac introduced its version of the type, named the Eldorado after the dream city of the Spanish explorers where roads are paved in gold. To blend in with such imagined surroundings, the earlier Cadillac Eldorado of 1958 had had gold-anodized wheel covers and trim; in the subsequent nine years standards of taste had fortunately improved at Cadillac, to the point where, in December 1967, *Car and Driver* called the new car "probably the most understated expression of taste Cadillac has ever exhibited."

The body style was a close coupled coupe, with fashionably long-nosed proportions and a heavy front overhang. The body contours were original and distinctive. Where other cars were rounded, as on the tops of the fenders, the Eldorado was sharply creased, giving the appearance of a "skin" stretched tightly over a framework. The trunk lid, for example, had a ridge between the deck and the drop-off running down to the bumper. The highlights on the surface and the beautiful detailing of the taillights and other parts persuaded many people to spend the necessary $8,000 to own one.

The Eldorado begat a new Continental in the following year. It was called the Mark III, though it was actually the second car to bear that designation: the lumbering rhinoceros of 1958 which had originally borne it had conveniently been forgotten. For the most part its styling, if undistinguished, was restrained and tasteful; exceptions were the dummy radiator in front and the spare tire shape stamped in the trunk lid. In the same vein was a new

1967 Cadillac Eldorado

Pontiac Grand Prix unveiled in 1969, which featured a garish, neo-Edsel hood and "radiator," and the 1970 Chevrolet Monte Carlo. The purpose of these cars was to attract attention at the country club, and in this they were generally successful, at the expense of subtlety. "Few have ever accused the Grand Prix of being beautiful," remarked *Car and Driver*, October 1969, "recognizable, yes. . . ."

Ever since the '20s domestic automobiles have reflected a belief among their makers that most Americans, if they could afford it,

1969 *Pontiac Grand Prix*

would drive a Cadillac. The average large sedan is a luxury car in spirit, and comes as close to the size and interior appointments of the real thing as its price will allow. Detroit's willingness to produce a large variety of luxury/personal cars in the '60s showed its continuing faith in this philosophy.

There were indications, however, that motorists were no longer as excited about big and fancy cars as they had been. The ordinary large sedan of the late '60s was larger, more powerful, and more luxurious than ever before, but nonetheless was losing its status. "To George F. Babbitt, as to most prosperous citizens of Zenith, his motor car was poetry and tragedy, love and heroism," wrote Sinclair Lewis in the '20s. But by 1970 its image was fading. In an interview with *Time* magazine, February 23, 1970, Henry Ford II remarked, "I think the glamour of the automobile is decreasing. . . . People are looking at it now as a machine to get from place to place to do something else."

Ford perhaps overstated the case, but there was certainly evidence of disenchantment with the usual "full-sized" car, with its heavy overtones of power and status. A market was growing for less pretentious cars which resembled the Volkswagen in size and price. Sales of imported cars increased by large annual increments, as they had in the late '50s, and Detroit was again faced with the problem of competing with them. The original compacts had grown larger, and by the late '60s all but the Valiant had become extinct. In any case, they were not small enough: a whole new series of cars was needed.

What should they be like? The most popular foreign cars gave no sure guide. Toyota and Datsun, the second and third best selling small cars, were square conventional sedans, attractive in an anonymous sort of way, but obviously designed with function foremost. Had they been the leaders in the small car field one might have concluded that small car buyers are sensible, practical people who care little about a car's looks as long as it does not actually look ugly. These were not, however, the most popular small cars; at the top was the Volkswagen, whose appeal (in spite of what its owners would claim) was largely irrational. It was a car for the individualist, though it sold in hundreds of thousands; it was supposed to be practical, though its owners put up with noise, uncertain handling, cramped accommodations, and feeble accel-

1969 *Ford Maverick*

eration for the privilege of being considered sensible. Whether small car buyers were more rational in their preferences than others was therefore an open question. Was the Volkswagen or the small sedan of the Datsun or Toyota type the pattern of the future?

The Ford Maverick, introduced in the spring of 1969, was nominally the first of the new generation of Detroit small cars. Yet in spirit it was more like a cheaper, smaller pony car. Rear seat headroom was sacrificed for a fastback roof, and for a car of its size (179.3 inches, or about the same as the original Falcon), its passenger and luggage space was very small. Also not really in the small car field, but closer to it in spirit, was the AMC Hornet which came out in the fall of 1969. In size and shape it was similar to the compacts of 1960, but its long wheelbase and short rear overhang gave it a roomy interior and unusual proportions. It was well received and in September 1969, *Car and Driver* reported that:

> [the] first and strongest of our impressions about the Hornet concerns exterior styling. It's very smooth and clean and its attractiveness lies in the basic body shape rather than in clever use of add-on trim.

1970 *AMC Hornet*

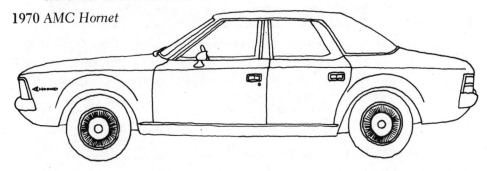

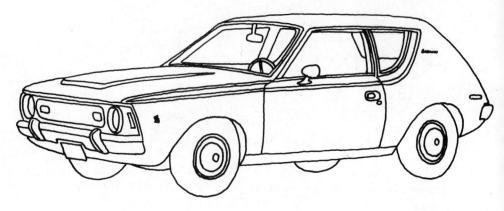

The Hornet was rational in concept; at the other end of the scale was the Gremlin, the first American Volkswagen-sized car, introduced by AMC in February 1970. The Gremlin was basically a Hornet shortened by 20 inches with a truncated station-wagon back, which other than its handy size had few practical features to boast of. Like the Volkswagen, however, it resembled no other car on the road. It had "a studied uniqueness in styling . . . probably the most conspicuous of its virtues is styling. It's brisk and efficient and it borrows from no one," according to *Car and Driver*, April 1970. Gremlin advertising promoted an image much like the Volkswagen's—the underdog, an ugly duckling with a good heart. It was a bid for the irrational small-car buyer, and early sales indicated that there were enough of them to meet AMC's modest goals.

The Gremlin, and the Ford and G.M. small cars which followed it, all showed a recognition by U.S. automakers of something they had not been aware of in 1960: that a small car, merely because of its size, unavoidably takes on a different personality from a big car, and the difference can be used to advantage. The compacts of 1960 apologized for being small: their shape was that of a scaled-down big car, and their styling—the Corvair's roof, the Falcon's taillights—mimicked their larger counterparts. Interiors were planned to maintain the illusion that six people could still be seated comfortably inside.

The new small cars were designed in a more positive spirit.

1971 *Chevrolet Vega (coupe)*

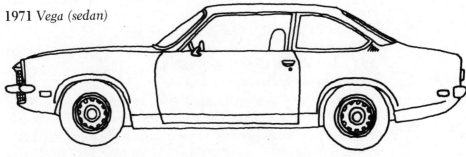

1971 *Vega (sedan)*

The styling of the Chevrolet Vega, for example, gave an impression not of a sedan but of a sports car. Most obviously in the fastback coupe, but also in the sedan, it had the basic shape of a sports car—two doors, longer hood than rear deck, windshield at a low angle—and the theme was supported by details like the "egg-crate" grille, slotted wheels, and dummy louvres. Like many other compromises in the past, such as the toy tonneau and the ponycar, this redefinition as a sports car (only implied in the Vega, not made explicitly) gave a more favorable interpretation of the passenger accommodations—it was roomy for a sports car, though cramped for a sedan.

The Vega borrowed heavily from styling on other cars. The front end was similar to the redesigned Camaro introduced earlier in 1970, and had a family resemblance to earlier Chevrolets, particularly the 1955 model. Its heaviest debt, however, was to Italian

cars designed by Pininfarina. The Vega sedan was almost an exact copy of the popular Fiat 124 in such critical things as its general proportions and its roof line. No one could dislike it, and many people shared *Road and Track's* opinion, of November 1970, that it was "one of the finest-looking compact sedans in the world."

In designing the Pinto, Ford stylists took advantage of its size in another way, not to emphasize its similarity to an existing type like a sports car but, instead, to escape from conformity. They recognized that small cars are a separate breed, with different (and relatively undefined) aesthetic values. Big car proportions, where a squarish greenhouse and plenty of rear overhang is the norm, rarely look as good on a small car, and often do not provide maximum seating and luggage space. Departure from the norm is difficult on a big car because the standard is so clearly defined—everyone knows what a big car should look like. With small cars the case is not the same, however: a wider variety of contours and proportions is acceptable.

The practical problem was how to provide enough head room for rear seat passengers without making the roof line ungainly looking by being too high. Behind the passenger's heads

1971 *Ford Pinto*

the roof could slope down; the further forward the passengers were, the more gradual the slope, but then they would have no leg room. Chevy designers took the easy way out by making two versions—the fastback, which deliberately sacrificed rear seating room for style, and the sedan, whose sensibly square roof gave more headroom but was less exciting to look at.

In the Pinto the rear seat was placed unusually far back, between the wheel wells, and the fastback roof was made fairly high in back to clear the passengers' heads. It looked unusual, but on a small car, not bad; carefully shaped rear side windows and a wide flattened-off back minimized the hump-backed look. Unlike the Vega, some people disliked it at first, but its appearance gave it a strong identity—something one could also say about the Volkswagen. Some commentators were outspoken in praise of it. In September 1970, *Road & Track* called it "Ford's best design since the 1961 Continental," and thought it was "especially satisfactory from the rear three-quarter aspect"—where the roof was most noticeable.

One heavily publicized feature of the new small cars was that no major appearance changes were planned for at least four years. This was hailed as the end of the annual model change, an event which many people saw as a symbol of the wastefulness of the American auto industry.

Responsibility for the idea of yearly style changes and the resulting national hysteria is traditionally placed on General Motors, which is supposed to have instituted it as a conscious marketing policy in the '20s. G.M.'s president at that time, Alfred P. Sloan, denies this (Sloan, *My Years with General Motors*, Doubleday & Co., New York, 1964):

> General Motors in fact had annual models in the twenties, every year after 1923 . . . but . . . we had not in 1925 formulated the concept in the way it is known today. When we did formulate it I cannot say. It was a matter of evolution.

Automobile literature printed before the '20s makes it clear that some sort of annual model change was in effect ever since the beginning. Seasonal use of cars, with a definite break every year in

midwinter, led naturally to an informal annual change comparable in some ways to present day fashions in clothing. Cars were
referred to by model year, as they are in this book, very early:
there was a "Winton for 1899," a "new Pope-Toledo for 1904," and
so forth. Model years were announced whenever the manufacturer felt like it. Most cars were introduced around New Year's,
but there was no set rule—some makers anticipated the new
calendar year by five or six months.

The wastefulness of frequent style changes was noted with
disapproval by *The Horseless Age* on December 13, 1905:

> It seems as if the automobilist who sells his machine after one
> season's use, in order to keep up to date . . . is paying dearly
> for the pleasure of following fickle fashion. Probably a large
> majority of automobile owners use their cars but one year,
> and by so doing they, of course, help to keep the manufac-
> turers going and stimulate . . . the continual making of
> changes in form and design. Not all of these changes are
> unqualified improvements, by any means.

Even in 1905 the main reason for trading in a year-old car
had little to do with its actual mechanical deterioration. The annual mileage covered in those days was usually quite small, and
(popular myth to the contrary) the basic mechanical components
of most cars built after the turn of the century were reasonably
sturdy. For want of precise information on how strong a part
needed to be, most makers provided a generous safety factor.
Tires were the only part whose bad reputation was deserved, but
they needed such frequent replacement that tire wear was not an
important consideration at trade-in time. No, said *The Horseless
Age*, March 2, 1904, the reasons for selling lay elsewhere: "These
vehicles, when 'cast off' by their buyers, usually are but little
worn. . . . The majority of them were discarded simply because
they were out of fashion."

Through the next sixty years, motorists continued to show
eagerness for novelty and boredom with cars which looked out of
date. In the 1960s, however, as the automobile's functions, both
expressive and practical, were separated into distinct categories,
this pattern was altered. The frequency of style changes no longer
had to be geared to an overall average preference, as it had in

earlier periods where the Great American Automobile had been built to be everything to everyone. In some kinds of cars constant variety in design was vital, in others it was not needed at all.

The value of "newness," visual evidence that a car is fresh from the factory, varied widely from one category to another. It meant most in intermediate-sized cars like the Ford Torino or Pontiac Tempest, particularly in the sporty or luxury versions of these cars. Much of the prestige of such a car depended on its age—when new, it was the object of envy, but by the time it was two or three years old its status value was greatly diminished. Visual details that showed that it was up-to-date were a necessity.

Appearance was still important to people who bought large expensive cars, but it was enough that the car looked rich; it did not have to look dramatically new. The Corvette was similarly exempt from the pressures of novelty: the model which came out in 1968 continued on through the '70s with very few changes. Some low-priced cars also had long model runs. The Valiant introduced in 1967 stayed virtually the same for a decade.

In abolishing annual model changes in the new small cars for at least a four-year term, automakers were simply making a virtue of an existing situation. Fewer people would buy Pintos and Vegas than would buy big Fords and Chevrolets, and a long model run would help to pay off the investment in development and tooling. With the pace of annual changes already nearly at a standstill in existing compact lines such as the Chevrolet Nova (formerly the Chevy II) and the Valiant, it seemed unlikely that the public would demand constant style innovations in the new cars, especially since their original designs did not rely on modish and short-lived features for their appeal.

The proliferation of automotive types in the '60s made it harder than ever to see a general direction of evolution. The waning importance of the annual model change and the growing proportion of smaller, simpler cars on the road indicated a cooling of the traditional American partiality for the automobile. Some people interpreted the situation this way, but there were also signs which pointed in the other direction. Car sales grew ever larger, and some cars became popular which carried the garishness, wastefulness, and frivolity of the American automobile tradition to ever-greater heights. Huge dummy radiators came into vogue which extended forwards a foot or more; paint schemes with lurid orange and black stripes became common; even paisley patterned vinyl roof coverings were offered.

The decade of the '60s saw very little that was wholly new, but the traditional automotive forms—sports car, pickup truck, van, off-road vehicle, luxury car, small economy car—were cross-bred to produce a vast progeny of mongrels like sports sedans and luxury trucks. There were even rumors of a small Cadillac. The traditional types that were not invigorated by cross-breeding, particularly the large, four-door sedan that was *the* car of the '50s, remained almost exactly as they were in 1960. Had a big Chevy or Ford of the early '70s been placed by a time warp on a city street in 1960, nobody would have paid it much attention.

Other than becoming fatter and longer and heavier, big cars had not changed much. The general movements that have acted in other periods, such as the movement toward lower cars in the '50s or toward wider bodies and integrated fenders in the '30s and '40s, had no counterpart in the '60s. Historically, the periods which have seen the greatest development in the shape of the automobile—the period before 1905, and the period from 1933 to 1950—have been those in which business competition has been most intense and in which functional requirements have been most pressing. In the comfortable '60s, by comparison, nothing much happened to the automobile's basic form.

7

The Real World Intrudes

Through most of the history of the American automobile the stylist has had only to please the buyer to be successful. And the buyer was, generally speaking, not hard to please. He was willing to put up with cars that had cramped accommodations for their size, that were wasteful of gas and of materials, and that were dangerous in an accident and expensive to fix. All he insisted on having was a car that pleased his eye. No outside forces seriously intruded on this lazy and tolerant relationship.

In 1973 two events occurred which forever changed this symbiosis of designer and consumer: through the bumper laws which took effect in this year, government made its first conspicuous alteration in the appearance of cars, and through the oil embargo and subsequent gasoline shortage, the world's natural resource limits first influenced the use of automobiles in this country. Government action and global conditions were suddenly added to public taste in determining the shape of cars.

The government's first interest in car design concerned the safety of a car's occupants in a crash. In June 1970 the Department of Transportation requested Fairchild and AMF (for a consideration of $7.8 million) to develop prototype Experimental Safety Vehicles (ESVs) which would meet a number of requirements: they should preserve the life of unbelted occupants in frontal or near-frontal crashes at any speed up to 50 mph, and should prevent serious injury to passengers in a series of other maneuvers—sliding sideways into a pole at 15 mph, rolling over twice at 60 to 70 mph, and so on.

The specifications pretty well determined the general design of the vehicles. To protect passengers, the seating area had to be very rigid, and unless fancy materials were used, this meant it must be heavy. A tank, after half a century of development, still depends on armor plate for protection; likewise the ESV, in effect. Injuries result from quick deceleration, and the more give there is outside the passenger cage, the more gradual the deceleration; hence, the larger the car the better, and this meant the addition of yet more weight. Prodigious bumpers were needed to absorb the specified abuse, and this added more weight still—the bumper system on the AMF vehicle added 800 pounds. The AMF ESV was more than 18½ feet long, over 80 inches wide, and weighed nearly three tons; the Fairchild ESV was similar in size, and not much lighter.

If $7.8 million could produce crude ESVs, presumably a huge increase in investment could provide better ones; but without an alteration in the laws of physics, the requirements would always produce enormous, heavy, expensive, and fuel-thirsty cars, and whether car users wanted such vehicles or the nation's economy or resources could afford them was doubtful.

On production cars larger bumpers were the only conspicuous product of the government's interest in vehicle safety, and indeed, safety was only secondary to reduced repair costs in the bumper laws that went into effect in 1973. The law required that, in a frontal collision at 5 mph or a rear collision at 2½ mph, no damage be done to "safety related" equipment such as steering, brakes, and lights, and that the body damage be minimal—the hood and trunk must still open, for example. Bumpers that would meet the requirements not only had to be stronger than before,

AMF ESV

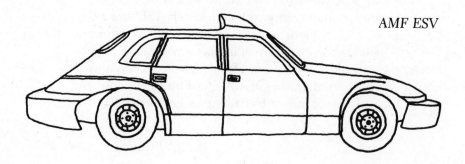

but they also had to stick out farther from the body so they had room to yield on impact.

In effect, this meant a return to projecting bumpers like those used in the '20s and '30s, but the necessary bulk of the new bumpers created aesthetic problems that the earlier ones did not. It is one thing to harmonize body shapes with a slender bar or two floating out ahead; it's another thing to hang a gigantic steel beam out there. Most automakers decided that filling the gap between the bumpers and the body with some sort of flexible material made them more acceptable looking, but few solutions to the problem were very imaginative, and the general consensus was that the new bumpers looked awful. "I keep wondering," wrote the editor of *Road & Track* in January 1974, "whether it's better to have a car that's ugly all the time or one that's ugly only after it has hit something or been hit."

Significantly, however, the bumper law caused the appearance of a few cars actually to improve. An outstanding example was the Corvette, whose new urethane nose not only gave better protection but also eliminated the bumper as a separate design element. Body design has always advanced by absorbing individual elements into simplified forms—hood shapes gradually blended into bodies, headlamps melted into fenders, fenders merged into body sides, and so on. In 1968 Pontiac came out with a rubberized paint that would withstand bumper abuse, and separate chrome bumper bars began to give way on some models to freer front-end designs painted in the body color. The bumper was still there, but was disguised as a body panel.

1930 *Jordan Speedway* *(detail)*

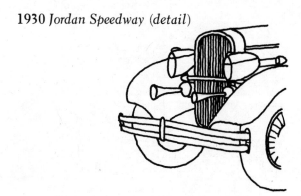

The 1973 Corvette simply continued this process. It showed, among other things, that the bumper laws were not inconsistent with good looks, at least on a big car; on small cars, big bumpers were harder to hide. It also showed that pressure for functional improvement, as so often in the past, could force aesthetic advances that might not otherwise be made. The real problem with the big bumpers was not aesthetic, at least in the long run, but practical: they cost more to make, they cost more to fix (in spite of the intent of the law), and, at a time when car weight was suddenly causing concern, they were much too heavy.

Roof design was another area where government requirements had some influence. A law took effect for 1973 which set minimum standards for roof strength. Pillarless hardtops could

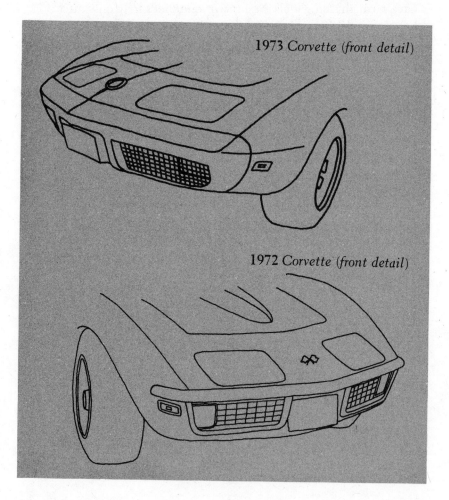

1973 Corvette (front detail)

1972 Corvette (front detail)

still meet the 1973 roof strength law, but probably wouldn't be able to meet increasingly demanding later versions of the law, and new body designs in the mid '70s such as the Ford Granada all had substantial center pillars supporting the roof.

The roof laws specifically exempted convertibles, but they were dying anyway. By 1974 convertibles were made only on big G.M. cars, and of those, only the Cadillac sold in worthwhile numbers. Many practical reasons can be given for the passing of the convertible: it was vulnerable to theft and vandalism, it was less safe than a sedan, it provided a less satisfactory way of keeping cool in the summer than air conditioning, and it was uncomfortable at modern highway speeds with the top down. Air conditioning had indeed grown much more common in the '70s, but except for this, there had been almost as few practical arguments for the convertible back in its peak years of the '50s and early '60s. Then, however, they were considered exciting and romantic, while in the '70s they had lost their appeal. As so often in this history, if we attend only to matters of function and practicality we will miss the main point: convertibles were popular because, for a time, they answered an expressive need in the people who bought them; when the fashion changed, and people began to regard them simply as machines to perform a practical function, they were finished.

While federal safety legislation and the recommendations of the Department of Transportation were influencing auto evolution toward ever larger, heavier, and more expensive vehicles, suddenly oil prices increased four-fold, the U.S. balance of payments went far into the red to pay for foreign oil, and the nation's economy slipped into a recession. In this changed world, 2½-ton cars were too expensive for most people to buy, and their appetite

1975 Ford Granada

for fuel was ruinous for both their individual owners and the nation as a whole. Not long after they had taken the first legal steps toward requiring all cars sold in the U.S. to be crash-proof (and thus necessarily heavy and expensive) safety vehicles, Congressmen began working on laws that would effectively ban such cars through minimum mileage standards.

American conditions in the late '70s and beyond would increasingly resemble those of postwar Europe, where high gas prices, urban space restrictions, usually less affluent buyers, and a tax bias against large cars were already normal, and in many respects, the direction of car design would follow the European pattern—toward cars that were smaller, cheaper, and more economical of fuel. In the 1980s, some American automobiles might come to resemble the German Audi 50, which is 11½ feet long and weighs less than 1,500 pounds.

American drivers were lured toward smaller cars by several new models introduced in the mid '70s. In the fall of 1973 Ford introduced the Mustang II, which was followed a year later by the Chevrolet Monza 2+2 (and versions made by Buick and Oldsmobile). These were latter-day ponycars not much bigger than the Pinto-Vega-Gremlin size. The 1975 Ford Granada and Mercury Monarch imitated Mercedes' appearance, smaller size, and luxury; comfort was no longer something you could have only in a huge car. Even Cadillac, in 1975, came out with a smaller model called the Seville.

The most imaginative of the smaller cars introduced in the mid '70s was the AMC Pacer. The Pacer (like the Audi 50) followed

1974 *Audi 50*

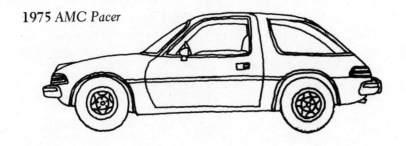

the pattern of small car design set by the BMC Mini in 1959. The Mini was either a lumpy fastback sedan or a slant-back station wagon, depending on how you thought about it; in any case, it was a visually pleasing and highly efficient package for carrying people. Like recent European variations of the theme, the Pacer had a rear door or hatchback, which further increased its utility. While the Gremlin could perhaps be called the first American imitation of the Mini, the Pacer, with its sloping nose, enormous glass area, and graceful roof design (reminiscent of the Chevrolet Nomad), was the first whose styling was greeted with general enthusiasm.

A trend toward smaller American cars was well under way before the oil shortage occurred, and had more to do with urban conditions and the obesity of "full-sized cars"—cars that were 18½ feet long and weighed well over 2 tons—than it did with gas mileage. Unfortunately, mere reduction in overall length does not give a car better gas mileage. Weight is perhaps the most important thing, followed by engine size and power; frontal area and aerodynamic shape are also significant at highway speeds. Partly due to the heavy bumpers and protective beams inside the doors which federal safety laws required, and partly to extra sound deadening material and power accessories, the new small cars were seriously overweight. The Pacer weighed 3,000 pounds, half again as much as some European sedans of similar size and seating capacity, and several hundred pounds more than any of the 1960 compacts, which were longer. The Mustang II and Monza 2+2 were also around 3,000 pounds.

Either fuel prices had to go down, or the government's dreams of armored crash-proof vehicles had to die, and it was not hard to see which was more likely. The safety vehicle concept developed by the Department of Transportation was not, on the balance, a worthwhile goal anyway, since the clumsy bulk of a car that could crash with little damage at 50 mph made it that much more likely to do so. The inflexibility of the oil squeeze made the general lines of American car evolution plain: future cars would have to use less gas, and to meet this end they would necessarily become smaller and lighter, and perhaps better streamlined.

Streamlining has given inspiration to American designers at regular intervals in the automobile's development. The rage for the torpedo body and smooth graduated shapes influenced almost every car made between 1910 and 1920; the great transformation in automotive form between 1932 and 1950 was also done in the name of streamlining. In the '60s the use of added-on aerodynamic aids—upturned spoilers at the rear, air dams under the front, wings, and other devices—on racing cars inspired a fad for such devices on production cars. The 1968 Dodge Charger, which showed racing car influence in its smooth overall shape, its roof design, and its vestigial rear spoiler, was one of the most attractive products of the fad; the 1970 Pontiac GTO shows a more outspoken allegiance to the theme.

Except in a few cases in the '30s, streamlining on American cars has been done purely for visual effect, without any serious effort to reduce drag. The wing on the 1970 Pontiac GTO probably had about as much aerodynamic effect as a row of gargoyles would have. And, as it turns out, swoopy streamlined shapes sometimes actually produce more drag than conventional boxy ones. With some serious work on streamlining for function as well as for appearance, improvement could be made in both areas, especially since virtually nothing serious had been done to improve aerodynamic efficiency on American sedans since the '30s.

1970 *Pontiac GTO*

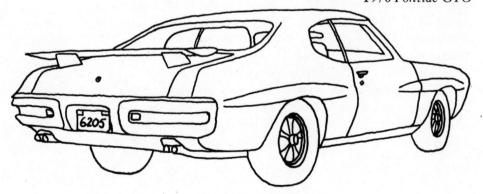

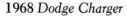
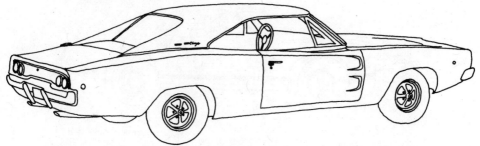

Although a smooth shape has little effect on gas mileage at low speeds, enough driving in the U.S. is done at turnpike speeds to make an improvement worthwhile.

Objective, rational analysis of America's car needs for the future yields the inevitable conclusion that cars must become vastly more efficient—particularly in their use of fuel, but also in their use of raw materials for their manufacture, and in their passenger capacity for a given external size. American cars, in other words, should become more like European cars. Many people, especially those who lived in large cities or those who felt most acutely the rise in fuel prices, were already moving toward small cars in the mid '70s and would welcome the change. Legislators in Washington, viewing the economic disruptions caused by rising oil prices, would pass laws making some shift toward smaller cars mandatory.

As I have tried to show in this book, however, the people's choice has always been guided as strongly by irrational impulse— the gut appeal of a car that is large, powerful, impressive, expensive-looking, and perhaps also beautiful—as it has by considerations of convenient size or good gas mileage. While planners in Washington, looking to the future, see cars like the Audi 50 as the only way out, and drivers in places like New York or Los Angeles, where automobile use has long since reached a crisis, have taken to small cars by necessity, these people are not typical of the majority of Americans who buy cars. If a poll were taken in 1975 to find which car the largest number of Americans wished to own, the winner would not have been the Audi 50 but would

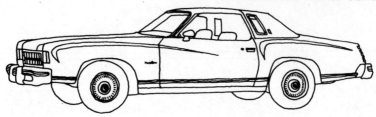

probably have been the Chevrolet Monte Carlo, a gas-greedy, 2-ton car which found an excuse for passenger accommodations no better than the Audi 50's by having an impressive long hood, flamboyant sculptured sides, fashionable opera windows, and an air of luxury. "Feel good about your taste," urged an ad for the Monte Carlo in *Time*, January 27, 1975, "If your eye, your instinct, and even your bones tell you Monte Carlo satisfies your taste, trust them." Eye, instinct, taste—American cars have traditionally been built to satisfy these, not to stand trial before the rational intellect. Until the influence of gasoline shortages and government regulations makes cars like the Monte Carlo either illegal or, from a practical standpoint, flatly impossible to run, millions of people will stubbornly continue to buy them. Why? Because, if history is any guide, when Americans go out to buy a car, their eyes and their instincts usually guide their choice.

Index

Note: In the text and the index a car's model year is used, rather than the year of its introduction and initial production. For example, the original Corvair, introduced in the fall of 1959, is called the 1960 Corvair, as people referred to it then. If the Pope-Toledo Company chose to call their new car, introduced in the middle of 1903, the 1904 model, the lead of the manufacturer is followed. Model years are in *italics*.

Speed, love of, 139–40
Speed craze, 25–6, 50
Sports cars, 213–4, 216–9, 250–1
Stafford: *1911*, 64–5, 68–9
Station wagons, 221–5, 250–1
Stearns: *1907*, 56, 80
Steering, tillers vs. wheels, 11
Sterling: *1916*, 111
Stevens-Duryea: *1912*, 96
Stout Scarab, 154
Straight-line body, 65
Streamlining: on Airflow, 157; development of, 140–44; effect of efforts towards, 183; necessity in future, 304–5; public reaction, 149, 153–4, 170–1; streamline body, 68–9
Studebaker: *1910* electric, 61; *1918*, 86; *1937*, 170; *1939*, 178; *1947*, 191, 206, 224; *1950*, 206; *1953*, 206–9, 215; *1959* Lark, 253; *1962* Hawk, 261–2; *1963* Avanti, 262–4
Stutz: *1915* Bearcat, 74; *1916* Bulldog, 83; Black Hawk speed record car, 144; *1928*, 125; *1929*, 157
Sundberg, Carl, 238
Sweep Spear (Buick trademark), 205

Tail fins: on 1948 Cadillac, 204; on Chrysler cars, 230–1; on Ford cars, 232; other references, 233, 239, 242, 244–5, 258, 262, 267
Teague, Richard, 278
Teague, Walter Dorwin, 170–1
Thomas: *1904*, 38; *1905*, 38; *1906*, 50

Tires: balloon, 150; doughnut, 150, 163; other, 294
Tonneau body: early problems, 31–5; first use, 18; Roi des Belges style, 33–4; toy (baby or pony), 56, 79, 252
Tops: California, 99; canopy, 39; early, 11; roadster, 118; sedan tops strengthened, 300–1; Springfield, 96–7
Torpedo body, 63–5, 68, 304
Touring Car, decline, 85–9
Toyota: in 1960s, 288–9
Trunk, development of built-in type, 171–4
Tucker: *1948*, 194
Tulsa: *1920*, 85

Van, breadloaf or slab-nose, 283–4
Velie: *1918*, 83
Ventiports (Buick trademark), 205
Victoria Lines, 77
Volkswagen: *1958*, 241; Microbus, 283; in 1960s, 288–9

Walker, George, 190, 260
Weather protection, 38
Weight distribution: 9, 49, 157, 163, 166
Wheels: wire, 69–73, 216; disc, 104–6; size, 108; hidden, 151
Window area, increased, 174–5, 188, 190–2, 197, 202, 241
Winton: *1914*, 69
Woods: *1916* Mobilette, 111